"It's a marvelous, beautiful book."

> Ursula Vaughan Williams
>
> poet, novelist, and widow of composer Ralph Vaughan Williams

"It was a fascinating study. Congratulations on a job well done."

> Andrew M. Greeley
>
> priest, sociologist, novelist

"I marvel at the scholarship, insight, compassion (of Passionate Holiness), and "pioneering" in a little understood or accepted area of life."

> --Sister Agnes Cunningham SSCM
>
> Former Head of the Catholic Theological Society of America

"Many thanks for sending me your book Passionate Holiness, which I enjoyed very much. It is a fascinating account of the cult of Holy Wisdom, mixed with stories of various 'distinctive people' and the roles they have played in the history of the Church. It is full of saints, sinners, heretics, martyrs, and those who persecuted them. Some of these people, and the ideas they believed in, have featured in my novels, though there was much that I was not aware of. The material in the Russian and Irish chapters were new to me. You say at the beginning of Chapter VII that the reader may cry out "Too much information". Not me! Passionate Holiness is a work of remarkable scholarship, and I wish it had been published before I wrote my Byzantine novels, rather than afterwards. If I ever return to Byzantium as a subject, I am sure I will find your book invaluable. The icons that illustrate the book are beautiful. You are lucky to have access to works by such gifted artists. If only my publisher had commissioned something similar for the cover of Theodore. Maybe next time!"

> Christopher Harris
>
> English novelist, author of "Theodore," "Memoirs of a Byzantine Eunuch," and "False Ambassador"

"Here's something the antigay modern Roman Catholic Church would like to forget: In the early years of Christianity, homosexual saints were worshipped too, as Dennis O'Neill reminds us. O'Neill is a Chicago-based Catholic pastor who 11 years ago founded The Living Circle, a spirituality center devoted to GLBT people and their friends. In 1995 the Circle hosted an art exhibit entitled "Passionate Holiness" that displayed such holy icons as Saint Boris and George the Hungarian and Saints Brigid and Darlughdach of Kildare. O'Neill's retelling of such stories, plus striking color illustrations, will surprise and inspire any reader, gay or not."

> Anne Stockwell
>
> Review from "The Advocate", May 24, 2005 issue, p. 82.

"Passionate Holiness is indeed a remarkable book, unlike any other that I know of. Its scope is amazing in its extent, both geographically and chronologically. Much of the subject matter is unfamiliar to theological historians, and it all needs to be generally known. The book gives historical meaning not only to numerous examples of all-male and all-female pairs of lovers, but also the details of the periods in which they lived and of their subsequent cults. In my own specialty, Russian literature and history, the book shows enormous erudition and a secure command of the material."

> Simon Karlinsky
>
> Professor Emeritus of the Department of Slavic Languages and Literature at the University of California, Berkeley

"I read Passionate Holiness with great interest. I am amazed by the scope and depth of the work, moved by the faith that motivates it. I am so thrilled to know more about The Living Circle (described in the book) as it seems a unique and effective ecumenical group."

> Mary E. Hunt Ph.D.

a feminist theologian and author of many books, who is co-founder and co-director of the Women's Alliance for Theology, Ethics, and Ritual (WATER) in Silver Spring, Maryland. A Roman Catholic active in the women-church movement, she lectures and writes on theology and ethics with particular attention to liberation issues.

"Passionate Holiness is a feast for the mind, the eyes, and the soul. Dennis O'Neill reclaims the many queer treasures that lie buried in Christian history. With impressive depth of scholarship, he traces Christ's feminine incarnation as Holy Wisdom. He details the stories of a bisexual martyr, cross-dressing nuns, saints who ministered in same-sex pairs, and other people of faith who lived outside gender norms. As O'Neill writes in the text, "When history reads like this, who prefers soap operas?" Color illustrations of contemporary icons bring the text to life. This book makes an important contribution to expanding human understanding of Christ and the saints who follow Her/Him."

Rev. Kittredge Cherry
author of "Hide and Speak", "Womansword", "Equal Rites: Lesbian and Gay Worship, ceremonies, and Celebrations", "Jesus in Love", and "Art that Dares"

"Passionate Holiness is one of the most beautiful books I have ever seen."

Thomas Moore
a leading lecturer and writer in North America and Europe in the areas of archetypal psychology, mythology, and the imagination. He is the author of "Care of the Soul", "Soul Mates", Rituals of the Imagination", "The Planets Within", and "Dark Eros".

PASSIONATE HOLINESS:
Marginalized Christian Devotions For Distinctive People

By Dennis O'Neill

Order this book online at www.trafford.com
or email orders@trafford.com

Most Trafford titles are also available at major online book retailers.

© Copyright 2010 Dennis O'Neill.
All rights reserved. No part of this publication may be reproduced, stored in a retrieval system, or
transmitted, in any form or by any means, electronic, mechanical, photocopying, recording, or
otherwise, without the written prior permission of the author.

Printed in Victoria, BC, Canada.

ISBN: 978-1-4269-2505-4 (sc)

*Our mission is to efficiently provide the world's finest, most comprehensive book publishing
service, enabling every author to experience success. To find out how to publish your book, your
way, and have it available worldwide, visit us online at www.trafford.com*

Trafford rev. 1/12/10

North America & international
toll-free: 1 888 232 4444 (USA & Canada)
phone: 250 383 6864 ♦ fax: 812 355 4082

ACKNOWLEDGEMENTS

Among the many people whose loving encouragement has helped nurture the writing of this book I would like particularly to thank Veronica Morrison, Barbara O'Neill, and Michael Reiniger, my associates in co-founding and developing The Living Circle, which is a place where stories like those related in *Passionate Holiness* are told, where the saints who appear among its characters are venerated, and where their images can be found. I am grateful to the late Alan Hovhaness and his dear wife, Hinako Fujihara, to whom I am beholden for obtaining the Armenian script of the Sts. Polyeuct and Nearchus icon. Thanks to Robert Lentz and William Hart McNichols for their wonderful icons and to the late Cardinal Joseph Bernardin and Fr. Henri J. M. Nouwen, both of whom encouraged me in this research and writing. Many thanks to Frances Hankins and Geraldine Boberg, librarians at Chicago's Catholic Theological Union, for their generosity, graciousness, and determination in helping to track down books. I am deeply grateful to Peter Awobolaji, Jim Barry, John Boswell, Stan Buglione, Kevin Bunten, Timothy Cain, Terry and Mary Childers, Larry Craig, Jeremy and Paulette Dale Roberts, Courtney Davis, Brian Donovan, Christina Cross Sedlak, John Fortunato (who suggested the adjective 'Distinctive'), Peggy Galus, Arlene Halko, Jonathan Hall, Richard and Nancy Harsch, Rosemary Haughton, Michael Jacobsen, Margaret Kahn, Simon Karlinsky, Pat Keenan, Matthew Kelty, Andrea Kaspryk, Carol Kottewitz, Edward Lally, Liza Martin, Larry McBrady, Michael McCabe, Brian Patrick McGuire, Sarah Farley McGrane, Dennis Moorman, Dorothy Noel, Larry Odegaard, Joseph Pawlowski, Joe Piszczor, Eduardo Ramirez, Larry Rolla, Frank Sasso, Randy Schultz, Melissa Sherman, Bill Stang, Steve Starr, Bill Stenzel, Pat Tucker, Ursula Vaughan Williams, Kevin Wood, and Mary Sue Wielgus for their editorial advice. Thanks also to the board of Grant Hospital, the Daughters of Charity at St. Joseph Hospital, and the staff of Light of Christ Lutheran Church for providing homes for The Living Circle as it has sojourned through its first decade and to the staffs of St. Benedict parish in Chicago and St. Martha parish in Morton Grove for their encouragement. Les Stahl especially devoted endless hours of help on the computer in his and Daniel Huey's home. His editorial suggestions, computer expertise, and astute observations led to the present ordering of this book's material. I will be forever grateful for his patience and constant encouragement during the many phases of this book's development. Thanks beyond words to Jim Gregory, whose home IS home – the home Wisdom built for me (Proverbs 9:1). Finally and foremost, to Christ, Holy Wisdom Incarnate, with praise and gratitude, this book is dedicated.

Lex orandi, lex credendi.
"As people pray, so they believe."
- a presupposition in Canon Law

TABLE OF CONTENTS

ILLUSTRATIONS

The originals of each icon with an * can be seen in the chapel of The Living Circle. For information, contact us at dennisboneill@aol.com or phone us at (847) 581-9136.

For viewing a complete selection of the icons of Robert Lentz or to order copies, the address is http://www.trinitystores.com The toll free number is (800)699-4482

For viewing a complete selection of the icons of William Hart McNichols or to order copies, the address is http://puffin.creighton.edu/jesuit/andre

INTRODUCTION

The Living Circle is a Chicago-based interfaith spirituality center and chapel for the lesbian, gay, bisexual and trans-gendered community and their friends. In the Autumn of 1995, over fifty items of sacred art from the collection in the TLC chapel were transported to Toronto. The icons, pictures, statues, and relics were displayed in Holy Trinity Anglican Church in an exhibit entitled "A Passionate Holiness: Gender, Desire, and Christian Spirituality".

One of the pieces was an icon by William Hart McNichols called "Holy Priest, the Anonymous One of Sachsenhausen". Placed on the wall next to it was the text which originally inspired its iconographer. This passage, from Heinz Heger's book, *The Men in the Pink Triangles*, tells the story of an unnamed priest who was interned in the camp as part of the Nazis' systematic attempt to exterminate homosexuals. It details both the terrible abuse to which the priest was subjected, throughout his passion and death, and the heroic faith he continued to show, both in Christ and in the basic goodness of humankind.

Because the narration included the coarse, sexually explicit language used by the priest's tormenters, before the exhibit opened, the sexton questioned whether some of the words should be deleted. I expressed dismay that anyone would be surprised to discover that some Nazi camp guards used crude language; and I requested that the text not be sanitized, especially since the icon honors all who are victims of homophobia.

It was wisely decided that we should not tamper with an eyewitness account. Instead, we placed next to it a sign warning viewers that crude language would be found in the adjoining text and advising any who might find it objectionable to skip the icon altogether and move on to the next image in the exhibit.

Despite this precaution, one person was mightily offended and complained that a church would allow obscene language in a text displayed in its nave. I asked him whether he had read the warning sign. Indeed he had, but he had ignored it and was now saying, "Well, I didn't expect the text to be **that** obscene!"

What I found most disturbing about the man's response was that he had just taken in the story of another human, brutally, sadistically beaten to a pulp by fellow humans – a priest who died professing his faith in Christ and in the basic goodness of humankind – and apparently all that disturbed the complainer was the use of sexually explicit language. What had nurtured such an imbalance of values in a seemingly otherwise decent person who clearly was interested in the exhibit? What led him to read the text anyway, when he had been given clear advanced warning about its contents?

The answer to the second question is easy enough. It seems that, for many humans, from Adam and Eve who were forbidden to eat specific fruit to a child banned from dipping into a jar of sweets, the most compelling way to guarantee that they will be drawn into doing something forbidden is to warn them against it. For Western Christians, there is no subject that has been more hemmed in with warnings than human sexuality.

The answer to the question of imbalanced values is more complex, but related to many branches of Christianity proclaiming the taboo that **every** sexual matter is considered "grave matter". It should not be amazing that some folks have skewed priorities when it comes to the relative seriousness of certain moral issues. I have been a Roman Catholic all my life. When I was a child, I was taught that any un-confessed mortal sin could send a person to hell. In those days, many sins were called mortal:

it was considered a mortal sin either to murder someone or deliberately to eat meat on Friday and **any** sexual activity outside of marriage was mortally sinful. Even as a child, I could see that these were not all matters of equal gravity. But I accepted what I was told and was saddled with a skewed ethic that in the question of a sin's relative gravity might have reduced the gravity of murder to the level of masturbation. Unfortunately, since every sexual matter was considered grave matter (it still is!), the reverse happened. Masturbation was elevated to the level of murder when it came to considering eternal repercussion. This is one way we trivialize serious matter: make everything grave and nothing remains serious.

There is another way. It sometimes happens that people trivialize important matters because they are so overwhelmed by the evil of which humans are capable that they lose the ability rationally to sort things out. The whole event of the Holocaust has affected many people in this way.

A combination of these things could have contributed to causing the man who was shocked at the obscene, abusive language he read in church to trivialize what happened to the original victim of that abuse.

Another dynamic operating in this story is the fact that it is never a neutral thing to combine written words and symbols, which demands that the masculine left-brain (written words) and the feminine right-brain (symbols) work in harmony. If they don't, it becomes quickly apparent when people are out of harmony. When they are combined, words and symbols have the power either to heal and bring peace or to agitate and bring alienation. The power stirred up by religious images and erotic language is great, and combining them can be like putting the flame to the fuse. The man in Toronto was not the first to demonstrate this point to me.

The Living Circle's first location in Chicago was in a public hospital, which was trying, over ten years ago, to introduce and make available a holistic program as a complement to the more ordinary treatments already being offered. We were invited to open our office and chapel there because the staff desired to make available a spiritual component to their already-existing program for the treatment of those living with HIV/AIDS. The chapel was dedicated at a lovely, well-attended ceremony in February of 1994; but it was shut down and the art was removed within four days.

There was more than one reason for this, but the primary one was as follows. Some of the nurses from my own denomination were so horrified at the thought that some of "their" saints were being honored as possible kindred spirits by lesbian, gay, bisexual, and trans-gendered folks that they stirred up a reaction among the hospital personnel. The icons had to be removed lest they be damaged. One nurse said, "These are not the saints I grew up with!" So the curious result was that a group primarily composed of Catholics succeeded in having icons and relics of our own saints removed from a public hospital because they couldn't abide having them in a chapel identified with people who make up over ten percent of the population – several of whom worked at the hospital!

This taught The Living Circle the power of our own images. If they could be catalyst to such negative reaction, imagine what power they must have to heal. The stories about to be told are drawn from the lives and writings of the saints – "our saints" as much as anyone else's since they are the spiritual ancestors of all of who believe. Included are stories of "other" saints and anything-but-saints as well.

The main thesis of a book recently published helps to explain why, particularly at this time in history, the combination of word and image, which is an essential component of The Living Circle's mission, has such a powerful potential for the healing of our planet. *The Alphabet and the Goddess: The Conflict Between Word and Image* was written and published in 1998 by Dr. Leonard Shlain, chief of laproscopic surgery at California Medical Center in San Francisco. Combining an explanation of the functions of the human brain with a large amount of historical research, Dr. Shlain demonstrated that a specific event in history very likely shifted humankind from an earlier matriarchal kind of religion and government, characterized by a high regard for women and for art, to the now predominant patriarchal mindset, characterized by tribalism, belligerence and a diminished appreciation of the critical value of women in every aspect of life and of art as a necessity, rather than a luxury.

The author pointed out that in the prehistoric phase of human development, when our survival needs required that there be both hunters and nurturer-gatherers, men usually took the former role and women, being the child-bearers, took the latter. Over a period of about a million years, the human brain split into two functions – a remarkable development necessitated by the fact that evolution had to "rewire" one of the brain's lobes to accommodate speech. Of the twin hemispheres of the brain, the right is the elder sibling, the "feminine" side, which integrates feelings, recognizes images, appreciates music, holistically expresses and embraces **being**, and perceives the world **concretely**. The right brain is also a major center of dream activity and intuition. The left "masculine" side of brain is more concerned with **doing** than with being. It is the perceiver of time and the agent of abstraction, of counting, of willing, and of speech. Shlain declares that "Words are tools, the very essence of action."[1] Since women have 10 percent to 33 percent more neurons connecting the two lobes of their brains than men, they can generally perform multiple tasks simultaneously better.[2] The ability to keep a broader view and to perform multiple tasks are skills particularly needed by nurturing, gathering mothers. The ability to focus on a single task and remain as unemotional as possible are more desirable tools for hunters.[3]

Along with the human brain, the eyes too evolved opposite but complementary functions. Older than the cones, the light-sensitive rods of the eye share the right brain's ability to perceive reality all-at-once. Rods are a key component in the state known as **contemplation**.[4] The cones of the eye help the viewer to appreciate color and to intensify clarity. The need for cones is particularly acute in predatory birds, mammals, and – the only truly predatory primate – the human; for cones allow the predator to **scrutinize** and to **concentrate**.[5]

Dr. Shlain draws the conclusion that if there was one historic event which fundamentally "rewired" the human brain in a way that shifted humankind to a patriarchal mode, with profound consequences for history, culture, and religion, it was the invention and the use of alphabetic writing. Since alphabetic writing and reading are horizontal, linear functions, they require constant stimulation of the side of the brain used for focus and concentration – the left, masculine, hunter side. It is said that a picture is worth a thousand words. The right brain helps a person to take meaning from the mere glimpse of a picture. But a similar glimpse at an entire page covered with words conveys little; for a page of words must be read to be understood. And reading requires the focus provided by stimulation of the left, hunter side of the brain. While one might think that literacy should broaden a human mind and lead to its becoming more embracing of life in its wide variety of experience and expression, the opposite seems to be the truth. Dr. Schlain demonstrates that a lopsided reliance on the left brain's attributes without the tempering mode of the right-hemisphere has, at several times in history, initially led society through periods of demonstrable madness.[6]

Having survived the 20th century, the most widely literate in history, but also the bloodiest, it is high time for those accustomed to being in control to acknowledge the spiritual imbalance of the status quo and to learn from society's often-overlooked wise ones: those in whom the masculine and the feminine are balanced and who realize that a parallel balancing of words with images is a vital necessity for the healing of this planet. Many lesbians, gay men, bisexuals, transgendereds, and people who are not sure where to place themselves in the wide spectrum of human gender identity or inclination, yet do not identify with the word "heterosexual", can be found among those whose wisdom society tends to discard. Throughout this text, they will be referred to as "distinctive people" - a neutral term intended concisely to embrace all people who either identify with the opposite gender or are erotically drawn to members of their own gender. The reason for this choice is that perfectly respectable adjectives like "queer," "gay," "odd," and "different" have all too often been used either pejoratively or condescendingly in reference to those who constitute the world's non-heterosexual minority. Even the word "minority" itself sometimes raises the hackles of some of the majority who feel threatened.

What special wisdom do distinctive people have? The wisdom that comes from having struggled with their very identity in such a way that they tend to take little for granted, even their own security. Their perpetual minority status makes them easy targets for bullies who love to scapegoat. On the other hand, their hard-won self-acceptance gives them the strength to resist victimization of themselves and of others. Many self-accepting distinctive people are naturally predisposed to becoming carriers and channels of balanced feminine-masculine erotic energy. Among indigenous people in several places throughout the world, distinctive people are regarded as members of a third gender — a mid-gender between feminine and masculine. They are considered people who in their very being are maintainers of balance. Because they stand midway between masculine and feminine, they are presumed to be natural marriage counselors and shamans, able to serve as menders of damaged relationships and bridges between this world and the Otherworld. They are considered particularly blessed and sacred. Among Native Americans, this phenomenon is documented in over 130 North American tribes.[7]

Even as the left brain is the realm of Christ the Word, the right brain is the realm of Christ-Sophia (Wisdom). Distinctive people often have dominant right brains, which is the reason many are artistic, musical, colorful and earthy. It is also the reason they are Sophia's children - and sometimes her prophets. While some make excellent specialists, many tend to be generalists, who are often inclined to take the broader view of things because so many different things stimulate them. While Logos (Word) Christology comes from above, Sophiology (Wisdom Christology) comes from below — from the lived experience rather than from ideas with which people try to shape, control, and judge behavior. Rather than words, images emerge from Sophia's realm — as does the cult and veneration of the saints.

Passionate Holiness is written to remind distinctive people of their important place in the Creator's ongoing effort to save Mother Earth and her inhabitants from the results of human folly. It will do this by telling the stories of forebears who pioneered this mission, some of them the spiritual ancestors of contemporary distinctive people. Just as the public worship in many Churches consists both of Word and of Sacrament — a telling of the Story and a rendering of the Reality Present - so this book will not only treat the lives some of Wisdom's prophets and prophetesses but also demonstrate ways their presence has been mediated to this day by skilled artisans, painters, sculptors, architects, composers, story tellers, preachers, and leaders of prayer. Through the resulting experience of communion with saints, kindred ancestors continue enthusiastically to help and guide us in our roles as healers and preservers of life.

PROLOGUE

According to an anecdote from the sayings of the wise abbots and abbesses who lived in the Egyptian desert in the fourth century,

> *A brother tempted by a demon set out to a certain old man and said to him, "These two brothers are together and they are of evil life." But the old man perceived that he was beguiled of the devil, and he sent and called them to him. And when evening was come, he laid down a mat for the two brethren, and happed them in one bed, saying, "The sons of God are great and holy." But he said to his disciple, "Shut that brother into a cell by himself: for the passion which he would fasten on them he hath in himself."*[8]

One striking feature of The Living Circle's chapel is its collection of original images by several artists. The icons of Robert Lentz alone constitute the largest collection of his work after the reredos in apse of the Cathedral of Santa Fe. The Living Circle icons were commissioned to serve as a permanent non-verbal reminder that all the children of God are great and holy - even those some of our churches are unable or unwilling to embrace unconditionally. It has never been easy for the Church adequately to represent the Lord, who thrice had to repeat to Peter in a vision, "What God has made clean do not call unclean." (Acts 10:15) In the Lentz icons of the TLC collection, some holy people are juxtaposed artistically for the first time in history. St. Boris can be seen with his dear friend and co-sufferer George the Hungarian. Sts. Brigid and Darlughdach, the first and second abbesses of Kildare, stand together, as do St. Elizabeth of Hungary and her beloved husband, Blessed Ludwig IV, Landgrave of Thuringia. And St. Polyeuct embraces Nearchus, just as he does in their story. These two soldiers were intimate friends, one of whom ended up a Christian martyr and the other, the recorder of his passion and death, having assumed something like the role the Beloved Disciple took in writing about his relationship with Jesus.

The story of Polyeuct and Nearchus is quite believable, not only because it is deeply touching but also because it is so messy in a human sort of way. It is clearly not fixed up to make the characters appear more noble than they were. Few people would commend Polyeuct for the unfeeling way he treated his wife. Compared to what is usually recorded in martyrdom accounts, Polyeuct's judge comes off rather sensible and well-intentioned. Also, even though the story begins with the likelihood of martyrdom for Nearchus, his beloved friend Polyeuct ends up the martyr instead. Nearchus apparently survives. There is nothing here of the heroic mutuality that will be apparent in the martyrdom account of the lovers, Sts. Sergius and Bacchus. The story even espouses what will later in history be considered a rather questionable theology of baptism,[9] which was never emended by later editors. So this is a martyrdom story that probably happened just as it is narrated. It is a text that approves of the desire of two men to be together for eternity - even though one seems to be discarding his wife in the process.

This book tells their story and shows the way devotion to Polyeuct in Constantinople became a catalyst to the spreading of other devotions – the most far-reaching being devotion to Christ-Sophia.

In the stories which are about to unfold, the ways the saints lived their lives were obviously considered acceptable, or these martyrs would never have been called "saints".[10] Indeed, the title of saint has been deliberately attached to the names of all those in this narration whom later generations would give feast days in the liturgical calendar. This is done in order to make it even clearer that the nurturing of intimate relationships was considered an acceptable component of a holy life, both to those who lived these lives and to other saints who held them up as exemplary Christians. Later in history, when a more rigidly disapproving majority would believe it had the right to condemn deviance, Europe would experience the persecutions and inquisitions characteristic of the Middle Ages against wise healing women (branded as witches), midwives, Jews, Moors, Cathars, Templars, lesbians, gay men and other minorities.

This kind of official disapproval of what was formerly either overlooked or considered acceptable behavior may be the reason why, in 1969, the Roman Catholic Church dropped Sts. Sergius and Bacchus from the official calendar of the saints, along with Sts. Barbara, Christopher, Eustace, Margaret of Antioch, Ursula and her Companions, and a number of others whose actualhistorical existence was considered highly doubtful.[11] St. Catherine of Alexandria was also dropped at this time. This means that, of the three heavenly voices who spoke to St. Joan of Arc and sent her on her mission to get the French king crowned, Sts. Catherine and Margaret were now no longer considered actual saints, leaving only the Archangel Michael. Apparently there was such hue and cry raised up among the faithful concerning the loss of St. Catherine of Alexandria that, in 2002, she was given back her old feast day. The Ordo declares that "This memorial has been newly included in the Universal Calendar of the revised Missale Romanum, edition typical tertia."[ii] We can only hope that, eventually, a similar restoration will be given to the feast of Sts. Sergius and Bacchus There is no reason to doubt that they existed. It will be seen that evidence for their cult stretches back almost to the time of their death, and the tomb of Sergius became one of the most venerated shrines in the East. It is difficult to avoid the conclusion that the decision to scratch them from the calendar of the saints was based on disapproval of the likelihood that they were each others' lovers.

By the fifth century when it arrived in Constantinople, a cult would develop around St. Polyeuct, which revered him as the protecting saint of solemn vows. Devotions to Polyeuct, to Sergius and Bacchus, and to Christ as *Hagia Sophia* (Holy Wisdom), were greatly enhanced by being nurtured in this city and symbolized in the churches which bore these dedications. Such buildings were visited by countless thousands of pilgrims and tourists. Since Constantinople was the capitol of the Byzantine Empire, devotions observed there spread quickly throughout the Christian world.

The story of the building of St. Polyeuct's church in the Byzantine capital involves tale of spite and subversiveness that typified the way three of the Empire's most famous citizens dealt with each other. All three were Christians engaged in the building of great churches. But they sometimes treated each other with an arrogance and vindictiveness reminiscent of some of the wicked characters in Robert Graves' historical novel,[12] *I Claudius*. Even though they treated each other appallingly at times, they saw to it that the three most remarkable churches in Constantinople were built - churches whose dedications reflect an acceptance of deviance which would disappear later in history. The first was dedicated to a martyr who was apparently bisexual; the second, to a pair of martyrs who were very likely each others' lovers; and the third, to Christ depicted sometimes as an androgyne, sometimes as a woman. When history reads like this, who prefers soap operas?

In the second century of the Common Era, there appeared a group of Christian teachers identified by future generations as the Apologists - writers who tried to persuade the persecuting Roman emperors to stop harassing their Christian subjects. The main purpose of the Apologists' writing was to neutralize slanders against Christians by explaining what they actually believed and how they actually lived, thereby demonstrating that Christians were good people and loyal subjects of the Empire, who prayed for its prosperity and desired only to live and worship in peace. Thus Quadratus and Aristides of Athens wrote to Hadrian; Justin Martyr to Antoninus Pius and Marcus Aurelius; Melito of Sardis to Marcus Aurelius; and Athenagoras of Athens both to Marcus Aurelius and to Commodus. Though their writings provided future generations with a priceless glimpse of the Church in that era, they didn't make much positive difference at the time. Actually, St. Justin's efforts led to his martyrdom.

In a similar manner, in the final quarter of the twentieth century, many apologists wrote on behalf of distinctive people. There are plenty of volumes already available, which amply demonstrate that the churches who persist in either treating gender minorities like second-class citizens or excluding them altogether should stop doing so, both because they are misunderstanding and misapplying the Scriptures[13] and because many distinctive people are lovers of Christ, deeply rooted in their faith traditions. Such apologies have the persuasive power to touch the minds and hearts of anyone open to learning the truth, exercising a healing influence on people getting in touch with their own gender identity or inclination - especially if they are not part of the heterosexual majority and have therefore likely been taught by religion and society to despise themselves. Except for the sole purpose of attacking such apologies, homophobic individuals and churches are generally uninterested in reading anything that might challenge their own prejudice.

But this book is not an apology. Its purpose is not to persuade bigots that their fears are unreasonable and their homophobic language is un-Christian. Its purpose is to help reacquaint us with some often overlooked aspects Christian history. African Americans and other groups seeking to reconnect with their identities are well aware that by separating people from their own histories oppressors found a particularly heinous and effective method of controlling them. As Desmond Tutu, Anglican Archbishop of Cape Town, once said with regard to South Africa's Apartheid policy, "One of the ways of helping to destroy a people is to tell them that they don't have a history, that they have no roots."[14] In a sermon he preached in London's Southwark Cathedral on February 6, 2004, Archbishop Tutu also said, "*I could not myself keep quiet whilst people were being penalized for something about which they could do nothing, their sexuality. For it is so improbable that any sane, normal person would deliberately choose a lifestyle exposing him or her to so much vilification, opprobrium, and physical abuse, even death. To discriminate against our sisters and brothers who are lesbian or gay on Grounds of their sexual orientation for me is as totally unacceptable and unjust as Apartheid ever was.*"[15]

The same anti-erotic sexism which has held women to be of secondary status in many Christian churches has also succeeded in holding churches in homophobic bondage. One way it has achieved this is by ignoring a great deal in Church history and the lives and writings of many of its saints, who honored both *eros* and friendship as essential components of the spiritual life. This book is a reminder that distinctive people have always been part of Christianity's history and have contributed significantly to its theology, spirituality, mysticism, art, music, architecture, and leadership.

Nor is this book a tabloid, whose prurient purpose is to "out" the saints. Indeed several of the saints who will be considered were clearly heterosexual. Unless they choose to reveal it to me, I cannot even know the gender inclination of some of my closest friends. So it's irresponsible to draw such conclusions about people, most of whom lived centuries ago. In the long tradition of hagiographical writing, only Sergius and Bacchus are clearly called each others' "lovers". In what is by far the most common version of their lives – that of the 10th century Metaphrastes – Sergius is referred to at the "sweet companion" and "lover" of Bacchus (ho glukē hetairos kai erastēs). While the Medieval St. Aelred of Rievaulx seems to have been drawn exclusively to people of his own gender, he would have had no understanding at all of homosexuality as an actual category of gender inclination. This notion was explored – and the term "homosexual" created – for the first time only in the nineteenth century. [16] In other stories from the early centuries of the Christian era, the close bonding between some pairs of males were described by writers who, for the most part, falsely presumed that women were incapable of such relationships with men, but could only serve as begetters of their children. The perceptions of those characterizing friendships such as that of Polyeuct and Nearchus and others were likely distorted by such sexism. Many of those who will be considered were monks or nuns; so their opportunities for forming heterosexual bonds – even if they were so inclined – were sometimes severely limited. Also the effusive expressions of passion typical of eras like the Victorian can make some relationships appear to have been more publicly passionate than they may actually have been.

The opinions of so-called experts can be badly skewed by their own prejudices. In 1964, a priest named Girolamo Moretti published a book entitled *The Saints Through Their Handwriting*. In it, he used his expertise as a handwriting analyst to draw conclusions about the characters of thirty-two canonized saints. According to the thinking of that time, he incorrectly presumed that being homosexual was a personality disorder and that "passive sensuality" and "homosexual inclination" were equivalent terms. With such presuppositions, he wrote about St. Joseph of Cupertino that "He also could have...some leanings toward homosexual love, precisely because he is not sexually active, but passive."[17] Of St. Aloysius Gonzaga, he wrote: "His sensuality is easily provoked...and tends to forms of abandonment, a type of sensuality I should term passive...and can easily go against nature.... It would be a grave misfortune if he were ever to acquire the habit of satisfying his sexual urges by himself."[18] These are hardly neutral, objective statements; and the criteria by which the conclusions were drawn are discredited and insulting. When this book discusses *eros* and friendship in the lives of the saints, it is mindful that saying anything on the subject is a potentially explosive, risky business, and that, in the future, readers will likely understand such issues differently and wonder what all the fuss was about. How I long for that day to come! For the present, the most that can be responsibly done is to look at what the saints said, wrote, and did, and also at what others wrote about them - ever trying to be mindful of their personal biases and ours - in order to honor those who were willing to risk forming intimate bonds of friendship with others and who, rather than try either to eradicate, suppress, or sublimate human *eros*, allowed it to be an important component of their spiritual lives.

As we reconnect with aspects of history often overlooked and find distinctive people to have had vital roles in the development of our various faith traditions, healing occurs. Our spirituality is enriched, fresh channels of grace are opened, life is enhanced, and there is more freedom for everyone.

Beyond this, it will be apparent that the sexual orientation which many people abhor in distinctive people is the facet in their lives through which they are revealed to be God's chosen prisms, contemporary reflections of Divine Glory. A cursory reading of the *Acts of the Apostles* might lead one incorrectly to conclude that St. Paul is the narrative's hero, when the real hero is, in fact, the Holy Spirit. Likewise a cursory reading of this book might lead one to conclude that the spotlighting of a few individuals from a vast assembly of saints and scoundrels is its primary purpose, when, in fact, the real thread which connects the saints whose lives I consider is Holy Wisdom, incarnate, acting throughout history in the abiding, liberating Presence of Christ.

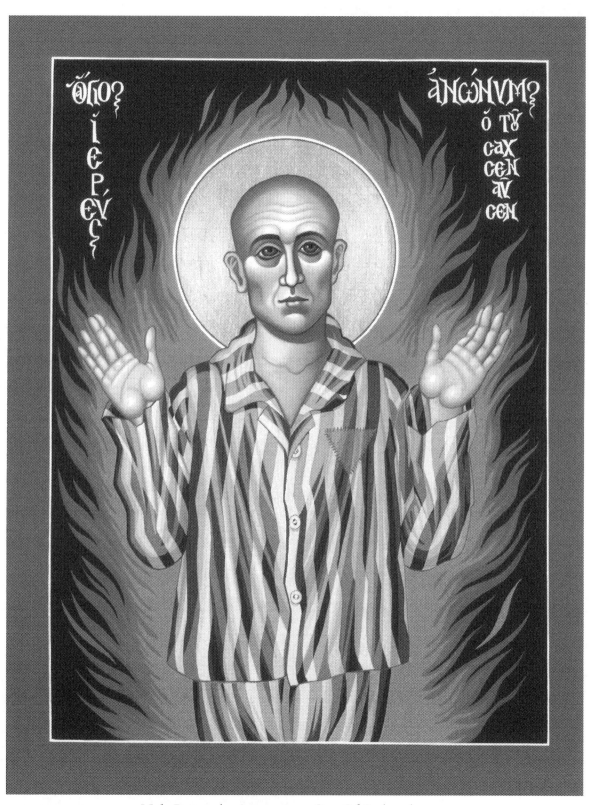

Holy Priest, the Anonymous One Of Sachsenhausen

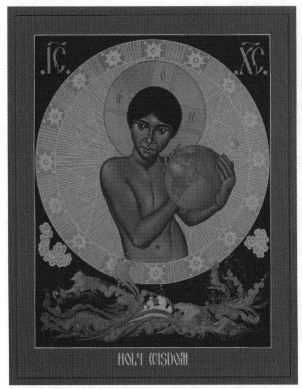

Holy Wisdom

Hagia Hesychia

CHAPTER I
HOW LADY WISDOM BECAME CHRIST THE SAVIOR

It all began with Wisdom. Every aspect of creation as it has unfolded from before the beginning of time, life in its infinite variety, the visible universe and everything unseen or yet to be revealed - all are manifestations of Wisdom, the playful master craftsperson and source of the Creator's delight in the dance of creation. Thus declares the prologue to the compendium of ancient sayings, which constitute the Book of Proverbs. This prologue was probably written sometime in the fifth century B.C.E. at the time when Proverbs was given its definitive form. The manner in which it presents Wisdom as an attribute of God makes her sound like a separate being.

> Yahweh created me when his purpose first unfolded,
> before the oldest of his works.
> From everlasting I was firmly set,
> from the beginning, before earth came into being...
> when he laid down the foundations of the earth,
> I was by his side, a master craftsman,
> delighting him day after day,
> ever at play in his presence,
> at play everywhere in his world,
> delighting with the sons of men. Proverbs 8:22-31[19]

This text reveals that there was a time when at least some Jews believed that God was not alone in bringing creation into being. Of the important Biblical concepts Wisdom, Word, Law, and Spirit, only Wisdom can confidently be said to have been regarded as a personal agent in creation, a belief which is expressed not only in the Book of Proverbs but also in the Wisdom of Solomon, written in the middle of the first century B.C.E.[20] The Hebrew word for "Wisdom" is *Hokmah*. Not only is this term grammatically feminine, but the Bible's depiction of *Hokmah* is also consistently female.[21] The Greek word for *Hokmah* is *Sophia*, also a feminine word.

Elisabeth Schüssler Fiorenza traces origin of the *Hokmah-Sophia* tradition to Egypt, pointing out that several scholars have suggested that Hellenistic Jews in Egypt conceived of Divine Wisdom as prefigured in the language and image of Isis, and other goddesses. Like Isis, Sophia is particularly invoked as a divine savior figure who promises universal salvation. The encomium preserved in the Book of Wisdom 9:18-10:21 begins with the statement that people were saved by Sophia. It summarizes her saving activity in 10:98: "Sophia rescued from troubles those who served her."[22]

After acknowledging that the ancient scholars were well aware of the grammatical rule that so-called grammatical gender was not identical with so-called natural gender,[23] Schüssler Fiorenza agrees with Dieter Georgi in identifying the Alexandrian Jewish philosopher-theologian Philo as the one who was responsible for a deliberate theological "sex change." Philo transferred the attributes of the feminine Wisdom over to the masculine Logos (the Word) who, in Wisdom 18:14-19, is still subordinate to Sophia. He taught that two worlds exist: Sophia's heavenly world of life and salvation and our earthly world of mortality and struggle. Whereas Sophia abides in the heavenly world, her son Logos (the Word) lives in our world, in order to clear the path of salvation for people. By restricting Sophia to the higher world, Philo deprived her of her place as mediator of salvation and as our advocate in this world. Through this turnabout, he attributed to the Logos Wisdom's functions and titles, thereby ultimately identifying the *Logos* with Divine Wisdom.[24]

This shift opened the way to St. Paul's sophiological (Wisdom) Christology. Schüssler Fiorenza has demonstrated that, as far as scholarship can determine, Paul's earliest Christology was sophiological.[25] In other words, when he made his earliest attempt to articulate who Jesus is in the light of the historically unprecedented event of Christ's Incarnation, Life, Passion, Death, and Resurrection, Paul desired to show Jewish Christians where in the Scriptures there is any evidence of Christ's eternal pre-existence. So he chose the one attribute of God presented in Scripture as though it has a separate divine personality of its own. He called Christ God's Holy Wisdom - a grammatically feminine word. This means that before Paul or anyone else identified Jesus with the masculine terms Word of God or Son of God, the Apostle to the Gentiles identified Christ with the feminine Wisdom of God. In Paul's thinking, Jesus of Nazareth did not close the Sophia tradition: he activated it.[26]

Making brilliant use of his training as a rabbi and Scripture scholar, St. Paul presented the God of Israel incarnate in Jesus Christ against a background of wisdom, Torah, creation, and redemption. He made his transition from the Hebrew Bible to the beginnings of Christian theology by identifying Divine Wisdom, described in Proverbs as the delighting and playful pre-existent companion of the Creator, with Christ, the incarnate "Wisdom of God," a Christ who possesses all the fullness of the Godhead and is the perfect image of the Deity. He calls Christ "the mystery of God, in whom every treasure of wisdom and knowledge is hidden" (Col. 2:2-3).[27] Even earlier in his writings, in the First Epistle to the Corinthians (1:24), Paul identifies Christ as "the power and the wisdom of God."

The authors of the later Synoptic Gospels record that Christ Himself made this identification. Jesus clearly identified Himself with Holy Wisdom in this passage in Matthew's Gospel:

> *The Son of Man came eating and drinking, and they say, "Look, a glutton and a drunkard, a friend of tax collectors and sinners!" Yet Wisdom is vindicated by her deeds (Matt. 11:19).*

The Gospel of Luke presents an earlier version of the same saying:

> *Wisdom is vindicated by all her children. (Luke 7:35)*

A modern allegorical treatment of Wisdom mirrors the playful, engaging Christ-Holy Wisdom of the above passages:

> *You never knew where she would be or what she would be doing. At one time she would be telling marvelous tales or singing strange songs to the babies. At another she would be found inexplicably and bitterly weeping, and the next moment swapping outrageous jokes with somebody. Sometimes she was inaccessible at the top of a turret, wrapped in prayer, after which she returned to the family with reports of marvelous visions seen from her window, which upset everybody and sent them off on quests and adventures.[28]*

Perhaps no one should be amazed that, at least on one occasion, Christ's own mother and family tracked him down to bring him home, because rumors about his behavior led them to think he was out of his mind (Mark 3:21,31-34)

The early identification of Christ with Holy Wisdom provides a portal through which distinctive people can discover that they always have a special access to Christ and a vital place in his Church. Christ-Holy Wisdom is a mirror in which they can recognize the presence of Christ in their own inability to fit into the molds others have constructed for them. Being Sophia's children, they cannot be other than they are without insulting their Creator whose very Wisdom is said to take continuous delight at creation as it unfolds according to divine plan.[29]

In the introduction to her book *The Catholic Thing*, theologian Rosemary Haughton explains that her theme is "something called Catholic" but that to call it the Catholic Church is not good enough because "this thing is wider than the boundaries of the vast community so described; and also, many times, parts of that Catholic Church have not been 'Catholic'" in the sense she wants to describe. She then offers an allegory of the twin sisters Mother Church and Sophia. The portion of her description of Sophia above comes from this allegory, as does her characterization of Mother Church who, despite her glory, her goodness, and her faithfulness, has a shadow side, which should be recognizable to any distinctive person:

> *She is extremely inclined to feel that her will and God's will are identical. In her eyes, there can be no better, no other, way than hers. If she is unshockable, she is frequently cynical. She is shrewd, with a thoroughly earthy and often humorous shrewdness. She knows her children's limitations so well that she will not allow them to outgrow them. She will lie and cheat if she feels it necessary to keep her charges safe; she uses her authority "for their own good" but if she seems to be questioned she is ruthless in suppressing revolt. She is hugely self-satisfied, and her judgment, while experienced, is often insensitive and therefore cruel. She is suspicious of eccentricity and new ideas, since her own are so clearly effective, and non-conformists get a rough time.*[30]

Haughton declares that her book is "largely concerned with the antics of Sophia," but that the strange relationship between Sophia and Mother Church is so essential that what she calls "the Catholic thing" acquires its special character from the interplay of that relationship. Put simply, the less any Christian church is inclined warmly to embrace everyone – including its distinctive members – the less catholic in the universal sense it is. The relationship of distinctive people to the Christian Church is therefore vital to its claim of catholicity.

In the first Christian centuries, Christ-Holy Wisdom appeared in the writings of various sects whose ideas about Christ came to be described as Gnostic. Gnosticism is a term which was used to cover a broad cluster of heterodox ideas which the Church had to confront even as early as the Apostolic era. One thing all Gnostics agreed on was a contempt for matter so great that they denied any possibility of an actual Incarnation. In the Gnostic text, *Pistis-Sophia*, Jesus is depicted as a heavenly wisdom figure who ascends and descends from heaven to the waiting disciples in order to disclose to them secrets that they are expected to understand and rituals that they are expected to perform. Nevertheless, the identification of Jesus with Wisdom-Sophia in this book is not accepted universally.[31]

The identification of Jesus with Sophia was much clearer in two other texts - neither of which contains overtly Gnostic teachings.

The *Gospel of Thomas* is the first. Its recovery was as spectacular an event in the twentieth century as the finding of the Dead Sea Scrolls. In 1945, two Egyptian peasants discovered a trove of ancient Christian texts buried in the desert near Nag Hammadi. Among them was a non-canonical Gospel, mentioned in passing by Origen (d. 254) in his first homily on Luke, which St. Hippolytus of Rome (d. 235) attributed to the Nassene Gnostics and St. Cyril of Jerusalem to the Manicheans.[32] By 348, Cyril was warning Christians not to read it. After this, it is no longer mentioned by the early Christian writers.

Now that scholars have had decades to discuss the origin and date of this Gospel, it is generally agreed to have been written no later than 140 - much more likely before 90. In fact, the Gospel of Thomas may be as old as, or even older than Q, (from *Quelle*, the German word for "source")[33] - a compilation of the sayings of Jesus, which was one of the sources for Matthew's and Luke's Gospels. The background of the *Gospel of Thomas* is that of Jewish Wisdom speculation. It is totally independent of the New Testament gospels and most probably was in existence before they were written. Several scholars opine that it should be dated A.D. 50-70.[34]

Like Q, Thomas is a compilation of the sayings of Jesus, some authentic and some not. While He is never called "Christ" in the text, it is clear that Jesus was understood to be the Divine One. Actually, the text may date from before the time before terms like "Christ", "Son of God", and "Word" were the preferred ways of characterizing Christ. While the Gospel, technically, lacks a Christology, it has Sophiology in abundance. As to the question of what constitutes salvation (Soteriology, which focuses on Christ as Savior, *Soter* in Greek) in this Gospel, there is no Soteriology of what is given, i.e., a "grace" Soteriology, but rather a Soteriology of what is found, i.e., a "Wisdom" Soteriology."[35] The Gospel of Thomas frequently speaks of people seeking the Kingdom, but what is actually being sought is Wisdom. "The identification of Kingdom and Wisdom is one key to the interpretation of the Gospel of Thomas."[36] Another key to understanding this gospel is "The identity between all-penetrating Wisdom in the present and primordial creative Wisdom in the past."[37] Thomas is thoroughly a Wisdom Gospel, linking the Jewish Wisdom literature with St. Paul's identifying Christ as the Wisdom of God. One example is Logion 77:

> *I am the light which is above (all things), I am (all things); (all things)*
> *came forth from me and (all things) reached me. Split wood, I am there;*
> *lift the stone up, you will find me there.*[38]

In this passage, Jesus is presented not as a messenger or friend of Wisdom, but as Wisdom personally creating, illuminating, permeating all things. Likewise, He is Wisdom with regard to human existence. He is the light within those who have light, Holy Wisdom, ever coming from the Undivided Father.[39]

In Logion 108, Jesus says:

> *He who drinks from my mouth will be as I am, and I will be he, and the*
> *things that are hidden will be revealed to him.*[40]

Since the metaphor characterizing Wisdom as a fountain appears in the older Wisdom tradition, the implication is that drinking from the mouth of Jesus is the equivalent of from the mouth of Wisdom.[41]

Something noteworthy in the Gospel of Thomas is that Jesus never mentions either marriage or sexual continence. So there is no anti-erotic aspect. On the contrary, for example, He seems to approve of the naked human body in Logion 37:

> Jesus said, "When you strip without being ashamed, and you take your clothes and put them under your feet like little children and trample them, "then (you) will see the son of the living one and you will not be afraid."[42]

This Gospel also has a passage which seems to address the subject of gender-dualism and calls for a frame of mind which should sound like a heavenly home to some distinctive people. Logion 22 says:

> Jesus said to them, "When you make the two into one, and when you make the inner like the outer and the outer like the inner, and the upper like the lower, and when you make male and female into a single one, so that the male will not be male nor the female be female, when you make eyes in place of an eye, a hand in place of a hand, a foot in place of a foot, an image in place of an image, then you will enter the (Father's) domain."[43]

If we recall that, for Thomas, Kingdom stands for Wisdom, then Christ-Holy Wisdom is here telling his followers that, as an aspect of the childlike state to which they must return in order to find Wisdom, they will also have to stop thinking dualistically about gender.

Another second text, which clearly identifies Jesus with Sophia and was also recovered at Nag Hammadi, is called the *Teachings of Silvanus*. It dates to the second or early third century and includes these passages:[44]

> For the tree of life is Christ. He is Sophia; he is also the Logos...

and:

> For since (Christ) is Sophia, he makes the foolish person wise. Sophia is a holy realm and a shining robe. For Sophia is much gold which gives you great honor. The Sophia of God became a type of fool for you so that she might take you up, O foolish one, and make you a wise person.

The image of Christ as pre-existent Word (*Logos*, in Greek) developed a little later than the image of Christ as pre-existent Sophia (i.e. the Wisdom who existed before creation came into being). This identification of Jesus as the incarnate Word then dominated the Christology of the second and third centuries. The most complete biblical picture of the pre-existent Christ as Logos can be found in the Prologue of John's Gospel, which was written after Paul's epistles and the Synoptic Gospels. Logos Christology bridged the earliest Sophia Christology of Paul, Matthew, and Luke and the subsequent Son Christology of the classic creeds,[45] though the attribution of Sophia to Christ remained an important concept to the Church fathers who framed these creeds.

There is a very minor tradition in the history of Christian theology which identifies Holy Wisdom with the Holy Spirit. Only two the Church Fathers, St. Theophilus of Antioch (d. 180) in the East,[46] and St. Irenaeus of Lyons in the West (d. 202-3)[47] both writing in the final decade of the second century, made this identification. This reflects a notion which appeared earlier in Syriac theology, which carried on the Hebrew tradition of the feminine Wisdom and translated it into a feminine image of the Holy Spirit.[48] This can be seen in Odes 19 and 36 of the third-century Syriac hymns called the *Odes of Solomon*,[49] in which the Holy Spirit is imaged as the female power of gestation and birth. It must be said, however, that, throughout these odes, all the Persons of the Trinity have feminine attributes. Ode 8:14 speaks of milk coming to the faithful from the breasts of Christ,[50] and in Ode 19:2-3, God the Father is likewise described having breasts that burst with milk like a nursing mother's.[51] Though these odes do not seem to be Gnostic in origin, since they show no signs of dualism, the complete texts of five of them are quoted as Sacred Scripture in the Coptic text entitled *Pistis Sophia*[52], which had its origin in Egyptian Gnostic circles.[53]

Other than these few exceptions, because the title of Wisdom had already come to be closely connected with the Son, the identification of the Spirit and Wisdom failed to secure general acceptance. [54] Following St. Paul's reference to "Christ who is the wisdom of God and the power of God", all the rest of the Church Fathers identified Sophia-Wisdom with Christ, the Second Person of the Holy Trinity.[55]

Among the Apostolic Fathers, Christ's pre-existence was generally taken for granted, as was his role in creation as well as redemption.[56] Following the logic of the Book of Proverbs imagery, Christ was understood to be identical with the Divine Wisdom ever-present with the Creator. The Greek Fathers considered Christian revelation to be the truest and highest philosophy (philo-sophia), because the content of the revelation **is** Christ, God's Holy Wisdom (Sophia).

Probably the earliest to use of the term philosophy in this sense was Justin Martyr (d. 164), the most important of the Apologists. Justin referred to Christian teaching as the "divine philosophy" (*philosophia theia*)[57] It is divine and surpasses all human wisdom because it is "inspired by the Divine Wisdom or Logos,"[58] i.e. Christ.[59] Justin also said that Christ, "is called Wisdom by Solomon".[60] Athenagoras of Athens (c.177) wrote that "the Son is the Intelligence, Reason, Wisdom of the Father..."[61]

In his treatise, *On Spiritual Perfection*, St. Clement of Alexandria (Titus Flavius Clemens: d.215) described Christ as

> *the Son of God, who was the Father's counselor before the foundation of the world, the Wisdom in which the Almighty God rejoiced. For the Son is the power of God, as being the original Word of the Father, prior to all created things: and he might justly be styled the Wisdom of God and the Teacher of those who were made by him.*[62]

Clement's successor as head of the School of Alexandria was Origen, who has been described as "the outstanding teacher and scholar of the early Church, a man of spotless character, encyclopedic learning, and one of the most original thinkers the world has ever seen."[63] Origen not only equated Sophia with Christ but also stated that Wisdom is the most ancient and most appropriate title given to Jesus.[64] For Origen, wisdom was not simply an inert group of revealed facts or speculations but rather one of the many aspects of Christ, the Wisdom of the Father, by which "the whole creation was enabled to exist." Wisdom was created at the beginning, according to Proverbs 8:22. Origen quoted this text repeatedly. And he insisted that to have wisdom, we must literally have Christ; we must in some sense share in him: "Each of the sages, in proportion as he embraces wisdom, partakes to that extent of Christ, in that he is Wisdom."[65]

Origen identified Wisdom with Christ again and again in his writings.[66] Commenting on a passage in the Song of Songs, Origen made a connection between the breasts of the beloved and the breast of Christ as the source of Wisdom:

> *"Thy breasts are better than wine" (Song 1:2b LXX) is interpreted as referring to ...the inner ground of the heart of Christ upon which John, the beloved disciple, reposed. The treasures of wisdom and knowledge (Col. 2:3) that the perfect soul drinks from Christ's breast are even better than the wine she received from the Law and the Prophets.*[67]

A man converted to Christianity by Origen and subsequently his devoted disciple was St. Gregory Thaumaturgus (d.268), who spent the latter portion of his life as bishop of Neocaesarea in Pontus. St. Gregory of Nyssa recorded that, at the beginning of his career as bishop, Gregory Thaumaturgus felt so overwhelmed by the responsibility and anxious about all the dangers arising from heresies that, for the first time in recorded history, the Virgin Mary appeared, accompanied by St. John the Evangelist, to set his mind at rest. At her request, St. John expounded the faith to him. Gregory recorded what he was taught, and Gregory of Nyssa preserved the text as the Creed of Gregory, a Creed whose teaching about Christ is clearly inspired by St. Paul's Sophiology:

> *One only God, Father of the living Logos, of the subsistent Wisdom, of the Power, of the eternal Impress, who has perfectly generated a perfect (Son), Father of the only begotten Son.*
>
> *One only Lord, the sole from the Sole, God of God, impress and image of the Divinity, active Logos, Wisdom which upholds the whole Universe, and Power which has made the whole creation...*[68]

According to Jaroslav Pelikan, *Proverbs 8:22-31* may have been more prominent in the background to the prologue of John's Gospel than theologians have thus far recognized. And it provided the Church with the basis for its fullest statement of the divine in Christ as Logos - even more than the obvious documentation of John 1:1-14.[69] Unfortunately, the fourth-century Arian controversy seems to have broken out primarily over interpretation the very same text from *Proverbs*.[70] Reflecting on the first line – "Yahweh created me when his purpose first enfolded" – the Alexandrian priest Arius (d.336), concluded and preached that "there was a time when he (the Word) was not." In other words, the Second Person of the Trinity was somehow inferior to the First Person. Perhaps the Arian heresy might not have occurred if this line had been translated more correctly. Bruce Vawter points out that, even though the translation of the Hebrew word *quiānānî* as "created me" is ancient and goes back to the *Septuagint*, a more correct translation is "acquired me" or "took possession of me" of me. This

> *was what Aquila, Symmachus, and Theodotion read out of the Hebrew of Prov. 8:22, beginning a translation tradition that was continued by the Latin Vulgate and the Syro-Hexaplar.*[71]

While the idea that God acquired Wisdom when the divine purpose first unfolded doesn't do much to clarify the Biblical author's exact understanding of the relationship between Wisdom and the Creator, it does remove any reason for concluding that Wisdom was somehow inferior to the Creator.

The historian Socrates wrote a history of the Church, which covered the period between 305 and 439. In it, he records an epistle written by St. Alexander, the Patriarch of Alexandria whose denunciations of Arius led to his condemnation at the Council of Nicaea. Alexander wrote:

> *How if the Son is the Word and Wisdom of God, was there a period*
> *when he did not exist? For that is equivalent to their saying that God was*
> *once destitute both of Word and Wisdom.*[72]

Alexander's chief assistant at Nicaea was his deacon, St. Athanasius (d. 373), who would succeed him as patriarch and who was the man primarily responsible for the wording of the Creed issued by the council. In his writings, he often identified the Son as the Wisdom of God.[73]

The Council of Nicaea was actually called by the Emperor Constantine, who once told a gathering of bishops that he considered himself a sort of bishop:

> *"You are bishops whose jurisdiction is within the Church: I also am a*
> *bishop, ordained by God to overlook those outside the Church"*[74]

Constantine's devoted friend, Bishop Eusebius of Palestinian Caesarea (d. 339), in writing about the relationship between the Word of God and the Emperor, described Christ as the divine Bestower of wisdom.[75] Other Greek Fathers who maintained the identification of Wisdom with the Son were Didymus the Blind,[76] St. Cyril of Alexandria,[77] St. Methodius of Olympus,[78] St. Hippolytus of Rome, who wrote in Greek,[79] St. Epiphanius of Salamis,[80] St. Sophronius of Jerusalem,[81] St. Maximus the Confessor,[82] St. Nilos the Elder (d. 430) a pupil of St. John Chrysostom,[83] the Persian Father, Jacob Aphraates, who describes Christ not only as the Wisdom of God but as the Steward of Wisdom,[84] and St. John of Damascus, whose writings summarized all the dogmatic developments of the Eastern Church.[85]

To this list must be added the Cappadocian Fathers -- St. Basil the Great,[86] his brother, St. Gregory of Nyssa,[87] and his best friend, St. Gregory of Nazianzus.[88] Ministering and teaching in what is now part of Turkey, these Cappadocians had a great deal to do with the final Orthodox formulation of the doctrine of the Holy Trinity, and it was by no means their intention to attribute only masculinity to God in their use of terms like "Father" and "Son". In attributing the feminine Sophia to the Second Person of the Trinity, they were acknowledging that there is a feminine dimension to Christ. However, it was probably inevitable that the male-dominated society in which Christianity developed gradually suppressed the image of Christ as Sophia in favor of Christ as the Son, intending the term to designate relationship rather than gender. Gregory of Nazianzus wrote that the Trinitarian terms "Father" and "Son" did not indicate natures or essences or actions, but are meant to be understood as metaphors for relations.[89] There is much in the writings of the Cappadocians to lead to a conclusion that the Unity of the Trinity is a perfect model of loving relationship, of friendship, and of faith community at its best —this being especially because God **is** Love. (I John 4:16).

As this story unfolds, it will be of interest to observe the way Christian artists' understanding of Christ and envisioning of him influenced the ways they would choose to depict him. At first, probably because of the persecutions, they didn't try to depict him at all. It was safer to use symbols like the cross or the fish. Many of these can be seen in the Roman catacombs. But there are also early depictions of Christ on the walls and ceilings of the same catacombs, which show him as a handsome, beardless young man who has displaced the older gods and demi-gods in some of their classic poses. There is a third century Christ-Orpheus fresco in the Catacomb of Domitilla and a mosaic of Christ as the Sun-God in his solar chariot (c. 300) depicted in the so-called Julian Tomb Necropolis under Saint Peter's in Rome.[90] There are also wonderful free-standing sculptures from the third-fourth century. Two of the most famous from Rome are Christ the Good Shepherd (Hermes) and Christ the Teacher (Seated Apollo).[91] The sculpted youthful Christ, dressed as a philosopher, continues to appear in later scenes which detail moments in the life of Christ, as can be seen on the fourth century sarcophaguses in the Catacomb of Domitilla and St. Peter's in Rome and at Sant' Ambrogio in Milan.[92] By the fourth century, bearded Christs begin to appear in Rome, as in a wall painting from the Catacomb of Commodilla. Because there was no city of Constantinople until the fourth century, and because of the massive destruction of religious art in the Byzantine Empire during the iconoclastic period, it is not very clear precisely how Christ was depicted outside of Italy during the period of persecution. One remarkable and very early exception is the Great Chalice of Antioch, which was fashioned in the final third of the first century and depicts a youthful, beardless Christ, seated and dressed as a philosopher, as well as the other apostles.[93] As will be seen, the earliest surviving attempt to depict Christ-Sophia could still be seen in the nineteenth century in the catacomb of Karmouz near Alexandria, Egypt, long since destroyed, of which we now have only drawings.[94] There, in frescoes which were painted not later than the beginning of the fourth century,[95] Christ-Sophia was depicted as a winged, angelic person. A curious thing is that, given the universality of the theological identification of Christ with Holy Wisdom - both in the East and in the West – there is no evidence that there was ever a church dedicated to Holy Wisdom in Rome, until September 27, 1969, when Patriarch Josyf Slipyj consecrated St. Sophia Ukranian Catholic Catherderal there.

CHAPTER II
THE STORY OF ST. POLYEUCT, A BISEXUAL MARTYR

Polyeuct [96] and his friend Nearchus[97] were both noble soldiers serving in the Roman army, stationed at Militene,[98] in Western Armenia. They were probably part of the Twelfth Legion, called the *Fulminata*, which was stationed in Militene at the time and which, according to St. Gregory of Nyssa (d. 395), included a number of Christians in its ranks.[99] As early as the second century, this Legion could be found in the area with Christian members.[100] Polyeuct was martyred there for his Christian faith, probably in the year 259.

It is not clear when Christianity first arrived in the area, though there are legends that the Apostles Thaddaeus and Bartholomew brought the Gospel to this part of Armenia and were martyred there. From those early days, the Armenians were drawn to the Holy Land as the cradle of their faith. They migrated to many parts of the country and established monasteries, theological schools, settlements and trade centers even before Christian Holy Places began to be recovered. It is recorded that Armenian pilgrims were seen along Roman roads when the army of Titus was approaching Judea. Large groups remained in and around Jerusalem in settlements, which quickly became important centers of religious and intellectual life. In addition to the pilgrims who came to Jerusalem in those days, there were many Armenian soldiers in the Roman army. The Tenth Legion was mainly composed of Armenians from Militene. After the fall of Jerusalem to the army of Titus in 70 C.E., the early Christians fled from there to Pella. The recently born Church was partly dispersed and persecuted in the sense that his short period of exile caused the destruction of all the Christian institutions in Jerusalem.[101]

Armenia became the first and the oldest Christian state when King Tiridates, converted by St. Gregory the Illuminator, established Christianity as its official religion in 301, some twelve years before it became an acceptable faith in the Roman empire.[102]

There was a martyr named St. Eupsychius, who was Bishop of Militene from 238 to 244. At that time, it had recently become a diocese and was considered a part of the Exarchate of Cappadocian Caesarea.[103] During the period Otreius was Bishop of Militene (374-84), his diocese was included in the area over which St. Basil the Great (d. 379), Archbishop of Cappadocian Caesarea, was metropolitan.[104] So during the time Polyeuct lived in Militene, the temporal and spiritual authorities were located in Caesarea.

The earliest account of Polyeuct's martyrdom is an exordium, a theme-setting discourse, first delivered by Bishop Mamas of Militene.[105] It probably dates as early as 363, for it suits the period (363-65), implicit in the narration, when Emperor Julian the Apostate was dead and Christian emblems once again appeared on the standards of the army.[106] The text, which has survived in Armenian, contains and explicitly quotes an earlier Greek account,[107] which was probably the original testimony of Nearchus. This exordium would have been recited annually on the martyr's feast, both at his tomb, and at other churches to which copies of the text had been sent around, as was the custom in those days.[108]

The narration opens by introducing the principal characters, Polyeuct and his fellow-soldier, Nearchus, who are "called brethren; not as being so by blood relationship, but as being so by choice and love of each other."[109] We are then informed that the Emperor's most recent edict against Christians has had a singular effect on Nearchus, so distressing him that he weeps continually and can't even talk to Polyeuct.[110] Since Nearchus will not tell him the cause of his distress, the exasperated Polyeuct finally asks whether he has unknowingly done something, which has so offended Nearchus that he has renounced their friendship.[111] Hesitantly, Nearchus replies that the Emperor's edict may cause a separation between them, which will prevent them from maintaining their old friendship for each other.[112] This astonishes Polyeuct, who responds that he wouldn't have believed that even death itself could have threatened the bond of their love. When Nearchus replies that the separation he has in mind is above and beyond human death, Polyeuct wraps his arms around his neck and implores him to explain the nature of this impending separation.[113]

The dialogue's dramatic effect is heightened by the pleading of Polyeuct, who becomes increasingly alarmed at the thought of any possible threat to his friendship with Nearchus. He even goes so far as to declare,

> *I am ready...to bear accusations and death for my true love of Nearchus. Nay, had I even a child, I would not spare him, if I could indulge my love of Nearchus. Faith, I would reckon it lower than my love of him, and would sacrifice all to keep my affection for him whole and unimpaired.*[114]

Finally and with continuing reluctance, Nearchus reveals that the cause of his distress is the fear that, since Polyeuct is a pagan, if Nearchus should die a martyr for Christ and Polyeuct should later die a pagan, they would be separated in the afterlife. Polyeuct reassures him that he has not only long been drawn to Christianity but that, concurrent with the issuance of the edict, he has had a revelation of Christ – a vision that has led him to identify himself as a Christian. Of course, Nearchus is delighted with this news; but then he begins to fret that the newness of Polyeuct's faith might lead to his backsliding under imperial pressure. Burning with the fervor of a new convert, Polyeuct begins both to recount all he is willing to endure for his faith and to goad Nearchus into making a similar profession. When Polyeuct expresses the concern that, if he should approach the Savior unbaptized, he would not be acceptable to God, Nearchus tells him not to worry about it, declaring that "the approaches to deathless salvation are not shut to anyone."[115] When Polyeuct presses the question, Nearchus replies that "Everything is holy to the holy."[116]

Polyeuct then asks to be shown a copy of the edict and is so outraged with what he reads that he tears it up, goes outside, and attacks a passing pagan procession, smashing the idols being transported. For this, he is promptly arrested and brought to appear before the magistrate charged with the enforcing of the imperial edict. The man turns out to be his own father-in-law, Felix.

Felix, clearly bewildered by his son-in-law's action, tries to dissuade him from doing anything to bring calamity to their house. He asks him to consider his wife and children, but to no avail. Revealing a remarkably cool detachment from his own family, Polyeuct responds that his wife is free to follow him if she likes. Otherwise he looks forward to the heavenly family prepared for him by Christ; and she can expect the same fate as her gods, implying that they are nothing and therefore have nothing to offer her.[117]

Then Felix has Polyeuct flogged, but this only moves the martyr to taunt him. The drama is heightened when Polyeuct's wife Paulina enters, hoping she can persuade him to change his mind. She appeals to Polyeuct to recant, if not for her sake, then for the sake of their son. But he will have none of it. Finally, and with great reluctance, Felix condemns him to death.

Polyeuct uses his little remaining time to converse with fellow-Christians in the crowd. Standing nearby is Nearchus, for, as the narration says, "they were in their bodies twain one spirit and one life." Polyeuct then gazes at Nearchus, bids him farewell, and addresses to him his final words before being beheaded.[118] The original Greek text, which reads, mnēmoneue tōn aporrētōn hēmōn sunthēkōn, translates "Remember our secret pledge."[119]

The Christian community buried his body with honors at Militene. Nearchus gathered up relics of his blood on clean napkins and, some time after the martyr's burial, he recorded that he brought the relics to Cananeots in Egypt. There is no mention made of such a village in ancient texts. However, the town of Coptos, an important port on the Nile River in Upper Egypt, was also called "Cana", or "Caana". B. Aubé concludes that Cananeots probably means "New Coptos".[120] In modern times, sacred oil lamps, inscribed with dedications to Polyeuct, were uncovered at Coptos. They confirm his cult there, indicating the likelihood that there was an oratory dedicated to the martyr at that location between the fifth and sixth centuries.[121]

It is unknown why Nearchus chose to make this long journey to Coptos. Even though there was great civil unrest in Egypt in the period immediately after the death of Polyeuct, which brought Roman military reaction, it is unlikely that a military transfer brought Nearchus to Egypt. He was likely a member of the Roman Twelfth Legion (the *Fulminata*), or possibly the Tenth Legion (the *Fretensis*), but neither of these legions was ever in Egypt.[122] We do know that, in 260, within a year after Polyeuct's death, Gallienus became emperor and stopped the persecution of Christians.[123] So it became generally safe for them to travel where they liked, at least during his reign. In any case, Nearcus was likely to have been in Coptos before Galerius supervised the town's destruction during a revolt in 293.[124]

Nearchus personally recorded the narration, in which the above-mentioned excerpts can be found. This included his conversation with Polyeuct and his friend's subsequent conversion, passion, and martyrdom. He wrote that he himself passed this document on to a certain Timotheus, the Cananeot, and to Saturninus. Timotheus received the record and deposited it in a church built in the martyr's memory in Coptos. It is this story which was preserved in the more extended exordium first preached by Bishop Mamas of Militene at Polyeuct's tomb. It was thereafter read to congregations annually, both on his feast day, January 10th, and on December 25th, the day his blood was deposited in the city of Cananeots.

This deeply moving narration has been heard with reverence by hundreds of thousands of Christians throughout the centuries. Its primary compelling force throughout is the desire of these two Christian men to be together eternally. They are never actually described as each other's "lovers", in the sense of some sort of exclusive committed relationship. Nevertheless the fact that they made their desire to be together for eternity a priority greater than any of their other commitments - greater even than the commitment to life itself - seems to indicate a bond deeper than what is ordinarily characterized as friendship.

Chapter III
The Cult of St. Polyeuct Spreads

Devotion to Polyeuct spread widely and quickly. Aubé points out that there were many fourth and fifth century churches dedicated to him.[125] A church and monastery already existed at his tomb in Militene by the year 377.

One of those who would have grown up knowing about Polyeuct and Nearchus was the famous desert father, St. Euthymius the Great (d.473), who was born and raised in Militene. The birth of Euthymius was said to have been due to the fervent prayers of his parents, Paul and Dionysia, at the tomb of Polyeuct. Apparently unable to have a child, they decided to spend several nights at the monastery there, praying, and perhaps working, for a miracle.[126] This story parallels the biblical narration of the birth of Samuel in several ways.[127] Just as Hannah fulfilled a vow she had made by presenting the child Samuel to be raised in the tent of the Lord, so Dionysia brought her son back to the tomb of St. Polyeuct in a similar act of oblation. According to Cyril of Scythopolis, Euthymius passed most of his years in Militene between the monasteries of St. Polyeuct and of the Thirty-nine Martyrs.[128] He was first educated by Otreius, who was Bishop of Militene from 374 to 384 and by the two young clerics Synnodius and Acacius, who would both succeed Otreius as archbishops of the same diocese. When his education was completed, Euthymius was ordained a priest and became a monk there.

Euthymius apparently brought devotion to this martyr with him to Palestine when at the age of twenty-nine he traveled to Jerusalem. He remained living in the Holy Land for the rest of his days, leaving Jerusalem eventually to live with his friend St. Theoctistus (d.467) in a cave in the desert near Jericho, where they bolstered each other in praying and fasting. Their friendship has been compared to that of David and Jonathan.[129] Cyril of Scythopolis describes Euthymius' friendship with Theoctistus in this way: "He came to love him and grew so united with him in spiritual affection that the two became indistinguishable in both thought and conduct and displayed, as it were, one soul in two bodies."[130] Eventually, Euthymius would establish several other monastic cells in the area. Theoctistus was elected abbot of one of them, composed of monks who had originally come to them from the community at Pharan. From that time on, Euthymius traveled with a young monk, a deacon whom later generations would call St. Domitianus (d.473), also from Militene, who remained his constant companion.[131] Another renowned monk who was a close friend and disciple of Euthymius and Theoctistus was St. Sabas, who founded the great monastery of Mar Saba. Since it is likely that devotion to the revered friends, Polyeuct and Nearchus, as well as the lovers, Sergius and Bacchus, was observed in some of the communities established by Euthymius and his associates, it is worth noting the close bonds that these desert monks formed with each other. They apparently viewed the nurturing of close friendships as an important component of their otherwise rigorous ascetical lives.

Among the monasteries of Euthymius was one built in 428 at Khan el-Ahmar in Palestine, which, after his death and burial there, became a venerated goal of pilgrimage. Domitianus, who ended up *oeconomus* (steward) of this monastery, seems to have died there the same year as Euthymius.

Euthymius was well-known for his opposition to the Nestorian and Monophysite heresies. Named after Patriarch Nestorius of Constantinople, who denounced the custom of calling Mary, the Mother of Jesus the *Theotokos* (God-bearer), insisting that she be called the *Christotokos* (Christ-bearer), Nestorianism is essentially a denial that God became incarnate in Christ. On the other hand, Monophysitism claims that Christ had only one nature (mono-physis) - a divine nature - thus denying him a human will. This deviation from orthodox doctrine was first taught by the old Archimandrite Eutyches, who had for thirty years been head of a monastery of over three hundred monks near Constantinople,

Towards the end of the year 455, while Euthymius was living with Domitianus in a cave at Ruba, on the Dead Sea,[132] the exiled Empress Eudocia paid him a visit. This led to his persuading her to convert from Monophysitism, which she may have embraced originally at least partially in reaction to the fanatical Orthodoxy of her pious sister-in-law and rival, the Empress Pulcheria. If Euthemius and Eudocia had previously been theological opponents, they became one with each other in their devotion to St. Polyeuct.

Eudocia began her career as the beautiful and well-educated Athenian maiden Athenäis. In the year 421, young Emperor Theodosius II chose her to be his wife and empress. Eudocia was the name she took at baptism. She quickly developed a reputation for a piety which was apparently as genuine as that of the saintly Pulcheria, Theodosius's sister. During her years as empress, Eudocia either founded or renewed numerous philanthropic establishments and endowed several monasteries and churches - among them the first church of St. Polyeuct in Constantinople, through which she brought this martyr's cult to the heart Byzantine world. Even though she and Euthymius both shared devotion to St. Polyeuct, there is no evidence that Euthymius knew her before her conversion to Orthodoxy. Since she remained in exile until her death five years later, she must have built St. Polyeuct church earlier in her life and, therefore, learned about the martyr from a different source.

Perhaps the most that can be said on the matter is that it is more likely she became aware of the martyr during an earlier visit to Jerusalem in 438. There were many Armenians and Armenian churches in Jerusalem in the fifth and sixth centuries.[133] Eudocia probably learned about Polyeuct through contact with this community.

A funerary chapel and adjoining monastery of St. Polyeuct was built in the Musrara Quarter of Jerusalem near the Damascus Gate in the middle of the sixth century. It is mentioned by name in a list of about seventy Armenian churches and monasteries in and around Jerusalem, recorded by the Armenian monk Anastas,[134] who came to the Holy Land at the end of that century.[135] A lovely mosaic from the apse of this chapel was discovered in 1894. It depicts many pairs of birds, of varying species, and has an inscription in Armenian, which reads: "For the memorial and salvation of all the Armenians, whose names the Lord knows."[136] Another mosaic was uncovered on this site when a road was being expanded in 1992.

When Eudocia returned from Jerusalem to Constantinople in 438, she brought with her the relics of St. Stephen, the first martyr.[137] She deposited them in the church of her baptism,[138] which had been built by Pulcheria and was dedicated to St. Lawrence.[139] Perhaps she brought relics of St. Polyeuct as well at that time. It is not known precisely when the first St. Polyeuct church was built in Constantinople, but it is likely to have happened during the period after Eudocia's return from the Holy Land in 438 and before 443. Eudocia died on October 20, 460.

Chapter IV
St. Polyeuct Church: the Gauntlet Is Flung

If it was devotion to Polyeuct and her connection either with the Armenian community in the Holy Land or with Euthymius that led Eudocia to dedicate her church in Constantinople to the martyr, it was resentment and spitefulness that seems to have motivated her great-granddaughter to replace it with the biggest, most splendid church the in the city at that time.

Anicia Juliana was likely the wealthiest woman in the Byzantine Empire, and hers was its most illustrious family. In 472, her father, Flavius Anicius Olybrius, became one of the last of the Western Emperors. Both of her maternal grandparents were direct descendants of Theodosius I. Her mother Placidia was daughter of Valentinian III and Licinia Eudocia, who was the daughter of Theodosius II and Eudocia. Juliana herself was born about 462 and married Flavius Areobindus Dagalaifus, a man of German descent. Their son, Flavius Anicius Olybrius, held the consulship as a child, preceding his own father in that role. In 476, the German chieftain Odoacer of Herule deposed the child-emperor Romulus Augustulus, thus formally putting an end to the Roman Empire in the West. Shortly after this, Theodoric, King of the Ostrogoths ejected and replaced Odoacer. At this time, the Anicii family moved from Rome to Constantiniople. Julia's son Olybrius married Irene, niece of Emperor Anastasius I, by whom he had two daughters, but no son. Juliana had reason to expect that her son, with all this imperial blood streaming through his veins, would eventually be emperor.

In the year 512, a popular riot broke out over the addition of a few words to the Trisagion prayer in the Liturgy. Citizens gathered in the Forum of Constantine, threw down statues of Emperor Anastasius, and cried out for Juliana's husband, Areobindus, to be made emperor. But when they arrived at his home, they found that Areobindus had prudently fled. The eighty year old Anastasius resorted to a desperate expedient. He went to the Hippodrome and took his imperial seat, without wearing his diadem and begged the people to refrain from rioting. It worked. They were so touched by his speech that they asked him to put on his diadem, and the riot was over[140]. Areobindus must have died shortly afterwards, for nothing more is heard about him.

Meanwhile, the family of Juliana had demonstrated their loyalty to Anastasius. Indeed, the only apparent area in which they disagreed was theology. While Anastasius was a Monophysite, Juliana remained, throughout her life, committed to the Orthodox faith proclaimed by the Ecumenical Councils. She was on close terms with the Roman Pontiff. She demonstrated her desire for closer ties between the Western and Eastern churches by supporting an embassy of clerics who, after a synod which met at Rome in 515, were sent with the agreement of the Arian Theodoric the Great to Emperor Anastasius. It was led by the Orthodox St. Ennodius Magnus Felix, Bishop of Pavia (d. 521), a relative and acquaintance of Juliana's relative, the philosopher Anicius Boethius.[141] In the year 510, Theodoric had appointed Boethius a consul and his master of offices.[142] That same year Ennodius had led an earlier unsuccessful embassy to Constantinople, accompanied by senators Faustus and Agapitus. During the second attempt at reconciliation, Ennodius received such ill-treatment that he was fortunate to escape Constantinople with his life. If "peacemaking" efforts could lead to such tumult, it is clear that it was risky business for Juliana to support such efforts.

When Anastasius I died in 518, leaving no designated successor, Juliana's son was overlooked in favor of a palace guard, an uneducated Illyrian peasant, who became Justin I. Juliana was not pleased.

Neither, apparently, was Pope St. Hormisdas, who sent her a letter in 519, reminding her of her imperial blood.[143]

The election of Justin marked a dynastic shift, ending the Theodosian line. It was also the last straw for Juliana, who decided to respond by making a dynastic statement – a concrete declaration of her own family's royal past and future in the form of the church of St. Polyeuct. Her new church served as a gauntlet flung down to Justin and picked up by his successor Justinian.[144]

Already well known for her charitable activities, she was said to have filled Constantinople with her good works and to have been responsible for the building of several churches. Among them was a church in honor of the Theotokos at Honorati, across the Bosphorus from Constantinople. In 512, the citizens of that town expressed their gratitude to Juliana by commissioning for her a splendid copy of the *Herbal* written by first century scholar Dioscorides. The manuscript contains 498 miniatures, and its frontispiece shows a portrait of Juliana herself - the only known portrait of this great lady to survive to the present. She also completed the building of the great church of St. Euphemia in Chalcedon, where an inscription recorded that her grandmother, Licinia Eudoxia, had begun construction in 462.[145] When Eudoxia died before anything but the foundations could be completed, the work was continued by her daughter Placidia and son-in-law Olybrius, Juliana's parents.[146] Juliana was also responsible for the building of a church of St. Stephen in Constantinople, probably during the reign of Anastasius (d. 518). Here she placed the relics of St. Stephen that her great-grandmother, Eudocia, had brought back with her from Jerusalem in 439. These relics had been reposing in the church of St. Lawrence, which had been constructed by Eudocia's rival, Pulcheria. It is possible that Juliana exercised a sort of right of "pious spoliation" when she moved these relics discovered by her great-grandmother some sixty years earlier to her new church.[147] St. Polyeuct was her last and greatest achievement.

In building St. Polyeuct Church, Juliana was making a powerful dynastic statement on behalf of the Theodosian line by nurturing a devotion first brought to the capitol by her imperial great-grandmother Eudocia and by constructing next to her own palace as a sort of "family chapel" what turned out to be a church amazing in its ornate, magnificent architectural design.

It was very large (about fifty meters square) and probably domed. But nothing remains of the superstructure. Only its foundations and a great number of carved marble fragments have survived to the present. The latter show the most bewildering variety of ornament: peacocks with tails opened fan-like, stylized palm trees, Sassanian designed palmettes, vine scrolls, basket-work, vases with strange vegetal forms growing out of them. The total effect must have dazzlingly and overwhelmingly opulent and probably inharmonious. It clearly represented a deliberate break with the classical tradition.[148] As far as can be deduced from fragmentary remains, the apse was decorated with mosaics depicting figures against a gold background. And there were other mosaics as well, pieces of carved architectural sculpture, and busts of Christ, the Virgin, and the Apostles, which must have made the interior of the church stunning.[149]

Under the large ambo, a pulpit-like stand from which the Scriptures were read, there was a crypt, which may have been part of Eudocia's original church, though there is no evidence of this. It is possible that some the martyr's relics, which had been transferred to Constantinople early in the fifth century, reposed there. According to a recently published documentary source,[150] the relic of the head of St. Polyeuct was still venerated in his church there in the eleventh century. By the beginning of the thirteenth century, Archbishop Anthony of Novgorod and a party or Russian pilgrims recorded[151] that they saw and venerated this relic in the nearby Church of the Holy Apostles.[152] The head of St. Polyeuct is now located and revered in the chapel of a nun's convent, the Holy Monastery Of the Dormition of the Virgin "Kleiston", near Phyli, in Attica, Greece. Archaeological evidence indicates that St. Polyeuct Church collapsed in an earthquake which is recorded to have happened in Constantinople on March 1, 1202.[153] It was never rebuilt.

Centuries later, a French traveler named Pierre Gilles (d.1550) kept a journal of many things he heard and observed during the years 1544-1547, which he spent in Constantinople. His *Antiquities of Constantinople* presented a sort of walking tour of the city, from ward to ward. In it, the author records an intriguing bit of information:

> *Some modern writers say that at the time of the Emperor Basileus there was a great earthquake that overturned the Church of St. Polyclete and killed all who were in it....the fall of the Church of St. Polyclete from an earthquake crushed to death all who were in it.*[154]

While St. Polyeuct Church was in the heart of the city, Gilles locates his "St. Polyclete" about two miles away, in the area of Hagia Sophia and the Hippodrome.[155] But since there is no "St. Polyclete" listed in any calendar of saints, nor was there ever a church by that name in Constantinople, it is possible that this Frenchman misunderstood the name of the church and recorded a confused version of a tragic loss of life connected with the collapse of Anicia Juliana's church. The two emperors named Basil were too early by centuries, though it is possible Gilles may have mistaken the name Basil for the title "Basileus", which means "emperor".

If there had been any intention of rebuilding St. Polyeuct, the Fourth Crusade of 1204 would have ended such an aspiration. The crusaders conquered Constantinople and drove out Emperor Alexis V, Mortzouphlos, replacing the Angelus dynasty with a Latin one, which lasted from 1204 to 1237. Their subsequent orgy of raping, pillaging and looting the people and city of Constantinople included even this ruined church, which was systematically stripped of its decoration.[156]

Outside the Porta della Carta, the south portal of San Marco Cathedral in Venice, there are two ornamental freestanding pilasters, misidentified for centuries as the *Pilastri acritani*, since they were believed to have come from the church of St. John of Acre. They face what was in the twelfth and thirteenth century the main ceremonial entrance to the Doge's Palace. The truth is that they were shipped from Constantinople, as part of an enormous haul of architectural bits and pieces from the ruined church of St. Polyeuct[157] and that they were originally placed flanking the Porta della Carta to serve as monumental trophies of Venice's having conquered the Imperial city. At least three other capitals on columns at the south-west corner of the facade of the basilica of San Marco are also clearly part of the loot from St. Polyeuct.

Through the following centuries, all trace of the church disappeared under later constructions in Istanbul. It began to resurface only in 1960, when a number of marble blocks were uncovered as part of grading operations around Istanbul's new city-hall at Saraçhane, in the heart of the ancient city. It was easily identifiable because of a flowery and somewhat tedious dedicatory inscription of 76 hexameter lines, which Juliana had carved around the parameters of the interior walls and at the entrance of the church, outside the narthex. This text had been preserved in its entirety in the *Palatine Anthology*, a collection of ancient verses and epigrams, which was compiled around the year 1000. According to a *scholium* on the verses of Juliana's inscription, the church took three years to build.[158] Since Juliana died in 527-28, and the reign of Justinian began in 527, the building must have been completed in 527.

In his *Life of Our Pious Father Sabas*, Cyril of Scythopolis writes about a gift which was sent to St. Sabas (d. 532) as an endowment from Juliana at the time of her death: she gave him her eunuchs. Sabas, the founder of the great monastery of Mar Saba, had been an intimate friend and disciple of Sts. Theoctistus and Euthymius. He had journeyed to Constantinople in 511 in an unsuccessful attempt to persuade Emperor Anastasius I to stop supporting the Monophysites.[159] During his visit, Anicia Juliana and her friend Anastasia, the wife of Anastasius I's nephew, Pompeius, visited Sabas frequently where he was staying to pay her respects and to benefit from his teaching.[160] After Juliana's death, her eunuchs came to Jerusalem and, being acquainted with Sabas since his visit to Constantinople, sought him at his monastery, bringing much money and asking to be enrolled in his community. Sabas had previously decided not to admit any adolescents or eunuchs into the lavra, for he could not bear to see a feminine face in any of his monasteries.[161] Nevertheless, since they were acquaintances, he did what he could personally to reassure and to edify them, after which he entrusted them to the blessed Theodosius for membership in his community.[162]

In his book, *Glory of the Martyrs*, St. Gregory of Tours (d. 594) recounted an anecdote which sums up the way St. Polyeuct Church was expressive of the relationship between Juliana and Justinian I. It also throws additional light on Martin Harrison's statement that "The gauntlet flung down (by Juliana) to Justin was picked up by his successor Justinian."[163]

Eager to get his hands on some of Juliana's legendary wealth, Justinian paid her a visit and tried to flatter her into loaning him her gold in order to finance his wars against the barbarians. He promised to repay her from a tax he would collect after securing the peace. And he promised that people would publicly chant her praises for supporting Constantinople from her wealth. She saw through his deception and shrewdly explained that her income was widely dispersed over her various properties but that, if he would allow her the time to gather it after the harvest, he could inspect what she had collected, after which he could discard or take whatever he pleased.

He went home thinking that he had outfoxed her. But she assembled her craftsmen gave them all the gold she could find in her storerooms, saying "Go, construct plates to fit the measure of the beams, and decorate the ceiling of the blessed martyr Polyeuct with this gold, so that the hand of the greedy emperor cannot touch these things."[164] She then ordered them to attach the plates to the ceiling, thus covering it with pure gold.

When the task was finished, she invited Justinian to come and see what she had collected, after which he could do with it what he pleased. When he arrived, she humbly met him and invited him to pray with her in the family church, which was adjacent to her palace. Since she was an old woman, he took her by the hand as he led her in. After they prayed, she invited him to look up and see what she had done with her wealth. At first he was amazed and then embarrassed. He was too proud of his reputation as a defender of the Christian faith to be thought of as one who to whom it would occur to loot a new church. To cover his embarrassment, he praised the craftsmanship, thanked her, and prepared to leave. To prevent his going away empty-handed, she removed a ring from her finger, with its jewel concealed in the palm of her hand. She handed it to Justinian with the words, "Most hallowed emperor, receive from my hand this small gift that is assessed at more than the value of this gold."[165] On the ring was a Neronian emerald of enormous value. The emperor received the ring with repeated thanks and returned to his palace satisfied.

Devotion to St. Polyeuct in Constantinople became so popular that there was a second church dedicated to him there. Called St. Polyeuktos en tois Biglentiou it was located near the Bronze Tetrapylon of Theodosius I in the Forum of Theodosius.[166]

Gregory of Tours (d.594), in his book *The Glory of the Blessed Martyrs* says that, in his day, in the imperial capital, Constantinople, the most solemn oaths were always sworn in the church of St. Polyeuct.[167] The martyr was considered the protector of vows and the punisher of perjurers. The reason for this would seem to derive more from his last words to Nearchus than from his marriage vows to Paulina; for he had been willing to leave behind a wife, to whom he had vowed marriage for the sake of an eternity with a man to whom his dying words were: "Remember our secret pledge". Gregory even mentions an occasion when Frankish kings Guntram and Childebert II swore an oath by St. Polyeuct, supported by the French saints Hilary of Poitiers and Martin of Tours, calling on them as witnesses and as punishers of either king who might perjure himself.[168] This is clear evidence that devotion to Polyeuct as the guarantor of formal oaths had spread to the West by then. Since this was now considered his special role, it should not be surprising that there were churches dedicated to him throughout the Empire. Members of the Imperial Court carried his cult abroad. The Hieronymian Martyrology mentions that in Ravenna there was an oratory dedicated to St. Polyeuct.[169] The feast commemorating the dedication of this oratory was celebrated annually in Ravenna on April 9.[170] There was also a St. Polyeuct listed among those stational churches which existed in the city of Metz in the eleventh century.[171] existed in the city of Metz in the eleventh century. It was reconstructed between the thirteenth and the fifteenth centuries and rededicated to St. Livier. Suppressed in 1791, it is now an impressive ruin.

During all the intervening centuries after the Fourth Crusade, both in the Eastern and Western Churches, little interest has been shown in remembering Polyeuct and Nearchus. Quite the contrary. The memory of Polyeuct and Nearchus has been carried to the present more by the Muses than by the churches.

Even though the prescribed manner for depicting Polyeuct is shown with a complete drawing in the Stroganov *Patternbook*.[172] and described twice in Dionysius of Fourna's manual,[173] with rare exception, artists seem to have stopped depicting Polyeuct centuries ago, and Nearchus has apparently never been depicted until now in the icon painted by Robert Lentz.

One of the most enigmatic of the masterpieces of tenth and eleventh century Byzantine metal craftsmanship looted from Constantinople during the Fourth Crusade, and currently in the treasury of San Marco in Venice, might originally have served either as a household icon or as a book cover. It is a beautifully executed depiction of St. Michael, enameled and raised in relief by tapping from behind. On the reverse, among the many other saints which frame a central cross, there is a tiny round depiction of St. Polyeuct.[174] Otherwise, the only icon of Polyeuct still extant depicts him with Sts. Eustratius and Artemius on one of the double-faced tablets painted for St. Sophia Cathedral in Novgorod from the end of the fifteenth to the beginning of the sixteenth centuries.[175] This set of tablets was produced by the Archbishop's workshop, the biggest icon-producing establishment In the city of Novgorod, most probably during the time of Archbishop Gennady. . Also, there is a fourteenth century fresco of St. Polyeuct on an arch in one of the churches in the monastic complex at the Patriarchate of Peć, the administrative center of the Serbian Orthodox Church. While the feast of St. Polyeuct remains on the calendars of most churches, his cult has been all but forgotten.

The text of Bishop Mamas' homily was evidently the source from which the principal representative of Byzantine hagiography, St. Symeon Metaphrastes ("the translator"), derived his account of St. Polyeuct's life, recording it in the latter portion of the tenth century. Symeon, who was secretary of state to Emperor Romanus II (959-963), had already gained fame as a writer from the collection of saints' legends (*Menologium*) he had undertaken at the request of Emperor Constantine VIII

Porphyrogenitus (912-19, and restored 945-59). Unfortunately Metaphrastes was more interested in the ethical than in the historical side of his work. So instead of compiling the ancient acts and lives of the saints in their original form, he rewrote and polished them, adding marvels and horrors from unreliable traditions.[177]

Cyril Mango places Symeon's work in the context of a characteristic tendency of the Middle Byzantine period to heap ridicule on the style and the detail found in original accounts of the saints' lives. Now, instead of appreciating the candor and the specific details that gave a flavor of uniqueness and authenticity to some of these narrations, "primitive" became an adjective for "ugly", and style became everything. Even though Metaphrastes wrote in acceptable Greek, what he did in effect was to take a corpus of texts that had all the liveliness and the particularity of a given milieu and reduce them to a set of pious clichés. He suppressed concrete detail and paraphrased inelegant terms. If he thought a martyr's answers to his torturers insufficiently resolute, he improved them.

> *It may be an exaggeration to say that the Metaphrast spelled the death of Greek hagiography, but he certainly contributed to its emasculation while also causing the disappearance of many earlier texts which he paraphrased.*[178]

Metaphrastes started a trend which led to centuries of wanton revision early Christian texts, often leading to irretrievable losses.[179]

This having been acknowledged, it is rather remarkable that Symeon still preserved much of the original flavor in characterizing the bond between Polyeuct and Nearchus, by writing that they

> *were bound to each other by a friendship which was much stronger than blood or relationship, from which passionate union their souls were tightly bound together, each believing that he lived and breathed wholly in the other's body.*[180]

Metaphrastes also states specifically that Polyeuct embraced death for love of Nearchus.[181] A translation of Symeon's narrative from Greek to Latin is contained both in a revision published in 1551 by the Venetian Aloïsio Lippomani and in the compilation *De Probatis Sanctorum Historiis* (Cologne, 1570), edited by the German Carthusian Surius and completed by another German named Mosander.[182] It is characteristic of the way St. Polyeuct was all-but-forgotten during this period that Pierre Gilles, who died the year before the publication of the first Latin translation of the martyr's life, could accidentally have substituted the name Polyclete for Polyeuct in his *Antiquities of Constantinople*.

Yet Polyeuct has never disappeared from compilations of saints' lives. Nevertheless, it is ironic that from the sixteenth century on, rather than the Christian Church, it has been, primarily dramatists, historians, librettists, and several composers who helped keep alive the story of Polyeuct and Nearchus.

In 1632, a play entitled *Polietto* was published in Rome, together with six other tragedies written by an Italian dramatist named Girolamo Bartolommei. It is unclear what source the playwright used and uncertain whether his play ever became known to Pierre Corneille, the more famous writer who next took up the theme. (Romain Rolland describes Bartolommei as a "musical dramatist" and opines that he probably did inspire Corneille,[vi] though it is not known which composer worked with Bartolommei to produce his own play.) It is noteworthy that Bartolommei's other martyrdom play,

Teodora, was based on a story also used by Corneille in *Théodore* – another reason for suspecting that an awareness of *Polietto* influenced the French dramatist's subject choice. Pierre Corneille also based his tragedy *Polyeucte* (1641-41) on the translation of Surius and Mosander. In his introduction to this play, Corneille admitted to introducing several novelties, most notably a supposed former boyfriend of Paulina's named Severus. He also greatly diminished the role of Nearchus, turning him into a minor character. Marc-Antoine Charpentier composed *Le Ballet de Polieucte* to accompany a performance of this play at the Jesuit Collège d'Harcourt on August 8, 1680. Heinrich Elmenhorst was a German hymnographer, who was best known for his defense of opera. It was mainly due to his efforts that the first opera stage in Germany was established in Hamburg in 1678. He himself wrote the librettos to a couple of operas and did a translation of Corneille's *Polyeucte*, which was set to music by German composer Johann Philipp Förtsch (1652-1732) and entitled *Der im Christentum biss in den Tod bestädige Märtyrer Polyeuct*. It was first performed in Hamburg in 1688. Johann Adolph Scheibe (1708-1776), a German music critic and composer to the Danish court, composed incidental music for Corneill'e *Polyeucte*. The original text of *Polyeucte* was fairly closely followed when it was later turned into a libretto by Salvatore Cammarano and became the successful opera *Poliuto*, composed in 1838 by Gaetano Donizetti. Charles Gounod also composed an opera *Polyeucte*, based on Corneille's tragedy, with a libretto by Jules Barbier and Michel Carré. First performed on October 7, 1878, it was so panned by the critics that it was ignored in operatic repertoire down to the recent present. This is especially unfortunate, because it was Gounod's favorite among his operas. This opera was recently recorded and finally made available to the public. In the April 22, 2005 issue of Opera News, the reviewer wrote that "There really is one valid criterion (for judging this opera in the present): Is the music beautiful? The answer to that question is a resounding "Yes!!!!" Flemish composer Edgar Pierre Joseph Tinel composed a beautiful *Polyeucte Overture*, which is now available in recording. He wrote three symphonic tableaux to Corneille's *Polyeucte* between 1872 and 1882. Consequently this Overture is not real theatrical music, but more of a symphonic poem. Paul Dukas also composed a programmatic overture for Corneille's *Polyeucte* in 1891. it had a successful first performance – his first success – at the Concerts Lamoreux on January 23, 1892 and is still performed and recorded.

The year 1894 marked the beginning of a century in which the remains of some of the churches dedicated to St. Polyeuct began to resurface under the observant supervision of archaeologists. The Musrara mosaic in Jerusalem was uncovered that year. In 1960, St. Polyeuct church in Istanbul was discovered accidentally and then systematically excavated. Another mosaic from the Jerusalem chapel was found in 1992.

In the Armenian Calendar, St. Polyeuct's feast is kept on July 12th,[183] though, according to John Boswell, the Armenians have celebrated his feast January 9th, probably since the fifth century.[184] In the Greek Church, it is on January 9th. According to the Roman calendar, his feast is on February 13th; the Syrian Martyrology remembers him both on January 7th and on February 14th; and St. Polyeuct's feast was observed on January 22nd in Nicomedia and on May 20th in Cappadocian Caesarea.[185]

CHAPTER V
MEANWHILE, ELSEWHERE IN TOWN: ST. MATRONA OF PERGE AND HER OTHER NUNS WHO DRESSED AS MEN

If St. Sabas was concerned about eunuchs and feminine faces in his monasteries, perhaps one of the reasons was his familiarity with stories of numerous women who had lived for years in male monastic communities, undetected because they had disguised themselves as men. Among them were the legendary St. Pelagia (also called Marina, or Margaret), who, after having begun a career as a dancer in Antioch, retired to Jerusalem, where she passed the rest of her life as a penitent on the Mount of Olives, passing as a hermit named Pelagius. She supposedly died c.457 and has been venerated in Jerusalem at least since 530.[186] There was also the story of the Alexandrian St. Euphrosyne. In order to escape marriage, she dressed as a man and got herself accepted into a monastery, where she passed as the monk Smaragdus until she died 38 years later in 470. Then there was the legend of St. Anastasia the Patrician, who is said to have lived in Justinian's court, until she was so harassed by Empress Theodora that she fled to Alexandria, where she established a community of nuns. She later retired to a cave dressed in men's garments. There she passed as the "eunuch Anastasius" until she died 28 years later in 567.

More fascinating than the others was St. Matrona, because she was unquestionably an historical figure who, in her old age, opposed the Monophysite policies of Anastasius I. The chronicler Theophanes (d. 818) includes the monastic communities of Basianos and Matrona among those who were pressured by the Emperor, acting through his patriarch, Macedonius II (d.511), to support him. When they refused, he decided to desist his harassing them.[187] This would have happened c. 500. Matrona is documented in the *Ecclesiastical History* of Theodore Lector (c.525), which narrates some of the details of her life and discusses the career of St. Basianos.[188] St. Sabas would surely have heard of her, since he visited Constantinople during a period when she lived there and was known to have exercised great influence. A contemporary biographer says that her story is a happy one, "because she succeeded in becoming all she wanted to be."[189]

Matrona was born in Perge, in the province of Pamphylia, Asia Minor. There she married Dometianos, by whom she had one child, a daughter named Theodote. When Matrona was twenty-five, the family of three moved to Constantinople. This move was her idea, because she was bored with being a conventional upper-class provincial wife. Once in the Byzantine capital, despite her husband's strong objections, she began to spend great amounts of time visiting various churches and saints' shrines and participating in all-night vigils. Because she was out all night, Dometianus accused her of behaving like a whore and tried to force her to stay at home. She badgered him into changing his mind and then went off to visit the church of the Holy Apostles. There she met two pious older women named Eugenia and Susanna, who befriended Matrona and began to initiate her into the ascetical life.

Matrona decided to withdraw from the world. Since her husband would never give his approval, she knew she would not be allowed to become a nun. So the three women plotted a means of escape for her. Eugenia devised a plan whereby Matrona would disguise herself as a man and present herself for membership in the community of St. Basianos, a Syrian Abbot and monastic entrepreneur, who, during the reign of the Emperor Marcion, had established his monastery near several other monastic communities, all located just within the walls of Constantinople.[190] Susanna agreed to take care of little Theodote, who died shortly afterwards. Later, when Dometianos accused Eugenia of masterminding the plot, she cooly denied ever having known Matrona.

Matrona passed herself off as the frail eunuch, Babylas, and came to be regarded as one of the most outstanding monks in this monastery during the three years before she was discovered to be a woman, because of her pierced ears.[191] When word reached Dometianos that she had been identified, he came after her. She fled to Susanna, who hid her in her home temporarily, while Basianos arranged to have her sent to the convent of St. Hilara in the Syrian city of Emesa.[192] Her determined spouse pursued her there. Assisted by women all along the way, she fled again, first to Jerusalem, and then to Sinai. Finally, he gave up the pursuit.

She then retired to Beirut and took up residence in a ruined pagan temple, where she developed a reputation as a holy woman and an inspired teacher. Between 472 and 474, she returned to Constantinople with a woman companion – both disguised as men. There Basianos eventually assisted her in founding, near his own monastery, the convent which she headed until her death.

> Basianos "ordained her bishop, one might say, of souls." And he gave her "authority to 'lay hands' on others." At the same time, the venerable abbot granted Matrona a unique privilege. She and the nuns of her convent were allowed to dress like monks. "He did not give her woolen girdles and veils such as women were accustomed to wear, but men's wide, black leather belts and men's white mantles. And these they wore continuously." At the beginning of her ascetic career she had disguised herself in monk's clothing in order to hide from her husband. Now she wore the monk's habit openly, with the blessing of Abbot Basianos.[193]

Since Basianos was not himself a bishop, he could not literally have ordained Matrona to the episcopal order,[194] but it is clear that he gave her an authority over her community which was considered most extraordinary.[195]* Since she no longer needed to disguise herself, she and her sisters would seem to have chosen to dress as men simply because they preferred it over dressing as women.[196]

During the time Anicia Juliana lived in Constantinople, Matrona was a well-known and revered abbess. She had been spiritual advisor to the Empress Aelia Verina, consort of Emperor Leo I (d. 474). The Augusta Verina was impressed with the "manliness of her purpose"[197] and with the fact that Matrona requested no favors.[198] In the next century, Matrona would also be visited by Augusta Euphemia, the wife of the former Roman Emperor Anthemios,[199] who valued both her advice and her healing abilities. Towards the end of her life, probably recalling her own past troubles with Dometianus, Matrona advised a wealthy young aristocratic woman named Athanasia on how she might best manage to get away from her husband - basically by biding time and telling him nothing of her plans.

Shortly before her death, Matrona had a vision of paradise, in which he saw beautiful mansions, surrounded by luxuriant gardens, and majestic women walking among the flowers. Since for most of her long life Matrona had lived in communities of women, her understanding of paradise would naturally be the same.[200] She died on November 9, 524, at the age of approximately one hundred years, and was succeeded as abbess by the deaconess Mosilia. Matrona's feast was kept on the date of her death at her convent in Constantinople at least until the twelfth century according to a twelfth-century manuscript of the *Synaxarion of Constantinople*.[201] Her story was recorded by an anonymous nun from her own community, relying both on oral traditions preserved in the convent and the memoirs of what she had seen and heard written by an eyewitness a nun named Eulogia, who was long associated with Matrona.[202]

* Appendix A Matrona's contemporary, St. Brigid of Kildare, is a more likely example of a woman ordained a bishop.

CHAPTER VI
STS. SERGIUS AND BACCHUS CHURCH: THE GAUNTLET IS PICKED UP

At the time Juliana tricked Justinian out of taking her gold, he and his Empress Theodora resided at their private home, the Hormizdas Palace. It had been Justinian's home while he was still heir presumptive to the throne. That same year, 527, Justinian and Theodora were crowned on April 4th. Consequently, during this period, they would likely have moved into the Imperial Palace and connected the Hormizdas Palace to the palace proper.[203]

In many ways an enigmatic man, Justinian was proud and opinionated and could be ruthless. In controversies, especially those of a religious nature, he would entrench himself on one side and persecute any opposition. Since he considered union with Rome vital to the interests of his empire, he supported the Orthodox cause and persecuted the Monophysites, even though he had a genuine respect for some of their leaders.

On the other hand, Theodora could get anything she desired from him. For, while Justinian generally gave an impression of self-possession and of great strength, in fact, he could be rather vacillating, indecisive, and easily influenced by stronger wills than his own. And Theodora clearly had the stronger will. She was beautiful and remarkably intelligent, graceful and witty, with a fine sense of humor. Most of all, she had a logical, firm mind. She was so sure of herself, she could be authoritarian and vehement. From the first moment they met, Justinian was completely smitten with love for her. And until the day Theodora died (of cancer on June 29, 548), Justinian remained true to the boundless passion for her that she had kindled in him when she was young.[204]

If we may believe Procopius's *Secret History*, Theodora's father, Acacius, had been a bear-keeper in the Hippodrome. Raised by her widowed mother to be a dancer in the same establishment and an actress like her sisters Comito and Anastasia, she became a well-known and widely-traveled courtesan and, eventually, Justinian's mistress. In order to marry her, he persuaded his uncle, Justin I, to abolish the existing law which forbade senators and other high ranking officials from marrying servants, daughters of innkeepers, actresses, and courtesans. Not only clever and charming, she could also be despotic, haughty, ruthless, and violent. But she had a softer and more generous side too and was always quick to intervene on behalf of wives mistreated or unhappily married. It was largely through her influence that laws were instituted making it a crime punishable by death to entice young girls into a life of debauchery.[205] Theodora was as opinionated as Justinian, and she knew she could rely on his devotion to her to remain intact even when she publicly ignored his edicts. In a patriarchal ploy used by men who feel that control has either been lost or given over to women, Procopius even went so far as to claim, in his *Secret History*, that Theodora was a lifelong student of sorcery, which she used to maintain her control over Justinian.[206]

Though opinions varied concerning the reasons, it was manifest to everyone that, while Justinian opposed Monophysites, Theodora loved them and did all she could to help them. Earlier in her life, she had been discarded by a lover and left destitute in the streets of Alexandria, forced to wander wherever she could to survive. One of the things she witnessed during this period was the severity of the Emperor Justin's persecution of Monophysites. Some of them had helped care for her during this difficult time, and one of them became a lifelong friend of hers. This was St. Severus, Monophysite Patriarch of Antioch, who was in Alexandria at that time, banished from his diocese.[207]

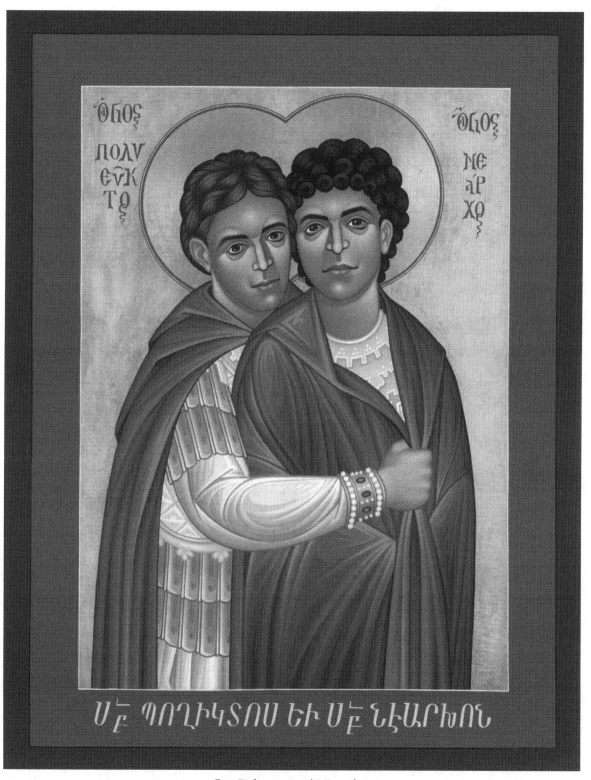

Sts. Polyeuct and Nearchus

Sts. Sergius and Bacchus

His career as a bishop had been launched by the learned and devout Monophysite Emperor Anastasius I. After a twenty year reign, during which he had made no significant changes, suddenly, in 511 he initiated a policy of making the Empire Monophysite, aided by Severus, whom many considered a great theologian as well as the inspiring leader of Syrian Monophysitism. Bishops were abruptly deposed in Constantinople, Antioch, and Jerusalem, and Monophysites put in their places. Severus was appointed bishop of Antioch,[208] replacing Patriarch Julianus, a man respected for piety, learning, and Orthodoxy.

One of the last things Julianus had done before being deposed was to dedicate the recently completed cathedral of Bosra to the Syrian martyrs, Sts. Sergius, Bacchus, and Leontius.[209] The Cathedral of Bosra's architectural importance lies in its innovative early attempt to make the transition from square plan to circular dome that characterizes Byzantine churches, most especially its direct successor, the Church of SS. Sergius and Bacchus in Constantinople. Another Syrian example of this sort of experimentation is the centralized church of St. Sergius at Resapha.[210] The Cathedral of Bosra was completed between September of 512 and March of 513, so Julianus may have been expelled from his See the same year the cathedral was opened.[211]

Emperor Anastasius I died on July 9, 518, and within a month everything was turned about. Justin became Emperor and drove Severus out of Antioch as part of the beginning of a persecution of Monophysites, which was vigorously to be continued by his nephew Justinian I.

One of the results of this persecution was a permanent schism in the Jerusalem Christian community. For about a century after the Council of Chalcedon in 451, which condemned Monophysitism, all the Christians in the Holy City remained under the authority of the patriarch of Jerusalem, sharing common places of worship. But Justinian's persecution of the Monophysites, among them by this time the Armenians,[212] led to many Monophysite clergy abandoning their monasteries in Jerusalem and going elsewhere in the Holy Land. Meanwhile, those who remained established a distinct episcopal hierarchy independent of the Greek patriarch, who was supportive of the Orthodox Chalcedonian position. Henceforward, the see of Jerusalem was split into the Greek patriarchate, which exercised authority over the Chalcedonian Christians, regardless of nationality or language, and the independent Armenian hierarchy, who had authority over the Monophysite communities, that is the Armenians, Jacobite Syrians, Copts, and Abyssinians.[213]

As Empress, Theodora added to her personal affection for Monophysites the sensible concern that Justinian's persecuting them might lead to the Empire's loss of Syria and Egypt. So she publicly disregarded her husband's edict, knowing she could get away with it, and gave refugee Syrian Monophysite monks asylum in the Hormizdas Palace, formally turning it into a monastery. This is mentioned in the *Lives of the Eastern Saints*, written by John of Ephesus, who probably resided in this monastery from 542 onwards,[214] and recorded that, at its height, this community numbered as many as 500.[215] Theodora's activities were such common knowledge that the only way people could explain them was by supposing that the Emperor was fully aware of what she was doing, and that both of them had decided on this scheme because they thought it would put them in a stronger position in dealing with both sides. [216]

These monks brought with them devotion to the two chief martyrs of Syria – Sts. Sergius and Bacchus - whose relationship appears to have had an intensity similar to that of Polyeuct and Nearchus.

Sergius and Bacchus had been Roman soldiers, officers in the household of Emperor Maximian (though it is possible that it was actually Maximinus Daia). Sergius is said to have been in charge of the school for young military recruits at Trieste, and Bacchus was a subaltern officer. They were martyred c.309 for refusing to be present when Maximian presided at the worship of Jupiter.[217] The earliest account of a big gathering to celebrate their feast can be found in the writings of Theodoret, Bishop of Cyr (near Antioch), who died in 466.[218] The precise date of the oldest Greek account of their martyrdom is uncertain, though the best guess is within a century or so after their death.[219] According to the narration, they were each other's lovers.[220] In an unsuccessful attempt to humiliate these soldiers, the emperor forced them to wear women's clothing and walk through the streets of Arabissus, in Cappadocia, after which they were tortured so severely that Bacchus died and was buried there. According to the account of their passion and martyrdom, after Sergius was returned to prison that evening, deeply depressed and heartsick at the loss of his lover,

> *Bacchus suddenly appeared to him with a face as radiant as an angel's, wearing an officer's uniform, and spoke to him: "Why do you grieve and mourn, brother?....If I have been taken from you in body, I am still with you in the bond....Hurry then, yourself, brother, through beautiful and perfect confession to pursue and obtain me when you have finished the course. For the crown of justice for me is to be with you."* [221]

This is a unique statement in the annals of the martyrs. Usually what is promised to a dying martyr is the beatific vision of God, union with Christ, the joy of heaven, or the communion of saints. Only in this account is the promised reward after death a reunion with the lover.

With nails in his boots, Sergius was then forced to run to Resapha (Augusta Euphratasiae) in Syria, where after more torture, he was beheaded.

Empress Theodora's friend Severus of Antioch was devoted to these lover-martyrs and would have acquainted her with the details of their story. When the tomb of Sergius, rather than Bacchus, began to gain international fame as the goal of Eastern pilgrimage, second only to the shrines in the Holy Land, some churches ended up dedicated only to Sergius. However Severus of Antioch insisted that he had to mention Bacchus and Sergius together because 'we should not separate in speech those who were joined in life.'[222]

This same Severus composed a beautiful homily in Syriac in honor of the two saints. In it, he preserved most of the details recorded in the Greek account of their passion and martyrdom: Sergius and Bacchus were, respectively, first and second in the emperor's service. Severus even gives the same number of miles as the Greek versions that Sergius was forced to run in boots with nails, between the place where Bacchus died, and the place of his own martyrdom. On the other hand, he expands some details, pointing out that they not only loved each other but actually resembled each other in size, appearance, greatness, and youth of body and soul. And he says that, in response to the emperor's forcing them to wear women's clothes their reply was that since wearing female attire does not prevent many women from honoring God, it should hardly impede them.[223] His narration of the rest of the story closely follows the earlier Greek account.

The tomb of Sergius became such a famous shrine that, in 431, Bishop Alexander of Hierapolis built a magnificent church there in the martyr's honor. In 434, Augusta Euphratasiae was raised to the rank of an episcopal see and renamed Sergiopolis. St. Sergius was apparently considered too important to be left undistrubed in his original tomb. Emperor Anastasius I had a relic of the martyr's thumb removed from the basilica of Sergiopolis to Constantinople.[224] Subsequently, relics of the two martyrs were widely dispersed to the innumerable churches dedicated to one or both of them throughout Syria, Arabia, Iraq, Iran, the Peloponnesus Crete, Caria, Isauria, and elsewhere. Sergius and Bacchus came to be regarded as the special patrons of Syria, with many churches there named after them. To this day, there is a Greek-Catholic St. Sergius (Mar Sarkis) Monastery at Ma'lula, Syria. It dates back to the fourth century, when it was also named an episcopal see. In those days it was called Seliocopolis. The church was probably built sometime between 313, when the Edict of Milan ended the persecution of Christians, and 325,[225] the year of the First Council of Nicaea, in which a Bishop Eutichius of St. Sergius in Maaloula is listed among the participants. The altar has been carbon-tested for age and dates back to 300 C.E., so Ma'lula may have been a Christian center already during the lifetimes of the two martyrs, and then subsequently dedicated to them some time after their martyrdom[226] One very early dedication to Sergius is at the site of the monastery at al-Hit in Hauran, north of Šaqqa (Maximianopolis). It was tended by an abbot and a deacon,[227] dates from the year 354,[228] and is, in fact, the earliest Christian monastic inscription to have been found anywhere.[229] It was the earliest basilica in history dedicated to a saint at a place other than the location of the saint's tomb.[230] In her book *The Barbarian Plain: Saint Sergius Between Rome and Iran*, Elizabeth Key Fowden includes a map showing thirty known locations of churches and monasteries dedicated either to St. Sergius or to Sts. Sergius and Bacchus in Syria and Mesopotamia. All but three of them were in existence before the year 750. Among them are the following: Jabiya, Damascus, Qara, Orthosias, Burj, Nawa, Raphaneae, al-Tuba, Tal al-Dahab, Chalchis, Sujin, Ikizkuğu, Söğütlü, Ehnesh, Qaraqosh, Mabrakta,[231] Deir-el-Kadi, Busr-el-Hariri, Selemîyeh, and Zebed.[232] The church of Sts. Sergius and Bacchus at Um is-Surab in Southern Syria was built in 489.[233] In the Syrian village of Dâr-Kita, which dominates the road from Antioch to Chalchis, a church of St. Sergius was built in 537.[234] The graffiti on the walls of its two baptisteries (one for locals; one for pilgrims) and of the church itself is a clear indication that it became a local center of pilgrimage. Also Built in the sixth century was a church dedicated to St. Sergius in Bamuqqa, Syria.[viii] There is a church of Sts. Sergius and Bacchus in Sadad, in the Diocese of Homs (Emesa), in western Syria. The number of churches built in Syria quickly declined at the beginning of the seventh century. The last registered building to be constructed was the church of St. Sergius in Babisqa. It is dated 609-10, four years before the Persian invasion and twenty-six before the Muslim conquest.[ix]

There is great devotion to Sergius and Bacchus in the Maronite community of Torza, in North Lebanon. Also in Lebanon is the Monastery of Sts. Sergius and Bacchus in Ehden, first built in the mid-eighth century. In the small village of Kaftoun there is a St. Sergius church which was originally built between 600 and 700. There is a Sts. Sergius and Bacchus church in Moncef, near Byblos. It was built in 1810. There is a church with the same dedication at Aslout, in North Lebanon. There is a St. Sergius Monastery at Bsharre. Kahlil Gibran was buried there in 1932. There are Sts. Sergius and Bacchus churches in Bashoukit, near Tripoli, in Bejen, in Ghbeleh, in Kobayat,[x] and in Dahr El Souan.

Abu Sarga, the oldest church in Old Cairo, Egypt, dating back to between the end of the fourth or the beginning of the fifth centuries, is dedicated to Sergius and Bacchus and cherishes some of their relics. The present building was constructed around 685 by Athanasius, the Coptic Christian secretary of the Arab governor 'Abd al-'Aziz ibn Marwan, who, with the governor's permission,[236] built the church over the original church, which is now called the "crypt". At that time, Abu Sarga served as the cathedral of the local bishop. The upper church was then burned in the fire of Fustat during the reign of the last Umayad caliph, Marwan II, in around 750, and then rebuilt shortly afterwards. It was rebuilt in 1171 after having been partially burned during the chaotic last days of Fatimid rule.[237] Since then, it has been restored several more times.

In the catacombs of Alexandria, Egypt, not far from Pompey's column near the southwestern extremity of the old city, wall paintings were discovered in 1864. They are stylistically similar to those found in the Roman catacombs, and their symbolism is of the same character. Though restored several times in later centuries, in their original form, these murals appear to have been painted not later than the first half of the fourth century. Among the saints depicted there, St. Bacchus is conspicuous, and it is certain that St. Sergius was depicted as well.[238] In Nubia, a cameo was unearthed depicting the imperial couple Honorius and Maria, later inscribed as Sergius and Bacchus (making Bacchus the wife) and an ancient lamp with the name of St. Sergius inscribed on it.[239] Elsewhere in Egypt, during the 13th or 14th century, the venerable Coptic monastery of Deir al-Baramus produced a lovely two-sided icon on one side of which Sergius and Bacchus are depicted as martyrs in ceremonial court costumes.[240]

The oldest icon of Sts. Sergius and Bacchus still in existence can be found in the Kiev Museum of Western and Eastern Art.[241] Painted in the seventh century, it is one of the few icons to have survived the disastrous iconoclastic ("image breaking") period of Byzantine history. This wanton obliteration of most of the finest religious art from the early Byzantine period was initiated in 730 with the decree of the Syrian Emperor Leo III (d. 741) ordering the removal and destruction of all images of Christ and the saints. Leo III was, in several other ways, a fine leader and an excellent general. He also considered himself another Justinian, in the sense of being a great and reforming lawgiver, because of his issuing of the *Ecloga* ("Selection"), a summary of Roman law written in Greek and revised to conform more closely to Christian morality than the old Latin *Code* of Justinian had done. The *Ecloga* gave the sacramental view of marriage added support by making fornication illegal, by requiring the bride's consent to a marriage as well as the groom's, and by severely restricting the grounds for divorce. In an effort to be more humane, the *Ecloga* prohibited abortion and considerably reduced the number of crimes punishable by death. However it also added one with a death penalty attached, the practice of homosexuality.[242]

There may have been a connection between Leo's simultaneous attack on the veneration and use of religious images and on sexually active distinctive people. He was trying to tighten his control over those elements of society who demonstrated in their manner of thinking, teaching, or lifestyle any independence from the imperial party line. The Church was responsible both for producing the icons and for the regulation of their use. Icons were a valued means of communion with the spiritual Otherworld -- a world over which the Emperor had no control. The veneration of the saints itself is something that has usually developed "from the bottom up", which means that it usually spread among common people before officially being sanctioned. So it has always been less susceptible to the restrictions of official scrutiny than officials might desire.[243] Religious and secular authorities at the top have often treated it with suspicion and tried to exercise control over it. This is one of the reasons the Catholic and Orthodox Churches developed the canonization process. Emperor Leo's attack on religious images can be understood as an effort to take over some of the control which the Church maintained over the minds and the imaginations of the Christian faithful.

Iconoclasm was a mania, which emerged among the educated class of Constantinople, not among the poor. It is an example of what can happen when linear, dualistic, masculine, left-brain, text-bolstered thinking feels threatened by right-brain, feminine, holistic thinking. Images and painting are entirely right-brain operations, emerging from the feminine side of the brain. Alphabetic writing is a masculine, a left-brain operation. It shouldn't be surprizing, therefore, that one of the ways the male iconodule ("image worshipping") theologians defended the use of images was by insisting on referring to their painters as "iconographers", which means "image writers". Only the masculine side of the brain could concoct the ridiculous notion of legitimizing painters by calling them writers. An iconoclastic attitude toward sacred images is characteristic of such sacred texts as the Torah, the Koran, and even the Communist Manifesto. During the Reformation period, several Protestant reformers bolstered their words with Bibles made much more widely available by the invention of the printing press in 1454 and were just as iconoclastic as their Byzantine forebears. Many of them insisted on dressing themselves and their places of worship in drab black and white, the colors of ink and paper.[244] The main defenders of the use of images during the iconoclastic controversy were the monks who painted them and women. At first, the iconoclasts sought out only religious images to smash. Later their targets also included painters, sculptors, and craftsmen. They even murdered those whose crime it was to love sacred art.[245]

Contemporary Russian icon painter Adolphe Ovtchinnikov, explains how the icon painters and their art are a revelation of Holy Wisdom:

> *If we ask a philosopher to expound his system without using words, he will realize we are being ironical at his expense. The same is true for the iconographer. Everything - crystals, minerals, and all his artistic means - constitute his words, whereby he expounds not just a separate understanding, but the whole of his conceptions concerning the deeds of Christ. And, of course, each deed recorded in the Gospels must be considered just as one would the facets of a crystal. This is why the paintings in the churches were disposed like the facets of a crystal. When Christ took flesh, all His activity, and each separate miracle or deed became integral parts of His image, the Image of God's Wisdom.*[246]

Like his father Leo III, Constantine V, was an able civil and military leader, but there was wide disapproval of his harassment of Church leadership and of his many and varied sexual activities. He had three wives and seven children, six of them boys, and he also had a taste for handsome young men.[247] Since Leo had surely been aware of his son's attraction for men, this could, in part, explain why the imperial father became such a persecutor of distinctive people.

Distinctive people are often seen by the heterosexual majority to be themselves icons of nonconformity. In other words, in a curious reversal, the majority often consider them to be "iconoclasts", in the sense that they violate the boundaries which have been established by the majority. Since the status of distinctive people in many societies often prohibits them from "fitting in," they end up on the "cutting edge" of what pushes the majority to stretch and to change. This happens both in the ever-changing areas of fashion and design and the more enduring areas of cultural and religious mores. Currently, they are challenging society to reconsider what sorts of relationship can be understood to be included when the word "marriage" is used. From prehistoric times, significant roles as spiritual counselors and as conductors of religious ritual. Since they are able to view life from the perspectives of both genders simultaneously, they can be natural "bridge builders" in the area of human relationships and "psychopomps" – i.e. spirit guides or channels for communication between this world and the Otherworld. A large number of distinctive people can be found among the artists and the religious figures in many societies.

If Leo III's iconoclasm was an attempt to centralize control by seizing it from the Church, it makes sense that he would not overlook the independence and the "iconoclastic" attitude towards orthodox mores represented by distinctive people. Of course, it cannot be demonstrated whether or not the majority of Byzantine icon painters were distinctive people, but the attacks on both groups did happen simultaneously. The artists and writers who were among the victims of the mass murders under Hitler and Stalin are twentieth-century examples of the way an attack on artists often accompanies an attack on their creative works. What is beyond doubt is that the Byzantine iconographers were monks and that monks and nuns quickly assumed leadership roles among those who supported the use and veneration of icons. Therefore, by the time Leo III was succeeded by his son, Constantine V (d.775), nicknamed *Copronymos* (i.e. also called Shit) by his enemies, the assault on icons had also become a full-scale attack on monastics, many of whom suffered martyrdom for their defense of holy images.

The first phase of iconoclasm lasted until 786, when the sainted Empress Irene attempted to reintroduce icon veneration. The government formally ordered the suppression of Iconoclasm in 787, its reintroduction in 814 and its final liquidation in 843, when the iconoclastic Patriarch John VII was deposed.

John VII had been born John Morocharzianus around the year 785. He was also nicknamed "the Grammarian" because he had been a schoolteacher. He began his religious career as a monk in the Hodegon monastery,[248] where his main task seems to have been the painting of icons. During this time, he had been in amiable correspondence with St. Theodore (d. 826), abbot of the monastic community of St. John Studios, which had strongly opposed iconoclasm during its first phase. When he and his community later also became involved with the internal quarrels of the imperial family, Theodore was first transferred to the Sts. Sergius and Bacchus monastery and was detained there, after which he was exiled to Thessaloniki and then eventually returned to the Studios community.

In his personal restatement of the rule of St. Basil for his monastic community, St. Theodore of Studios included this requirement: "Do not contract same-sex unions with or become spiritual kin (i.e. godparents) to the laity, you who have left behind the world and marriage. For this is not found among the fathers, or if it is, only rarely; it is not legal."[249] This requirement says nothing against contracting a same-sex union with a fellow-religious: and, of course, it implies that same-sex unions were common enough in society for St. Theodore to bother bringing up the subject at all.

Not long after Theodore Studites's return to Constantinople, John the Grammarian became abbot of the Sts. Sergius and Bacchus community. At first, he still had the reputation of being an iconophile ("icon lover").[250] But shortly after this, he shifted to the opposite camp and began to plot with Emperor Leo V "the Armenian" (d. 820) to revive iconoclasm. This led to his becoming the last of the iconoclastic patriarchs.

When iconoclasm was over, all the vast churches of Constantinople had to be redecorated.

> *The task was so great that its accomplishment had to be spread over half a century: in St. Sophia the first figural mosaic, that of the Virgin and Child in the apse which is still extant, was made in 867; the church of St. Sergius and St. Bacchus was redecorated between 867 and 877, that of Holy Apostles between 867 and 886.*[251]

Sts. Sergius and Bacchus was the smallest of the three churches listed, but it likely took ten years to redecorate it because, during the controversy, it had ended up supporting the iconoclastic cause, under its Abbot-Patriarch John VII (d. 843).[252]

To return to the story of the construction of this church, it should come as no surprise that the Monophysite chapel and monastery which Empress Theodora allowed her Syrian protegees to establish in the Hormizdas Palace were both dedicated to St. Sergius.[253]

Even though Anicia Juliana died shortly after the occasion when she tricked Justinian out of taking her gold, he was determined to get even anyway. First of all, the historian Procopius mentions that, after the completion of St. Polyeuct Church, Justinian henceforth would allow churches to be built only with public money or at imperial instigation[254] - "a clear reaction to Anicia Juliana's pretensions".[255] Simultaneously, he decided to build a church even more impressive than hers.

This was not the first church he built. Early in his career, he may have recalled that, in 499, the Pope's legate had complained to Emperor Anastasius that the patron saints of Rome should be more solemnly honored in Constantinople. So in the period before he became Emperor, to nurture the support of the Roman Pontiff, Justinian had a church built next to his Hormizdas Palace, which he had dedicated to Sts. Peter and Paul. This dedication would have been especially appropriate for him, since his baptismal name was Peter (Flavius Petrus Sabbatius). The project was probably well under way by July 29, 519, when he wrote an imperious letter to Pope St. Hormisdas requesting relics of Saints Peter, Paul, and Lawrence.[256]

He placed the church that he was determined would outshine Juliana's in between the Hormizdas Palace and St. Peter and Paul Church. Thus all three buildings were perfectly adjacent to and interconnected with one another. He had it dedicated to Sts. Sergius and Bacchus and he deposited in the church the relic of the thumb of St. Sergius, which had been brought to Constantinople by Anastasius I.[257]

> *In this church, the square-domed Byzantine type definitely replaces the oblong flat-roofed basilica. The church has been compared to an octagonal reliquary in a square box; the awkward angles of the square under the domed vault are avoided by columned exedras, and the round dome with the sixteen flutings rests on an octagon of piers.*[258]

Practically nothing remains of the rich mosaics and marble revetments that decorated the interior, but Procopius characterized the church as "outshining the sun by the gleam of its stones, and adorned throughout with an abundance of gold."[259]

Redecorated after iconoclasm in 867, Sts. Sergius and Bacchus was then vandalized in 1204 by the Latin crusaders. One of its most prized relics somehow escaped their grasp, for the skull of St. John Chrysostom was still mentioned as one of its treasures in 1427.[260] Although it remained Christian for about 50 years after the fall of Constantinople to the Ottoman Turks in 1453, the church was converted into a mosque between 1506 and 1512 by Huseyin Aga, Chief of the White Eunuchs of Sultan Beyazit II.[261] It is such an architectural delight that it has survived through the centuries as a mosque, appropriately nicknamed by the Turks *Kutchuk Aya Sophia* ("Little Hagia Sophia"), because it turned out to be the model for the building of the great church of Hagia Sophia.

Sts. Sergius and Bacchus church was a perfectly tasteful jewel of ecclesiastical construction and a major architectural breakthrough, built by the Emperor to spite Anicia Juliana's church, which was bigger in size but older in design and overdone in decoration.

Justinian began the building of Sts. Sergius and Bacchus in 527, which was both the first year of his reign and the year that saw the completion of St. Polyeuct Church. His new church was finished by the year 536. During part of the period of construction, there had been a truce between the imperial government and the Monophysites. It lasted from 531-36, during which time, many of the Monophysite hierarchy had taken advantage to this period of less persecution to come to the capitol and plead their cause. Imperial policy shifted back to open hostility the same year Sts. Sergius and Bacchus church opened. The change may have been occasioned by the arrival of Pope Agapetus I there that year.[262] The Pope arrived in late February or early March of 536. He had come to the imperial city ostensibly to conduct an embassy on behalf of the Ostrogothic King Theodahad, but he had his own agenda and was determined to strike at recent developments.[263] In the previous year, the holy ascetic Anthemius had been appointed Patriarch of Constantinople. Since the man was a known Monophysite, Agapetus refused to enter into communion with him and so pressured Justinian and Theodora that they both withdrew their support from the Patriarch. Thus Anthemius was deposed and Agapetus had the satisfaction of consecrating his successor, Menas. Agapetus achieved nothing on behalf of Theodahad, so he probably considered it wise to remain in the imperial city, which he did until he died the following April.[264] Meanwhile, Anthemius also lived on in the capital, hidden by Theodora in her palace, and it was believed that Justinian only became aware of this after his wife died.[265]

So even though Theodora may have been pressured into withdrawing public support from the Monophysite patriarch, she privately took care of him anyway. That same year, right in the face of the aggressive Roman Pontiff, she shrewdly managed to have her new church dedicated to the two favorite saints of the Monophysites. And it was built in such a way that they could enter the church from the Hormizdas Palace, without having to risk security by stepping outdoors. As an additional twist, this symbol of the Monophysite presence in the capitol was lodged between Sts. Peter and Paul church, the symbol of their Roman enemies, and the persecuting Justinian's original palace.

As if this weren't enough, she managed to get Justinian to dedicate the first church he built as Emperor to a pair of male lovers at the same time that he was becoming the first Emperor in history to outlaw homosexual behavior.[266] It was not until 533[267] that any part of the Empire first had to deal with legislation flatly outlawing homosexual behavior, even though Christianity had been the state religion for more than two centuries. In that year, following what had been standard ecclesiastical opinion since the fourth century, Justinian placed all homosexual relations under the same category as adultery and subjected them for the first time to civil sanctions (adultery was at the time punishable by death.)[268]

While this sort of law was clearly consistent with the increasing hostility to distinctive people being nurtured by some Church leaders at that time, it was also characteristic of Justinian's growing antagonism to all minorities and his deliberate program to curtail the rights of Jews, Samaritans, astrologers, and persons involved with the theater, as well as distinctive people, and several other groups.[269] His assault on theater people is ironic since Theodora and her sisters had been actresses. Justinian and the other autocrats ruling several great cities at the beginning of the sixth century disliked social deviance. The Emperor's antagonism went to the point of conducting a pogrom against distinctive men, many of whom he had tortured and castrated.[270] So his willingness to dedicate his church to Sergius and Bacchus, who were known to have been lovers, is rather amazing.

Despite its Monophysite beginnings, Sts. Sergius and Bacchus church shortly became a favorite church for use by clergy of the Roman rite, remaining thus for centuries. During the years 579 to 586, while he was a Papal Envoy to Constantinople, the future Pope St. Gregory the Great,[271] officiated there. Since he was a "scion of the house of Anicii,"[272] he was also very likely related to Anicia Juliana. Touché, Theodora!

Even though the building of Sts. Sergius and Bacchus provided Justinian a means of thumbing his nose at Juliana's memory, he had greater plans, which would go far beyond merely getting even with her. After all, Sts. Sergius and Bacchus church may have been architecturally better than her church, but St. Polyeuct was still bigger.

The building of St. Polyeuct church was the immediate catalyst not only for the building of Sts. Sergius and Bacchus church but also for the more rapid spreading of their cult all over the Empire. If Juliana's primary desire had been to see her own family outshine and outlast the dynasty begun by Justin and Justinian, a little glance at the future will reveal that her wish was granted. Theodora and Justinian died childless. When the Emperor died in 565, the crown passed to his nephew, Justin II, and after his death, on to other relations until the dynasty shifted.

Juliana's family had a long and continuous history of producing powerful Christian figures. The Anicii had been one of the earliest of the great fourth-century Roman families to take advantage of the conversion of Constantine by becoming Christian themselves.[273] Two beloved fourth-century Anicii were St. Melania the Elder (d. 410) and her contemporary and great friend, St. Paulinus of Nola - Pontius Meropius Anicius Paulinus (d. 431).[274] The famous philosopher and martyr for justice, Severinus Boethius (d. 524), who was Juliana's exact contemporary, was also a member of her family.[275] Some historians claim that their even more famous contemporaries, St. Benedict of Nursia, the Father of Western Monasticism (d. 547), and his twin sister, St. Scholastica (d. 543) were also Anicii. [276] In addition to Pope Gregory I (d. 604) after the Anicii became the Conti family, they numbered four more Roman pontiffs among their progeny: Lothario de' Conti, Pope Innocent III (d.1216) who, as cardinal deacon of Sts. Sergius and Bacchus in the Roman Forum, completely restored that church. After Innocent would come his grandnephew, Ugolino de' Conti, Pope Gregory IX (d.1241), during whose reign, the Syrian Jacobite Patriarch, Ignatius II, would reunite the Syrian Monophysite Church with Rome.[277] Later in the century would come Rinaldo de' Conti, Pope Alexander IV (d. 1261). And he would be followed centuries later by Michelangelo de' Conti, Pope Innocent XIII (d. 1724).

CHAPTER VII
THE CULT OF THE LOVERS SERGIUS AND BACCHUS SPREADS

As you read this chapter, whose purpose is to testify to the universality of the cult of Sts. Sergius and Bacchus, when you begin to feel enveloped by a cloud of details so dense that you want to cry out "Too much information!", you are ready to skip to the end of the chapter and pause at the spot where the Roman Church drops their feast from the calendar, claiming as its reason that Rome never had a significant devotion to the martyred lovers and that they had no cult at all there prior to the high Middle Ages.

There was another church dedicated to St. Sergius in Constantinople, located near the Cistern of Aetius.[278] In addition to honoring Sts. Sergius and Bacchus with a new church in the capitol, Justinian is said to have built a church in their honor near Škodra, Albania. (The city has also been called Scutari and, currently, Shkodër.)[279] He also expanded Sergiopolis in Syria, having the area surrounding the shrine of St. Sergius literally turned into a town by building fortifications and giving it a water supply, houses, colonnaded plazas, and the other sorts of buildings which are usually found in a city.[280] He also adorned the shrine with priceless gifts, as did Theodora, who contributed a magnificent jeweled cross. During the same period, Theodora had a bishop named Theodoros appointed for the region of Damascus. He bore the title, bishop of Bosra, but he did not reside there. Actually he lived among the Arab nomads at an encampment named Jabiya in Jawlan. The importance of this center was enhanced by the fact that it also included a sanctuary erected to the cult of St. Sergius.[281]

The main shrine at Sergiopolis survived the ravages of an attack by the Persian Sasannian dynasty early in the 7th century. It exercised a great attraction not only to the Arabs in the region of Damascus but also to those in Iraq. It was perpetually visited by bands of nomads. The commemoration day of the dedication of St. Sergius Church on November 15 was not only a great religious affair, but this annual gathering around the tomb of Sergius also provided an occasion for contacts on political matters, allowing the government's representative to meet the chieftains of the clans and tribes of nomads, to settle quarrels and to make business transactions.[282] The church was restored by the Umayyad Caliph Hisham, but assaulted again after the Abbasid conquest of 750. A final assault by the Mongols in 1247 left it in its present desolate condition.[283] The restoration by Caliph Hisham is an example of the way many Muslims syncretized devotion to the martyr into their own beliefs. Hisham so revered Sergius that he also built a three aisled mosque, which he incorporated into the preexisting north courtyard of the basilica at Resapha, to make it easier for pilgrims to pray in both shrines. He made the mosque simple, so it wouldn't rival the shimmering beauty of the basilica.[284]

In his *Ecclesiastical History iv. 28*, Evagrius wrote about an occasion when Sergiopolis was preserved from an assault of the forces of the Persian King Chosroes I (d. 579) through "the apparition on the walls of a multitude of armed defenders, a revelation of St. Sergius' vigilant protection"[285] A bishop famous for his missionary activities under Chosroes I was St. Ahudhemmeh. Early in his career, he was Nestorian bishop of Nisibis. After converting to Monophysitism, he was first consecrated bishop of Beth-Arbaie (between Nisibis and the Tigris River) by Armenian Catholicos Christophoros I. At a place called 'Ain-Quen'y', he built a great and beautiful complex, including a church and an impressive monastery, both of which he dedicated to Mar (Saint) Sargis.[286] The tribe of the Taghlib and other Arabic tribes and clans in that area were so devoted to St. Sergius that they carried his icon on raids with them.[287] In 559, Ahudhemmeh was appointed Metropolitan of Taghrit, east of the Tigris, after which he earned the honor of being apostle to the Arabs of Mesopotamia. His success as an evangelist also led to his death. When he converted and baptized a son of Chosroes, he was arrested and imprisoned. After languishing in prison for two years, he was executed on August 2, 575.

For centuries, Sergiopolis would continue to be enriched by the gifts of grateful suppliants. Among them was the Zoroastrian King Chosroes II of Persia. Largely estranged from the Persian nobility, Chosroes had been put on the throne with the help of Byzantine mercenaries. In gratitude to St. Sergius, he sent to his shrine a cross of beaten gold, encrusted with pearls and other jewels.[288] He was surrounded with Christians, among them his two wives, Maria the Roman and the beautiful Shirin. His financial wizard, under whose direction Persia became the financial power of the Near East, was Yazden of Kerkuk, a Nestorian Christian. Early in his reign (591-628), Chosroes not only tolerated his Christian subjects but he shrewdly addressed his propaganda to the Christian populations on both sides of the frontier, "ascribing his successes to the protection of St. Sergius, the patron saint of the Syriac-speakers and of the Arabs of the Fertile Crescent".[289] As a sign of his sincerity and gratitude, he continued to send rich votive offerings to the shrine at Sergiopolis.[290] The birth of Queen Shirin's son, Merdanshah, was another occasion when he sent votive treasures.[291] Shirin was an Aramaic Christian from Huzistan. At first a Nestorian, she became a Monophysite, following the influence of the chief court physician, Gabriel of Sinjar, who was also a Monophysite.[292] It was likely at Shirin's request that Chosroes had Qasr Shirin church built in Hulwan in honor of St. Sergius.[293] Also in Persia at this time, there was a St. Sergius cloister which the physician Gabriel had enough authority to transfer from Nestorian to Monophysite control.[294] This was done so high-handedly that, when a well-born Persian convert from Zoroastrianism, a Nestorian monk named George, protested it, he was seized and, after eight months in prison, put to death.[295] After the death of Gabriel, and probably because of the aggressive efforts of the Emperor Heraclius (d. 641) to regain portions of his empire from Persian control, Chosroes II became a severe persecutor of Christians, adding several martyrs to the calendar of the saints. One of the most famous was a soldier named Magundar, who, when he converted to Christianity, was given the name Anastasius. After he was martyred by strangulation and then beheaded at Bethsaloe (Kirkuk in modern northern Iraq) on 22 January, 628, the remains of St. Anastasius the Persian were buried in a nearby monastery of St. Sergius.[296] It is also recorded in the life of an earlier Persian martyr, St. Gulanducht, that, during a pilgrimage to the city of Nisibis, she visited the shrine of St. Sergius in Resapha. At that time, the great silver shrine there contained relics of both Sergius and Bacchus. After her torture and martyrdom by the Zoroastrians in 591, she was buried in a chapel dedicated to St. Sergius between Nisibis and Dara, in order to intercede on behalf of all of the region. In 615, Iranian aristocrat named George of Izlap, who had converted to Nestorian Christianity, was martyred and buried in a monastery dedicated to St. Sergius at Mabrakta, near Seleucia Ctesiphon.[297] In the chaos which resulted from all the turmoil of this period, Byzantine architectural and artistic activities in Syria ceased altogether. The last registered building to be constructed was the church of St. Sergius in Babisqa, which is dated 609-10 – four years before the Persian invasion and twenty-six before the Muslim conquest.[298]

After the death of Chosroes II, St. Maruthas was consecrated Metropolitan of Tagrit. During his twenty years in this role, he proved himself a great pastor. One of his accomplishments was the building of the large monastery of Mar Sargis, between the Tigris and the Euphrates rivers.[299] When the Islamic invasion came, Maruthas acted resolutely, opening the citadel of Tagrit to the Arabs, and thus saving the town from the calamities of war and destruction. He lived long enough to make Tagrit Both a safe place for Christians and the mother church of the East. He died on May 2, 649.[300]

Edessa (Urfa) had two chuches dedicated to St. Sergius. The earliest was built by Nestorian Bishop Hiba some time before 457. It was outside the East gate of the city and was later called the Church of St. Sergius and Simeon (after Simeon Stylites the Elder). This was not to be confused with another church dedicated to St. Sergius, built inside the city walls.[xiii] After Islam spread throughout the area, some churches belonging to the (Nestorian) Assyrian Church of the East were converted into mosques. One of them, the *Circis Peygamer* mosque, was originally Edessa's Church of St. Sergius and St. Simeon.[xiv] There is still a double church of Sts. Sergius and Bacchus in Bos Vatch, eight kilometers south-west of the city of Urmiah, Iraq.[xv] Beneath the church is an incubation room still used today by both Christians and Muslims, in which the mentally unstable are healed overnight in the presence of the relics concealed in the walls.[xvi]

Early in the twentieth century, a trove of 56 silver liturgical objects was discovered in the village of Kaper Korson, southeast of Antioch, in what had been part of Roman Mesopotamia. The items all had belonged to the village church of St. Sergius and were created from 540 to 670, which is evidence both that the church had been built in an earlier generation and was still thriving that late in history.[301] Similarly discovered during the same period was a silver treasure of three chalices and a paten, dating from the sixth to the seventh century and belonging to the church of Saint Sergios in the small Syrian village of Beth Misona,[302] The ruins of a church of St. Sergius (*Quasr Serij*) can be seen sixty kilometers northwest of Mosul, in Iraq. It was built by Monophysites in a basilica style and probably dates from the sixth century.[303] The missionary activities of Syrian monks led to the establishment of churches and monasteries dedicated to Sergius and Bacchus in Mesopotamia, an oratory between Nisibis and Dara.,[304] and among the Arabs and other nomads of the Arabian desert, who accepted these two martyrs as their special protectors along with their conversion to Christianity.[305] One group of monks specifically credited with this enterprise came from the community of Euthymius the Great.[306]

There was a St. Sergius monastery near Bethlehem.[307] In 502, at the time of Emperor Anastasius I, the Banu Ghassan Arab nomads, who lived in the steppe to the east of the cultivated lands along the Jordan, and the Roman Empire of the East signed a treaty, successively reconfirmed during the reigns of Justin and Justinian I, which specified that the Christianized Bedouin tribes were entrusted with the defense of the immense territory which extended to the Euphrates River, the border of the Persian Empire.[xix] The weakening of the Christianized Bedouin confederation at the time of Emperor Maurice Tiberius (r.582-602) paved the way for the Persian invasion of Syria Palestine in 613. During the time when this confederation was at its strongest, the Ghassanid ecclesiastical complex at Nitl, in Jordan, was built. It included a church dedicated to St. Sergius. Several beautiful floor mosaics remain, the work of a mosaicist named Ammonis. Another mosaic inscription declares that it was "built by Arethas, son of al-Arethas," the King of all the Arabs. This was very likely a Ghanassid sepulchral church.[xx] Along the Mediterranean coast, there were churches dedicated to these martyrs at Ptolemaïs and Mount Cisseron.[308] One of the two largest churches in Gaza was dedicated to St. Sergius. Choricius of Gaza[309] described it as a domed building with a square central bay, reduced by squinches to an octogon. Its pictorial decoration was very elaborate and included an apse mosaic of the Virgin Mary as Theotokos, attended by St. Sergius and Governor Stephen of Palestine, the founder of the church.[310] Relics of Sergius and Bacchus were venerated, by the beginning of the sixth century, in the Monastery of Holy Sion, near Myra, in Lycia. St. Theodore of Sykeon in Galatia (d. 613,), a great promoter of the cult of St. George, was responsible for the building of a large, three-aisled basilica of St. George, in which could be found a chapel of Sts. Sergius and Bacchus.[311] Theodore was a famous ascetic who traveled widely. While he was visiting Constantinople, the Patriarch Thomas I became "so attached to him and had such confidence in him that he begged him to enter into ceremonial union with him and to ask God that he would be together with him in the next life."[312]

There was a church of Sts. Sergius and Bacchus at Mamistra, the second most important town of Cilicia.[313] In this church the Armenian Catholicos (Patriarch) Hakob was elected to succeed Kostadian I in February of 1268.[314] On the upper Tigris River, in what is now southeastern Turkey, the Syrian Patriarch George of B'eltran (758-790) erected a new conventual church in 788/89 for the monastery of Sts. Sergius and Bacchus outside of Hah. In the same area at that time, there was a church dedicated to the two martyrs at Beth S'virna. In the twelfth century, during the period of the Second Crusade, Cistercian monks established a monastery of St. Sergius at Byblos (Gibelet), in Lebanon.[315]

Through Nestorian missionary activity in the East the name of Sergius eventually even reached China, where a Nestorian Christian named Mar Sargius ruled over the province of Kian Su in the years 1278-80. He was appointed to an office in Kublai Kahn's household and, in 1281, built as many as seven monasteries.[316] The easternmost extension of St. Sergius dedications was a church in Mongolia.[317]

The Assyrian Church came into contact with the Turkic and Mongol peoples quite early, beginning towards the end of the fifth century. In the year 1007, the conversion of the Kahn of the Keraits led to the baptism of 200,000 new Christians. According to the historians Mari ibn Suleiman and Bar Hebraeus, the Kahn, whose homeland stretched from modern central Mongolia to the South into the Gobi Desert, lost his way while hunting in a snowstorm. St. Sergius appeared to him and promised to rescue him if he would have himself baptized. The Kahn agreed and kept his promise.[xxii]

Sergius and Bacchus are honored in the calendar of the Armenian Church, but a consideration of their Armenian cult is complicated by the fact that there was also an Armenian soldier/martyr of the fourth century who bore the name Sargis (Sarkis), the Armenian equivalent of Sergius. This saint is probably the subject of most Armenian Sergius dedications, and it is to him that the Armenian Cathedral of London is dedicated.

Sergius and Bacchus can also be found included among the saints painted in the damaged frescoes still visible in some of the cave churches of Cappadocia (in modern Turkey), among them the tenth century Direkli Kilise, the eleventh century Almali Kilise ("Church of the Apple-Tree") at Göreme,[318] and another at Belisirma. In the late-twelfth century Karanlik (Dark) Church at Göreme, they appear as a couple two times. They can also be seen in the church at Yusuf Koç Kilisesi and in the church in the Karabas Kilise Monastic Complex.

The above-mentioned most ancient surviving icon of Sts. Sergius and Bacchus was one of a group of several beautiful images which survived iconoclasm because they were part of the collection kept at St. Catherine's Monastery on Mt. Sinai - a place so remote from the capital and so isolated in the wilderness that the iconoclasts apparently didn't bother to spend much time there trying to enforce their decrees. This particular icon dates from the seventh century and shows the martyrs, each wearing the gold and jeweled torque (*maniakion*) traditionally associated with them, and joined by Christ, who is depicted in the traditional Roman position of *pronuba/us* ("matron of honor" or "best man," often a deity) overseeing the wedding of a husband and wife.[319]

Another outstanding item in the collection at Mt. Sinai can be found among the large group of thirteenth century icons painted during the so-called Paleologan Revival in Byzantine Art. Among them is an icon depicting St. Sergius on horseback with a kneeling female donor. It was painted at Saint-Jean d'Acre ca. 1260s and is an example of Veneto-Byzantine Crusader style painting. Very similar, and also from Saint-Jean d'Acre in the same collection can be found a double-sided icon, with Sts. Sergius and Bacchus on horseback on one side and the Virgin Hodegetria on the other. It was painted ca. 1280s.[320] In the following century, in Constantinople, Theodore Metochites undertook the restoration of the Church of St. Savior in Chora during the years between 1315 and 1321, repairing the destruction wrought by the Crusaders. Alas, this same church was the first to be pillaged after the Turks took the city in 1453 and was turned into the Kariye Kamii mosque. Nevertheless many glorious mosaics and frescoes somehow survived, among them damaged mural depictions of Sts. Sergius and Bacchus in the Parecclesion, the funerary chapel which Metochites added to the church, and a lovely mosaic of either Sergius or Bacchus in the narthex, where they were surely both depicted originally. The Paleologan revival had a powerful influence on one of the greatest phases in the development of Russian iconography – the 15th century school of St. Andrei Rublev.

There is a famous mosaic of St. Sergius in the Church of St. Demetrius in Thessaloniki, Greece, installed there just after a fire in 620.[321] They are depicted both in eleventh century frescoes and in mosaics in the monastery in Daphni, Greece. Also in Greece, there was a church of Sts. Sergius and Bacchus built at Kitta in the twelfth century.[322] Theophanis Strelitzas-Bathas, also called Theophanis the Cretan, and his son Symeon, painted lovely frescoes in St. Nicholas Church at the monastery complex of Stavronikita on Mt. Athos between 1545 and 1546. There Sergius and Bacchus are beautifully depicted, facing each other from opposite sides of an arch.[323] There is also a beautiful icon of Sts. Sergius and Bacchus standing together in the Monastery of Simonas Petras on Mt. Athos. In Mani, the southernmost and middle peninsula of the Peloponnese or Morea, there is a beautiful Byzantine church of Sts. Sergius and Bacchus. Kythera is an Ionian island opposite the eastern tip of the Peloponnese peninsula. According to a tenth century Life of St. Theodore of Kythera (d. 961) written by a contemporary named Leo, when the saint, accompanied by a fellow-ascetic named Antonios, fled to Kythera, in order to lead a cenobitic life, they resided at an existing church dedicated to Sts. Sergius and Bacchus. [324]

The monastery of Sopaćani was founded by King Uroš I of Serbia in the mid-thirteenth century. Sts. Sergius and Bacchus are depicted in the frescoes painted there from 1264-68. In 1290, Queen Jelena (the Catholic Helène of Anjou), the widow of Uroš I and mother of King Milutin, built the church of Sv. Srdj i Vakh (Sts. Sergius and Bacchus) on the Bojana River, along the coastal region of Montenegro. As a younger woman growing up in Angers, the capital of Anjou, she would have witnessed the construction of the great Gothic choir in the monastery church of *Sts. Serge et Bach* in that city and carried the memory with her to Serbia. During the crusader period, the town which grew up around Queen Jelena's monastery was known to the Venetians as the port of San Sergio. This particular monastery has disappeared under the waters of the Adriatic. In Montenegro, about 20 km from Škodra, Albania, there is a church of Sts. Sergius and Bacchus, also built c 1290 in Romanic-Gothic style. It was a favorite place for the weddings of the Montenegran princes The church of St. George at Staro Kagoričino was built by King Milutin between 1312-13. Sts. Sergius and Bacchus can be seen among the saints depicted in the frescoes there in 1315. They are also depicted on a pilaster in the southwest corner of the church in Lesnovo, built in 1341. There is a church dedicated to Sergius and Bacchus at Nove Sad in Monetnegro. And at the fifteenth century

Serbian monastery of Curtea De Arges, there is a coffin containing their relics. An unfinished church dedicated to Sts. Sergius and Bacchus (begun in 1912) can be found at Degrmen in Serbia. And St. Sergius is depicted in a 1641 icon in the Church of the Holy Archangels in Sarajevo, Herzegovina.

Sergius and Bacchus were also the patron saints of Dubrovnik (Ragusa), until St. Blaise replaced them in 931, when his relics were stolen from the East and brought there by Ragusan sailors. The reliquary containing the arm of St. Sergius in the museum of Dubrovnik's thirteenth century Dominican monastery serves as a reminder of the city's earlier patronage. From at least the fourteenth century, Franciscan friars in the same part of Dalmatia (modern Croatia) were employing A rite for creating sworn brothers among Latin Catholics – an Ordo ad fratres faciendum Many other similar rites have survived to the present, and most invoke Sts. Sergius and Bacchus as models for such unions. The Dalmatian ritual was found in the library of the Catholic parish church of St. John in Trogir, Croatia, on the Adriatic coast.*xxv* According to a note at the end, the manuscript was complete in 1394. The Franciscans had arrived in the area around 1370. The opening sentence of the missal containing this rite reads, "*Incipit ordo missalis canonicorum secundum consuetudinem romane curie,*" (Here begins the order of the proscribed Masses according to the usage of the Roman Curia). So apparently these Franciscans presumed that they were using the rituals of the Roman Missal.*xxvi* The Dominican scholar O. Antonin Zaninović appended documents from the historical archives in Dubrovnik in the second half of the fifteenth century, describing the use of the rite (including a kiss of peace) by two Dubrovnik musicians earlier in the century.*xxvii*

Sts. Sergius and Bacchus can be seen among the saints depicted in the murals painted in the 1180s on the ceiling in the crypt of the cathedral of Aquilea.[325] Because St. Sergius had been a tribune in charge of training the young military recruits in the XV Apollinare Legion in Trieste, there is an ancient devotion to him in that city. The coat of arms of the city displays his lance, which the cathedral claims to possess as a relic in its treasury. While the cathedral is dedicated to St. Justus, another soldier martyred there, St. Sergius is also the city's patron. His image appears in stone beside the cathedral door, subtly converted from a memorial to a Roman lady by the addition of a halo, which probably gives the heavenly Sergius an occasional chuckle. [326]

Elsewhere in the Byzantine world, near Ravenna, Italy, there was a church called St. Sergius in Classe.[327] In the year 402, Emperor Honorius changed the capital of the Western Empire from Milan to Ravenna. Classe, or Classis, was a port established by Augustus Caesar five kilometers from Ravenna, on the road to Rimini. Ravenna had become a fine city under the governance of the Ostrogothic King Theodoric the Great (d. 526), who was an Arian. Named after the fourth-century Alexandrian priest Arius, Arianism was a heresy which considered the Son to be of secondary status to the Father in the Trinity by declaring with regard to Christ that "there was a time when he was not." Since King Theodoric was tolerant of his Orthodox subjects, Ravenna was a place where these usually antagonistic Christians could co-exist peacefully. It had many beautiful churches, built either by Arians or by Orthodox Christians. St. Sergius in Classe was originally an Arian church. In his book, *History of the Goths*, Herwig Wolfram claims that the Goths erected an Arian church consecrated to St. Sergius in Caesarea,[328] which was a third city in the Ravenna area, built between Ravenna and Classe; but this church is likely the same as the one located in Classe by an early chronicle. Both Caesarea and its churches now no longer exist. St. Sergius in Classe also no longer exists. A chronicler mentions that St. Sergius in Classe was sequestered during the vigorous persecution of Arians under Justinian I and consecrated as an Orthodox church by St. Agnellus, the Archbishop, who died in 579. *xxviii* Earlier in his career, Agnellus had been the priest at the sixth century church of

Sta. Agatha Maggiore in Ravenna. [xxix] His tomb can be found there in a shrine at the head of the aisle in the front of the church on the right, as you face the high altar. Enshrined along with the remains of Agnellus are relics of St. Sergius. [xxx]

Tradition has it that Ecclesius, Bishop of Ravenna from 521 to 531, brought from Constantinople the plans of the church of Sts. Sergius and Bacchus for the building of his own famous church of St. Vitale. [329] While the resemblance between the churches is obvious, the one does not derive from the other because St. Vitale may actually have been started first. [330] Ecclesius visited Constantinople in 526, the year Anicia Juliana's team of sculptors were hard at work decorating St. Polyeuct Church. Part of her team seems subsequently to have traveled to Ravenna where the church of St. Vitale has in its main order fourteen capitals of Preconnesian marble, carved with designs strikingly similar to the split-palmette capitals of St. Polyeuct. [331] Though St. Vitale was not completed until 547, its columns and capitals of the main order were part of the earliest phase of construction, so its capitals were very likely carved by the St. Polyeuct team of sculptors.

In the museum of Verona's Castelvecchio, there is an old sarcophagus covered with well- sculpted reliefs depicting Sts. Sergius and Bacchus and different scenes from their lives and deaths. Though its provenance is apparently not traceable prior to1179, it is called the tomb of Sts. Sergius and Bacchus, which is indicated by its Latin inscription. Its lid depicts them bearded on horseback. The vault shows details from their martyrdoms. In the 18th century, it was transferred from the monastery church of St. Sylvester in Nogara, where there had been altar dedicated to them, to the Museo Maffeiano, and thence to Castelvecchio. [332] It was originally in a church of Sts. Sergius and Bacchus, but which specific church is unknown. [333]

When the Italian city of Venice first came into existence in 726, it was part of the Byzantine Empire. [334] According to a popular tradition, supported in the Chronicle of Andrea Dandolo (Doge from 1343 to1354), as early as the fifth century, a Sts. Sergius and Bacchus Church could be found where Venice would later emerge. [335] Demus points out that this claim has been largely discounted but that there was likely a wooden church built there either in the seventh or eighth centuries, which was dedicated to the martyred lovers. [336] When the Cathedral of Olivolo, an island near Venice, was either built or rebuilt by Bishop Ursus in the first half of the ninth century and dedicated to St. Peter, Ursus deposited in the church the relics of its former patron saints, Sergius and Bacchus, whose church was said to have existed there since the seventh century. Their relics are still present behind a golden panel on the altar of St. Peter there. The *Chronicon Gradense* says the former church of Sergius and Bacchus was located where the church of St. Peter the Apostle is now. [337] The new dedication of the Cathedral of Olivolo to St. Peter was intended to woo Rome, while the transferring of the relics of Sergius and Bacchus was intended to lead to their becoming the principal patrons of Venice, along with St. Theodore. The whole attempt was derailed by the Venetian theft of St. Mark's relics from Alexandria in 827 and the city's adopting him as their principal patron. As a permanent reminder of the importance of their cult and the veneration of their relics in San Marco, Sergius and Bacchus gaze at each other from mosaics on opposite sides of the arch that forms the entrance to the St. Clement chapel, which is adjacent to the south of cathedral's main sanctuary. These mosaics were installed in the thirteenth century by Lorenzo Bastiani. According to an eleventh century inscription, among the several relics contained in the altar of St. Clement's chapel can be found those of Sts. Stephen, Clement, Blaise, Sergius and Bacchus, which may all belong to the original stock, and perhaps even date back to the period prior to the foundation of San Marco. [338] Meanwhile, the old church of San Pietro di Castello (Olivolo) remained the cathedral of Venice until San Marco took

Its place in 1807. Close to Venice is the city of Chioggia. In the sacristy of the church of Santa Maria Assunta there can be found fourteenth century arm reliquaries made by Venetian jewelers. Inside are relics of Sergius and Bacchus.

In the city of Urbino, very close to the house in which the great Renaissance painter Raffaello Sanzio was born, stands the church of San Sergio. Built on the site of a Roman piscina (fish pond) both in the fifth and in sixth centuries, and refurbished in the fifteenth century, it is the oldest place of worship in the city and possibly the oldest dedication to Sergius in Italy. In it can be seen a painting of the Martyrdom of St. Sergius by Claudio Ridolfi.

The cult of Sts. Sergius and Bacchus came to Rome from Constantinople, probably during the sixth century.[339] At that time, and in the period which followed, several churches with strikingly Eastern and Byzantine dedications were erected in Rome in the area centered around the Forum, the Via Sacra, and the Palatine. A Roman church dedicated to the martyred lovers was built prior to 750, in the south corner of the ruins of the Temple of Concord in the Forum.[340] It had a *diaconia* attached. A *diaconia* was a welfare center, from which alms were distributed. Each *diaconia* was under the supervision of one of the deacons of Rome. When the temple's ancient wall threatened to collapse, around 790, and the alms-distributor tried to topple it in a safe direction, it fell on the basilica, obliterating it to its foundations. Since there was no way the alms-distributor could afford to rebuild it, Pope Hadrian I himself (d.795), who was devoted to the martyrs, restored and enlarged it to a state of great beauty.[341] The *diaconia* was shifted to the nearby Arch of Septimus Severus and the church came to be called called *SS. Sergio et Baccho de Formis*. By the Middle Ages, the Anicii (the family of Anicia Juliana) had become the Conti family.[342] In the final decade of the twelfth century, Lothario de'Conti (d. 1216) was the Cardinal Deacon of *SS. Sergio et Baccho de Formis*.[343] As was the custom, he refurbished the church, completely restoring the crypt, redecorating the upper church, and adding a new altar, baldachino, and sanctuary furnishings. At this time, there were two towers built on top of the Arch of Septimus Severus, the southern of which served as the tower of SS. Sergio et Baccho.[345] When Lothario became Pope Innocent III in 1198, and because he attributed his election to the intercession of these martyrs,[344] he added a colonnade to the front of the church. In 1206, the title of *SS. Sergio et Baccho* was given to Lothario's relative, Cardinal Octavian. By this time, it was regarded as an "old Conti church."[346] This twice-rebuilt church stood until it was demolished in 1536 to make way for the triumphal procession of Emperor Charles V.[347] There was also a *diaconia* and a small oratory of Sts. Sergius and Bacchus in the north transept of the old St. Peter's basilica (perhaps identical with a later-mentioned church of "St. Sergius palatii Caruli").[348] Pope Gregory III (d. 741) enlarged this oratory, which had already existed there "long since," and he gave all the other support needed "and laid down that it should be at the service of the deaconry's ministry to support the poor for all time."[349] Despite this declaration, it was very shortly afterwards turned into a palatial residence for the imperial envoy.[350] This is the earliest mention in the *Liber Pontificalis* of a dedication in Rome to these two martyrs. In his floor plan of the old St. Peter's, Alfarano places this oratory in the north transept of the basilica. Pope Gregory III, who had the chapel enlarged, and the Byzantine Emperor Leo III, who began the iconoclastic controversy in 730, both died the same year. There was also in Rome a convent of nuns named *SS. Sergio e Bacco*, which could be found "behind the Lateran Patriarchate's aqueduct."[351] Pope Pascal I (817-24) removed the nuns and replaced them with monks who could join other monks in singing the Office at St. John Lateran.[352] There was another men's monastery attached to the church of *SS. Sergio e Bacco de Subura*,[353] and called by that name (as well as called "*in Callinicum*").[354] The earliest reference to this church appears in the *Liber*

Pontificalis, which mentions a donation it received from Pope Leo III (795-816). Whereas there were several Eastern monasteries in Rome at this time, these two were Latin rite, which is an indication that the cult of Sergius and Bacchus was no longer considered either new or foreign in eighth century Rome.[355] In all, then, there were six Roman establishments dedicated to these martyred lovers - two churches and a *diaconia*, a *diaconia* and chapel in old St. Peter's, and two monasteries. The one Roman church of Sts. Sergius and Bacchus to survive to the present is *SS. Sergio e Bacco de Subura*. At the time of the treaty of Brest-Litovsk in 1596, when the western part of the Ukranian Orthodox Church reunited with Rome, Cardinal Barbarini gave it to the Ukranians as their Roman headquarters; and so it remains, adjacent to the Ruthenian College. In this little church there can be seen a large painting of the martyrs painted by Ignazio Stern. It is clear from the way they are shown gazing at each other that the artist knew their story well. In 1967, *SS. Sergio e Bacco de Subura* church was renovated by Patriarch Josyf Slipyi and established as the first Ukranian Greek Catholic parish in Italy. The relics to the two martyrs venerated in this church were brought to Rome during the crusader period. Earlier in history, in 872, Pope Hadrian II sent a portion of their relics, which were obviously already in Rome, to the Emperor Louis II and Empress Angilberta for the new monastery of Sts. Sergius and Bacchus which they were building in Piacenza. There were also relics of the two martyrs in the church of St. Felix in Pavia.

Eastern monks and nuns had been fleeing to Rome for varying reasons since the beginning of the seventh century. A Persian onslaught on Palestine in 613 and subsequently the permanent Muslim conquest of the East and North Africa drove refugees to the West. Pope Theodore I, elected in 642, was the son of a bishop from Jerusalem.[356] In 645, a group of monks fleeing the great monastery of Mar Saba in the Judean Hills came to Rome and established the St. Saba church and monastery there. In the years between 678 and 752, eleven of the thirteen Roman pontiffs were of either Syrian or Greek descent. The Easterners brought with them the relics of saints like Anastasius the Persian and George of Lydda, the veneration of other Eastern saints, and devotion to St. Anne, the mother of the Virgin Mary. At the end of the seventh century, the Syrian Pope St. Sergius I (d.701) introduced three feasts of the Virgin Mary to the Roman calendar - the Annunciation, her Nativity, and her Dormition. He also introduced the *Agnus Dei* into the Eucharist as an antiphonal prayer. In the next century, iconoclasm would drive so many Eastern refugees to Rome that Pope St. Paul I (d.767) ordered Greek to be introduced into the Eucharistic liturgy to make it easier for Easterners to follow the prayers.[357]

The oldest surviving frescoes of Sergius and Bacchus in Rome date back to this same period and were discovered in 1900. In that year, the church of Santa Maria Liberatrice was taken down. Beneath it were the recovered and excavated the remains of the older church of Santa Maria Antiqua, first mentioned as early as 636-42. This church had been built up and decorated by Pope John VII (d.707), whose father, Plato, had been a high Byzantine functionary in Rome. Intended to serve as a mausoleum for his family and a monument to their name, it was then buried under the walls of the palace of Tiberius, in an earthquake of 896. When the church was excavated, many eighth century frescoes were recovered. Among the saints depicted were Sergius and Bacchus, Euthymius the Great, and Sabas.[358] There also can be found the oldest surviving Western image of St. Nicholas of Myra and a depiction of St. Erasmus of Antioch (St. Elmo).[359] It is likely that these frescoes were painted by Eastern monks fleeing persecution under the iconoclastic emperors. The monastic painters revealed by their choice of subjects that they were devoted both to the two martyred lovers and to the Palestinian fathers, Euthymius and Sabas, whose followers had helped spread devotion

** See Appendix B

to Sergius and Bacchus in the fifth century. The inclusion of St. Erasmus is a confirmation of Emile Male's suggestion that Eastern refugee monks and Latin monks collaborated together on these frescoes, some of which had Greek and some Latin inscriptions.[360] The Erasmus depicted was actually a bishop of Formiae, in Calabria, who had been martyred in 303. A later legend made him a Syrian bishop of Antioch. His being depicted in Santa Maria Antiquae is an example of the blending of traditions which was going on as Eastern and Western monks began to live together in Rome.

In the fifth century, St. Philip of Argira, the Apostle of the Sicilians, was born of a Syrian father in Thrace. One of the miracles attributed to him was the cure of a nun in a Sicilian monastery dedicated to Sergius and Bacchus.[361] Sicily and Southern Italy remained Byzantine until the end of the tenth century. One of the churches built among the ruins in the ancient forum of Naples in the mid-eighth century was dedicated to Sts. Sergius. There was likewise a Byzantine monastery there dedicated to Sergius and Bacchus. A further proof of local devotion to Sergius in the area during this period is the fact that a glimpse at the long lists of dukes of Naples and Amalfi will reveal that most were named Sergius. In Calabria, about five kilometers from Tropea, at Drapia, a Greek monastery of Sts. Sergius and Bacchus was built c. 700. It became a Franciscan monastery in 1421. The site is now marked with a little shrine to St. Sergius, and there is an annual festival there in his honor on the first Sunday of October. At Martignano, in the diocese of Otranto, there was also a church of Sts. Sergius and Bacchus.

For the next two centuries, Southern Italy and Sicily were ruled by the Normans.[362] In a fine mosaic, Sergius and Bacchus are depicted facing each other from opposite sides of an arch in the church of St. Mary's of the Admiral in Palermo, Sicily. It was built in 1173 by George of Antioch, the Great Admiral and Prime Minister of Roger II, Sicily's first Norman king.[363] Sergius and Bacchus also appear in the mosaics in the enormous basilica of Monreale, begun by King William II of Sicily before the year 1189.

An attaché of the English Embassy in Cyprus, writing in 1815, recorded that, three hours journey from Kakotopia, Cyprus, there was a very large Greek convent on the shore of the sea, dedicated to Ss. Sergias and Vaccha (sic).[364] They are depicted in frescoes in the Early twelfth century Church of Panagia Phorbiotissa at Asinou, Cyprus. There is also a church named after them in the town of Ayios Seryios in Cyprus. Their icon in this village church is a fine example of late sixteenth/early seventeenth Cypriot iconography.[365] Also in Cyprus is the church of St.Sergius in Neta, which contains some fine thirteenth-century Byzantine frescoes.[366] They are also depicted in the early eleventh century church of St. Nicholas of the Roof near Kakopetria, Cyprus, and in one of the finest Cypriot wall paintings of the second half of the fifteenth century in the church of the Holy Cross of "Agiasmati".

Monasticism in Gaul[367] can trace its origins to St. John Cassian (d. 433), whose training took place in Egypt, Palestine, and Constantinople. With the Western Roman Empire crumbling during the sixth century, the Gauls increasingly looked to Constantinople for inspiration and assistance. It is probably no coincidence that Sts. Sergius and Bacchus dedications began to appear in Gaul in the same century that Justinian and Theodora built their church in Constantinople. Already in the sixth century, an oratory in Paris was dedicated to them.[368] It was eventually replaced by the church of Saint-Benoit-le-Bestorné, which was destroyed in 1854 to make room for the Rue des Écoles.[369] They also had a church in Chartres, built near the cathedral, to the north. It was demolished in 1703.[370]

*** See Appendix C
**** See Appendix D

An important sixth century Italian cleric and historian was St. Venantius Fortunatus. He was educated in Byzantine Ravenna and then moved to Gaul for the rest of his life, becoming a dear friend of St. Gregory, Bishop of Tours. Gregory mentioned "the priest Fortunatus" in his *History of the Franks* (V.8), identifying him as the author of a *Life of St. Germanus of Paris*. Fortunatus may also have been one of Gregory's sources for information about Sts. Sergius and Polyeuct, since they both had dedications in Ravenna at the time. Gregory himself, the greatest historian in Gaul in that era, recorded the story of the ridiculous attempts of a man called Gundovald the Pretender to obtain a wonder-working finger-bone of St. Sergius for the city of Bordeaux, from a Syrian merchant named Eufronius,.[371] This effort was instigated by the city's conniving bishop, Bertram. Gregory also wrote that he himself placed relics of St. Sergius in the new baptistry which he had added to the church of St. Perpetuus in Tours.[372] Parenthetically, Gregory was one of several writers who recorded that the Church of Gaul had a pair of its own martyrs, who were venerated as beloved and inseparable companions: Sts. Epipodius and Alexander (d. 178).** In 654, King Clovis II of the Franks established the Benedictine monastery of *Sts. Serge et Bach*, in Angers, France.[373] He dedicated it to Sergius and Bacchus because he attributed his earlier military successes to their intercession.[374] The monastery closed in 1802; but the eleventh century crossing and transept remains, and the beautiful vast thirteenth century choir still exists as the most perfect example of Angevin (also called "Plantagenet") gothic architecture in existence. St. Serge Abbey had two daughter houses in Great Britain - St. Mary's Priory at Totnes in Devonshire and St. Andrew's Priory at Tywardreath in Cornwall, both alien priories, established c. 1088 and closed centuries ago.[375]

Also in France, there is an eleventh century chapel, which was part of a Cluniac priory in the Burgundian town of Berzé-la-Ville. In the twelfth century, St. Hugh of Cluny directed his artists to paint Sergius and Bacchus in the choir of this chapel.[376] The surviving mural in the apse owes a tremendous debt to contemporary Byzantine painting and depicts a Christ Pantocrator ("All-Ruling") together with Sts. Sergius and Blaise.[377]

There were churches dedicated to Sts. Sergius and Bacchus at least in two places in Germany. The church in the deserted medieval village of Vöhingen, in Baden-Württemberg was dedicated to them. Sts. Sergius and Bacchus were revered in the Benedictine Imperial Abbey of Weissenburg, on the German border of Alsace, founded in the seventh century by King Dagobert I. (Dagobert was the father of Clovis II, who founded Sts. Serge et Bach in Angers.) From the mid-ninth century, Weissengurg Abbey owned a manor on the Asperg, near Vöhingen. This is likely the reason for the dedication of the parish church. All that remains of the church is its foundation, but it is likely that it had a tower at the east end, above the chancel.[xxxi] There is also a Sts. Sergius and Bacchus church in Kreuzebra, in Thuringia.. It was rebuilt from 1738-1740 and probably received its dedication from the fact that Bishop Otgarius brought relic of the martyrs to Kreuzebra in 826. Otgarius was Archbishop of Mainz from 826-839.[xxxii]

During the tenth century, devotion to Sergius and Bacchus was introduced along with Christianity by the Byzantine missionaries who evangelized Kievan Rus' and the rest of what would eventually become Ukraine and Russia. In the first generation after that nation's conversion, the bond of these martyred lovers would find its parallel in the love borne for each other by St. Boris and his friend George the Hungarian - both assassinated for dynastic reasons in 1015.***

The devotion of the Eastern Slavs to Sergius and Bacchus was demonstrated in the new name given to a young man named Bartholomew when he was tonsured as a monk. According to his disciple and biographer, the monk-priest Epiphanius the Wise, who had been educated in Greece, when Bartholomew asked the abbot-priest Mitrofan to consecrate him a monk, he "consecrated Bartholomew to the angelic life on the seventh day of October, feast day of the holy martyrs Sergius and Bacchus. Hence he was given the name of Sergius."[378] This young monk would become the greatest of Russia's saints, Sergius of Radonezh (d.1392),[379] founder of the Holy Trinity Monastery, near Moscow. This same St. Sergius would help to launch the career of the greatest of medieval Rus's artists, St. Andrei Rublev, the outstanding icon painter of the Moscow school.**** In the sixteenth century, an artist in the archepiscopal icon studio of Novgorod produced an icon of Sergius and Bacchus of remarkable tenderness, which depicts them astride their horses, riding side by side, as one lover kisses the other on the cheek. In the wooden church of the Trinity, which was built in the Smolensk Cemetery of St. Petersburg between 1824 and 1825, there were three altars. The first two were dedicated to the Trinity and the Archangel Michael. The third was dedicated to Sts. Sergius and Bacchus.

A Russian *Iconographers' Patternbook* compiled by those artists working for the Stroganov family c. 1600 shows the specific pattern to be followed when depicting Sts. Sergius and Bacchus.[380] This pattern is later also described in the Greek *Painter's Manual* of Dionysius of Fourna (c. 1670-1745/6).[381] They are to be depicted as beardless young men. They wear either military or Byzantine court garb; and often, as a sign of their status, they wear the gold torques traditionally associated with them.

In many Syrian churches, Sergius and Bacchus are depicted on horseback. Thus they can be seen painted in the twelfth century in the nave of the church of Mar Musa al-Habashi (St. Moses the Ethiopian), seventy kilometers north of Damascus. Similar in style and date are the depictions of the two martyrs in the church of Sts. Sergios and Bacchos in nearby Q'ara. A bit further northeast is the church of St. Sergios in Sadad, which contains a splendid depiction of Sergius painted in the eighteenth century.

Two of the finest equestrian icons of Sts. Sergius and Bacchus can be seen in the most ancient church dedicated to them, Mar Sargis in Ma'lūlū, Syria. On the wall behind the ancient altar in the sanctuary is an icon depicting them facing each other, with Christ between them in the classical role of *pronubus* (best man) in the manner of their ancient icon from Mt Sinai. The other icon, over the central gate of the iconostasis, was painted by Michael the Cretan in April of 1813. It shows the two of them facing each other, crowned with martyrs' laurels by angels, and blessed by the Holy Trinity.

Sts. Sergius and Bacchus have a full office in the Greek, Coptic, and Syrian churches. In ancient Syrian Menologies, their feasts were celebrated separately, on the dates of their death. St. Bacchus was celebrated on October 1st, while St. Sergius was remembered on October 7th. In the Assyrian Nestorian Church, they are remembered as Mar Sargis and Mar Bacchus, having feasts both on April 25th and on the first Monday of November. In Russia and in most other churches, their feast day is October 7th.

In the Roman Calendar, the feast of Sts. Sergius and Bacchus was October 7th. Thus reads the Roman Martyrology, which was published by Gregory XIII in 1583, revised by Urban VIII in 1630, and augmented and corrected in 1749 by Benedict XIV:

The Seventh Day of October

> *The feast of the Most Holy Rosary of the Blessed Virgin Mary, and the commemoration of St. Mary of Victory…In the province of the Euphrates, the holy martyrs Sergius and Bacchus, noble Romans, in the time of*

emperor Maximian. Bacchus was scourged with rough sinews until his body was completely mangled, and breathed his last in the confession of Christ. Sergius had his feet forced into shoes full of sharp-pointed nails, but, remaining unshaken in the faith, he was sentenced to be beheaded. The place where he rests is called after him Sergiopolis and, on account of the frequent miracles wrought there, is honored by large gatherings of Christians...At Rome, the holy martyrs Marcellus and Apuleius...[382]

The feast of Sts. Sergius and Bacchus was quietly removed from the Roman Calendar in 1969 – ironically, the very year New York's Stonewall Riots launched the gay liberation movement - along with those of several other saints whose stories had become so obscured behind fabulous Medieval embellishments that the very existence of the original person was no longer considered historically traceable or provable. This is the wording of the decree as it is promulgated in *The Roman Calendar: Text and Commentary:*

A twelfth century addition to the Roman Calendar, the memorial of Sergius is abolished. The cult of this Syrian martyr is not part of the Roman tradition.

The memorial of Marcellus, martyred at Capua, was placed on the Roman Calendar in the thirteenth century. His cult is not part of the Roman tradition and is left to particular calendars. The Acts of the lives of Bacchus and Apuleius are legendary and their memorials, which entered the Roman Calendar in the eleventh and twelfth centuries, are abolished.[383]

Unlike Marcellus and Apuleius, the widespread cult of Sergius and Bacchus is traceable very nearly to the time of their death; and the story of their passion seems to have been recounted consistently and with little embellishment back to at least a century after the date of their death. Centuries after the spread of Islam drastically reduced the traffic of western pilgrims to the East, the tomb of Sergius at Sergiopolis remained a primary object of pilgrimage, second only to the shrines in the Holy Land, until it was destroyed by the Mongols in 1247. Never, until the document was issued ending the observance of their feast in the Latin Church, had Bacchus been separated from Sergius and paired with Apuleius. According to liturgical calendars, the proper pairings were Sergius with Bacchus and Marcellus with Apuleius. It has been demonstrated that the cult of Sergius and Bacchus in Rome is traceable at least to the eighth century – at which time they even had a chapel in St.Peter's! Also, they can still be seen in the frescoes of Santa Maria Antiqua in Rome painted on the wall of the left aisle during the reign of Pope Paul I (757-767) There they are depicted standing on either side of Pope Gregory the Great, who used their church as his headquarters during his sojourn in Constantinople. In this fresco, they stand among a group of saints and popes "representing the city and Church of Rome," rather than among the also-depicted saints representing the Eastern Church.[384] This means that veneration to Sergius and Bacchus had a long enough history in Rome for them to have been considered as properly depicted among the saints of the Roman Church at least as early as 767. Also, depicting a third saint between them is extremely rare. The likely reason the artist put Gregory the Great between them is that he was known to have been the Pope who introduced their cult to Rome when he returned in 586 after having spent the previous seven years as Papal Envoy to Constantinople and officiating there in their church. The cult of Sergius and Bacchus is demonstrably even older in Gaul and other places in the West. According to the principal *"Lex orandi, lex credendi,"* (As people pray, so they believe.), the number of dedications to Sergius and Bacchus in Rome long before the Middle Ages reveals either the ignorance or the duplicity of those who claim that they were not venerated in Rome until the eleventh and twelfth centuries.

Not only were the given reasons for dropping the feast of Sergius and Bacchus from the Roman Calendar demonstrably spurious, the dropping of their feast was also gratuitous. On October 7, 1571, Don Juan of Austria and the forces he led resisting the Muslim effort to begin the conquest of Europe had a terrific victory at the naval Battle of Lepanto. Pope Pius V (d. 1572) was a Dominican who attributed the victory to the praying of the rosary. So he instituted the feast of Our Lady of Victory – now called Our Lady of the Rosary, to commemorate the event. Since this became the primary feast for October 7th, the memorial of Sergius and Bacchus was so overshadowed by it that many Roman Catholics of later generations would never have even heard of the martyrs. This is a peculiar and ironic turnabout. Since Sergius and Bacchus had been considered special heavenly protectors of the Byzantine army for over a millennium, in an earlier era, a Christian victory on that date would have been credited to **their** intercession. The Emperor Justinian I, Evagrius the historian, King Chosroes II of Persia, Pope Innocent III, and King Clovis II of the Franks made precisely that claim. And, as a matter of fact, the Eastern Church did indeed credit Sergius and Bacchus with the victory at Lepanto. On the Greek island of Corfu in the Ionian Sea is a fifteenth century church called Our Lady Mary Antivouniotissa (Antivouniotissa = opposite the mountains). In it, there is an icon originally painted for the church of Trimartyros (Could these "three martyrs" have been Sergius, Bacchus, and Justina?) by Michael Damaskinos, a leading post-Byzantine Cretan painter who lived in Venice for years and studied painting there. The icon shows full-length images of Sergius and Bacchus, with St. Justina of Padua between them. The icon was commissioned to celebrate the victory at Lepanto. The feast of all three martyrs is October 7th. Justina of Padua would also have been included, because Padua is very close to Venice; and Corfu was part of Venetian territory in 1571.

Since their being reduced to secondary status on the calendar rendered Sergius and Bacchus virtually unknown in the West, their complete removal from the calendar in 1969 appears gratuitous. It makes it difficult to avoid the conclusion that homophobia had such a grip on those in the Vatican entrusted with the care and consideration of saints' causes that they rendered Sergius and Bacchus the only case in history where even martyrdom for the faith was no longer considered enough to deem the subjects worthy of the Church's veneration. Additionally, in dropping Sergius and Bacchus from the calendar the Vatican was discarding the only two saints who for centuries provided a link – albeit tenuous at times – between Christianity, the Arab world, the Persian world, and Islam.

It is interesting the way some contemporary volumes of saints' lives cover the matter of the Vatican's shabby treatment of these two martyrs. *The Birthday Book of Saints* calls Sergius and Bacchus "patrons of desert nomads and (unofficially) gay men" and concludes the article about them by saying "The image of these two husky centurions sashaying around in drag started giving people the wrong idea, and their Feast Day has been removed from the Calendar of Saints."[385] In this case, people would have come to the right conclusion for the wrong reason.

CHAPTER VIII
MEANWHILE, ELSEWHERE IN EUROPE: THE COMMUNITY OF NUNS WHO INCLUDED A CROSS-DRESSED MAN AND A EUNUCH

Venantius Honorius Clementianus Fortunatus was born about 535, during the time Sts. Sergius and Bacchus Church in Constantinople was being built. His birthplace was Duplicabilis, near Treviso, Italy, and he was educated at Ravenna. There he became acquainted with the devotional life of a thoroughly Byzantine community, which had its own churches of St. Polyeuct and St. Sergius. There too he would have been nurtured in the tradition of Holy Wisdom as an attribute of Christ - something he himself taught in his commentary on the articles of the Nicene/Constantinopolitan Creed.[386] In 565, he traveled to Germany, perhaps fleeing the violence of the Lombards. From there, he moved to Gaul. At Poitiers, he became acquainted with St. Radegund (d.587) and eventually became her advisor, secretary, and intimate friend.

As a child, Radegund had been abducted as one of the few survivors of the pagan Thuringian royal house, most of whom were murdered in 531 by King Clovis of the Franks and his sons. She had been kept as a hostage, baptized, educated, and, at the age of twelve, forced to become a queen of King Clotaire I, who won her from his brothers as a gambling prize.[387] Clotaire's ill-use of her, culminating in the murder of her brother, led to her fleeing the king and succeeding in her escape. She received the veil from St. Medard, who also ordained her a deaconess, after which she established her famous Holy Cross convent in Poitiers. She appointed her adopted daughter Agnes as the first Abbess and dwelt there with her until Agnes died in 586. Venantius Fortunatus stayed with them for twenty years (567-87), until Radegund died. During her years at Holy Cross, Radegund continued to be involved in the politics of her day, ever taking the role of mediator and peacemaker. Fortunatus assisted her in this. During Radegund's years there, Holy Cross convent provided a haven for a remarkably varied assortment of people. One of them was a woman named Clotild, who claimed to be a daughter of King Charibert. She resented being under the authority of Abbess Leubovera, Agnes's successor, and tried to lead a revolt, the goal of which was to have the abbess deposed and herself appointed abbess instead. This happened during the time Radegund lay dying. As part of this plot, Clotild leveled several accusations against Leubovera. Among them were the following:

> She maintained that the Abbess kept a man in the nunnery, dressed in woman's clothing and looking like a woman, although in effect there was no doubt that he was a man. His job was to sleep with the Abbess whenever she wanted it.[388]

Clotild noticed this man in the assembly and pointed him out. He stepped forward, and indeed he was dressed as a woman. While everyone stared at him, he explained that he dressed himself in this manner because he was impotent. He added that he had never so much as seen the Abbess, though he knew her by name. Since he lived more than forty miles from Poitiers, the accusation against him was ignored. (Apparently, the dressing as a woman part was no big deal in their estimation.) Clotild then accused Leubovera of having had men castrated and kept near her as eunuchs, in the manner of the Imperial court. When the Abbess denied any knowledge of such a thing, Clotild gave the name of one of the servants who was a eunuch. A physician named Reovalis then stepped forward and declared that, as a young lad, this servant had suffered from terrible pains in the groin, which no one could remedy. In desperation, his mother brought him to Radegund, who referred him to Reovalis, who removed the lad's testicles, following a procedure he had seen done by a surgeon in Constantinople. After this, he returned the boy to his mother. Since Reovalis swore that Leubovera knew nothing of this, she was declared innocent of Clotild's second charge.[389] For these two distinctive men had been originally welcomed into her community by St. Radegund herself.

At the time Venantius Fortunatus first arrived in Poitiers, Radegund was negotiating with Byzantine Emperor Justin II and Empress Sophia to obtain a relic of the True Cross for her convent. When the relic arrived in Poitiers, Fortunatus composed a poem not only thanking them for the relic but also praising Justin and Sophia for their orthodoxy. This poem was commissioned and then sent to them by a grateful Radegund. By the time the relic mission was accomplished, Fortunatus had sent a total of four poems to Constantinople in an effort to speed up the negotiations. The first three had been sent to Radegund's relatives in the Eastern capital. It was at this time also that Fortunatus composed his famous hymn, *Vexilla Regis* for the formal installation of the relic at Poitiers. By the time the relic was installed, Fortunatus had begun to acquire a reputation for the positive role he took in international diplomatic relations between the East and the West.[390]

By 573 Fortunatus had gained the friendship and patronage of Gregory, elected and installed as bishop of Tours in that year. Gregory, born in Clermont-Ferrand in 539, was of distinguished Gallo-Roman descent. In political and in ecclesiastical circles, he was a vigorous and highly influential figure throughout his career. He was also regarded as the foremost historian of his day.[391] Gregory was highly knowledgeable about contemporary Byzantine matters. His *History of the Franks* is the primary source of information about sixth-century Frankish devotion to Sts. Polyeuct and Sergius.

Venantius Fortunatus would become the only other contemporary historian of any importance in Gaul.[392] At the time of Gregory's installation as bishop, Fortunatus declaimed a panegyric in his honor, congratulating the citizens of Tours on his election. The eleven books of the *Carmina* of Fortunatus include many poems to Gregory. In addition to the panegyric,[393] Book V includes twelve other poems to Gregory. There are eleven more in Book VIII and one in Book IX.[394] In *The History of the Franks*, Gregory refers to him as "the priest Fortunatus."[395] Indeed Gregory himself may have ordained Fortunatus.[396] The only other likely candidate for ordaining prelate was Plato, who preceded Fortunatus as Bishop of Poitiers. The support Fortunatus gave Gregory of Tours was significant and constant. Many of his letters to Gregory convey greetings from Radegund and Agnes, and many show that both men shared a broad interest in literature. Gregory clearly had an appreciation of the political value of Fortunatus' support. But his informal poems to Gregory also reveal a more relaxed, intimate, and long-lasting relationship than the poet had with anyone other than Radegund and Agnes.[397] These poems indicate that they shared a lot of humor. One particular poem (8.[19]) is much more than a tribute from a poet to his patron. In its literary echoes of the ascetics' use of erotic terminology to express loving friendship, it is a tribute of great feeling for Gregory, which includes respect for him as pastor and patron, but also personal love.[398] The depth of personal feeling and intimacy was clearly mutual. As a token of his friendship, Gregory gave Fortunatus a villa and its surrounding lands. In about 600, Venantius succeeded Plato as bishop of Poitiers; and there he died around 603.

In addition to the volumes of Fortunatus' poetry, there are his metrical lives of Sts. Martin of Tours, Hilary of Poitiers, Germanus of Paris, Radegund, and others, and several outstanding hymns, most notably *Vexilla Regis*, and *Salva Festa Dies*. His epistles reveal that he was in communication with most of his eminent contemporaries. His letters to the much older Radegund are rhetorically playful and affectionate. He was unusually sensitive to the difficulties women had to face during that era. Additionally, as Brian Patrick McGuire points out, "Fortunatus was the first of a number of early medieval writers to posit a direct link between friendship with men and friendship with God."[399]

Not only was he affectionate with Radegund, Agnes, and Gregory. He was also very close to Sigoald, a companion provided by King Sigibert when he first arrived from Italy, as well as to Rucco, a deacon when he first met him, but afterwards a priest, to whom he composed a poem which is the most complete expression of male friendship prior to the epistles of St. Boniface and of Alcuin.[400] Fortunatus wrote a second poem to the same man after he became bishop of Paris (576-91). Since he is called Ragnemod here, "Rucco" must have been an intimate name that Fortunatus shared with him.

He wrote another poem to an unnamed cleric, which gained him a place in the *Penguin Book of Homosexual Verse*. The details hint that it was probably written to the same Ragnemod.

> *"Written on an Island off the Breton Coast"*
>
> *You at God's altar stand, His minister, And Paris lies about you and the Seine:*
> *Around this Breton isle the Ocean swells, Deep water and one love between us twain.*
>
> *Wild is the wind, but still thy name is spoken; Rough is the sea: it sweeps not o'er thy face.*
> *Still runs my love for shelter to its dwelling, Hither, O heart, to thine abiding place.*
>
> *Swift as the waves beneath an east wind breaking Dark as beneath a winter sky the sea,*
> *So to my heart crowd memories awaking, So dark, O love, my spirit without thee.*[401]

Though he was never formally canonized, Venantius Fortunatus was honored as a saint in the Middle Ages. His feast is December 14th.[402]

CHAPTER IX
HAGIA SOPHIA CATHEDRAL: THE GAUNTLET IS USED FOR OVERKILL

For the Roman Empire, the fourth century was a period of incredible religious shift. In 305, Christians were suffering a severe persecution under the Emperor Diocletian. In 313, Constantine I put an end to the era of persecutions with the Edict of Milan. This change was motivated as much by political expediency as by any genuine conversion on his part. More and more citizens were becoming Christian. He began slowly but steadily to suppress paganism; but he himself accepted Christian baptism only on his deathbed May 22, 337. By the year 392, the Emperor Theodosius I had completed the process of making the oppressors the oppressed by declaring it an illegal offense punishable by death for anyone publicly to practice pagan religion. Meanwhile, the Empire was getting a splendid new Christian capital.

In 326, Constantine had renamed the ancient city of Byzantium "Constantinople" and declared it his capital. If the city of Rome represented the best that classical pagan Roman architecture had to offer, Constantine's "Second Rome" would reflect his conversion to Christianity, with Rome's fine temples replaced by great Christian churches. Before his death, he managed to complete the building of several churches in Constantinople. The first was Hagia Irene (Holy Peace), built as the place of worship for the community center of Christians who were already living in town.[403] Another was that of the Holy Trinity, soon to be dedicated to the Holy Apostles, because the central drum under which he placed his tomb was surrounded with emblems and relics of the Apostles - the implication being that Constantine was a sort of thirteenth apostle. This was the church where he and most of his imperial descendants would be buried. A third church was dedicated as Holy Power, and called simply Dynamis (Power).[404] This dedication probably refers to Christ, who in I Corinthians I: 24 is called the "Wisdom and the Power of God," though it may refer to God the Father. Constantine also started the building of the first cathedral of Hagia Sophia (Holy Wisdom, referring to Christ), but he died before its completion, having endowed it in his will. It would be left to Constantine's son and successor, Constantius II, to complete the building, which was dedicated in 360.[405] Until then Hagia Irene had served as the cathedral.[406] Henceforth, these two churches, which were right next to each other, would constitute essentially one unit.

There are several possible reasons why Constantine chose these titles for his greatest churches. Like his father, Constantius I Chlorus, Constantine had a predilection for philosophers and rhetoricians and used to host a regular salon, a sort of religious-philosophical debating society. During his reign, Constantinople itself was sometimes called 'Platonopolis', because to his admiration for Plato. Constantine also at times described the Christian clergy and monks as 'philosophers'.[407] Words like "Peace", "Power", and "Wisdom" are as Platonic sounding as they are Christian. He dedicated his famous palace church in Syrian Antioch, known as the "Golden Octogon," to Harmony or Concord, under which dedication pagan temples could be found throughout the Empire. However the dedications in Constantinople also reflect his theological concern over what would come to be called the Holy Trinity, and the roles of the individual divine Persons. In this Constantinian Trinity, the Father seems to have been assigned Power, the Son, Wisdom, and the Holy Spirit, Peace.[408]

The first Hagia Sophia cathedral was destroyed by fire in 404, during the outbreak of social unrest which followed the second exile of the Patriarch, St. John Chrysostom (d.407). By 408, the Patriarch's old enemies, Emperor Arcadius and Empress Eudoxia were dead, leaving the throne to their children, the nine-year-old Pulcheria and her little brother Theodosius II. The restored Hagia Sophia was rededicated under Theodosius II in 415, six years before he married the empress who would bring the cult of St. Polyeuct to the capital. The restored Constantinian Hagia Sophia served as the cathedral until it, in turn, was severely damaged by fire in the Nike riot of January 15, 532, which nearly cost Emperor Justinian his throne.

Justinian viewed the Nike riot as an attempt by the family of Emperor Anastasius to replace him on the throne. As well as Anicia Juliana's son Olybrius, other potential rivals for the imperial diadem had been the two nephews of Anastasius, Hypatius and Pompeius. Anastasia, the wife of Pompeius, and Juliana had been good friends. Together they had visited St. Sabas frequently, when he was in Constantinople in 511-512. During the Nike riot, the mob attempted to crown Hypatius in the Hippodrome. Whether or not he participated in the event willingly, Justinian had trusted him and his brother enough to let them live on in the imperial city unharmed. Now Justinian felt betrayed, so he had Hypatius and Pompeius executed and sent Olybrius into an exile, from which he was recalled the following year.[409]

Meanwhile, on the verge of completing the construction of Sts. Sergius and Bacchus, Justinian saw in the burning of Hagia Sophia an opportunity not to be missed to outdo himself in getting even with Juliana for tricking him out the possibility of taking of her gold.[410]

He decided to replace the ruined cathedral with what would be for over nine hundred years Christendom's grandest place of worship. In order to do this, he decided to bypass his own architects in favor of the two greatest known practitioners of the art of design. They were masters of all the relevant architectural design theory, especially geometry and mechanics, and were able to bring imagination to their design and fresh theoretic insight and solutions to any new problems which naturally surfaced.[411] He chose Anthemius of Tralles and the elder Isidorus of Miletus, who produced for him a new Hagia Sophia, which would be known as the culminating architectural achievement of late antiquity and the first great masterpiece of the Byzantine world.[412] These two architects created a building whose form surpassed any preconceived idea up to that time.

The interior view is still overwhelming. The structure of the building is simple enough in construction. Four immense piers rise at the corners of a square whose sides are 100 Byzantine feet each. Seventy feet above the floor, they are joined, by four great arches. Those on the north and south are imbedded in the walls of the nave; those to east and west are free-standing, opening into semicircular extensions of the central square. The arches are connected by pendentives. From the arches and the pendentives rose, originally, a flattish dome 100 feet across. Semi-domes resting on the main piers and on pairs of subsidiary piers are adjacent to the main dome at a lower level to the east and west. And smaller conchs fill in the four spaces between the main dome and the semi-domes.[413]

Construction of Justinian's Hagia Sophia began on February 23, 532. The cathedral was completed and dedicated on December 27, 537, by the Patriarch Menas.[414]

According to legend, when he first entered the church at the dedication ceremony, Justinian was enraptured by the sight of its columns and side galleries sheathed in the rarest marbles, gathered from the far reaches of the empire, a vast nave filled with glittering golden candelabra, whose light reflected on the breathtaking mosaics which covered every inch of its ceiling and its colossal dome. He was then moved to exclaim: "Glory to God who has thought me worthy to finish this work. Solomon, I have outdone you."[415]

There is a context in which we can place Justinian's boast, and it has only indirectly to do with comparing Hagia Sophia to Solomon's temple. Here is the beginning of the text which Anicia Juliana shamelessly had inscribed in Greek at the entrance of St. Polyeuct Church, outside the vestibule:

> *What quire is sufficient to chant the works of Juliana, who after Constantine, the adorner of his Rome, and after the holy golden light of Theodosius, and after so many royal ancestors, in a few years accomplished a work worthy of her race, yea, more than worthy? She alone did violence to Time and surpassed the wisdom of renowned Solomon by raising a habitation for God.[416]*

A careful examination of the ground plan of this church reveals that Juliana's architects copied exactly the measurements of Solomon's Temple in Jerusalem, according to the details mentioned in the Bible.[417] They even used the "royal" cubit, the principal Scriptural unit of linear measurement.[418] So the allusion to Solomon in the inscription was not exaggerated poetic whimsy. Juliana had deliberately built a Christian version of Solomon's Temple.

We now know the identity of Justinian's "Solomon". As has been pointed out by Steven Runciman:

> *It is no wonder that the Emperor Justinian, when his architects completed the even vaster and more splendid (than St. Polyeuktos) church of St. Sophia, exclaimed with complacency 'Solomon, I have vanquished thee'. This formidable old lady was the Solomon that he had in mind.[419]*

Hagia Sophia retained its original splendor for centuries, despite the fact that portions of the dome collapsed and then were rebuilt and reinforced in 558, in 989, and again in 1346. But two major blows have reduced it to being a glorious shell, gutted of nearly all its former splendor. On April 13, 1204, Constantinople fell to the mixed Venetian, French, and Flemish forces of the Fourth Crusade. For three days these western Christians pillaged, raped, and massacred their eastern fellow Christians. They completely looted Hagia Sophia and destroyed whatever they couldn't steal. Nearly 250 years later, the cathedral witnessed a similar nightmare. On May 29, 1453, the city fell to the Osmanli Turks, better known to Westerners at Ottomans and Hagia Sophia was likewise looted. When the Turkish soldiers forced their way into Hagia Sophia, they either slaughtered or enslaved the many men, women, children, monks, and nuns who had taken refuge there and stole and desecrated everything they could touch. That afternoon, when Mahomet the Conqueror rode into the city, he went first to Hagia Sophia and had the ruined building turned into a mosque. The final stage of its history thus far began when, in 1935, Mustafa Kemal Ataturk turned it into a museum. Since that time, the experts who have removed layers of paint and plaster have been delighted to discover that some of the mosaics have survived, giving today's visitors a taste of how splendid it must have been in its first centuries.[420]

CHAPTER X
THE CULT OF HOLY WISDOM SPREADS

Just prior to the building of Justinian's cathedral, an anonymous author began to circulate a body of spiritual writings which would have a profound effect on the development of Christian mysticism. It seems clear that he was a Syrian. Because he chose to attribute all his works to St, Paul's friend Dionysius the Areopagite, he is now identified either as Dionysius the pseudo-Areopagite or, more simply, Pseudo-Dionysius. Though every contemporary expert on the subject is in agreement that we are not yet able to identify the person behind the name, in 1928, Joseph Stiglmayr made the possibly erroneous but tantalizing suggestion that the only known Christian writer in approximately the time and place of these works whose genius was equal to that of the great unknown author and whose Neoplatonic-Christian spirituality closely paralleled that of the Pseudo-Dionysian corpus was Empress Theodora's great friend, the Monophysite Patriarch Severus of Antioch.[421] In one of Pesudo-Dionysius's most famous works, entitled *The Divine Names*, the author identified the Logos of God with Divine Wisdom.[422]

In analyzing the structure of *The Divine Names*, Endre von Ivánka has suggested that the treatise was composed of a series of essays on divine predication based on Plato, Proclus, and the Greek Fathers.[423] In a diagram showing his actual breakdown of these proposed essays, the "Greek Fathers" section begins with Chapter 7:4 and goes to the end of the treatise. What von Ivánka proposed as a possible original title for this "Greek Fathers" section was "Treatise on the Constantinian Triad (Wisdom-Power-Peace)," with the Father characterized as Power, the Son as Wisdom, and the Holy Spirit as Peace.[424] Striking is the appearance in this triad of the very names chosen by Constantine for three out of four of the great churches either begun or completed by him during his reign - though it does not solve the question of whether Constantine intended his Holy Power (Dynamis) Church to honor the Father or the Son.

If Severus of Antioch's authorship of *The Divine Names* is considered highly questionable, it is much more probable that he was responsible for the historical innovation of establishing at Antioch a rite of public Communion utilizing Presanctified Gifts.[425] It is also likely that he brought and introduced this Liturgy of the Presanctified to Constantinople between 531 and 536, the period during which Justinian invited him and other Monophysite leaders to Constantinople for conciliatory discussions.[426] The Liturgy of the Presanctified, the Liturgy of St. John Chrysostom and the Liturgy of St. Basil the Great are the three primary liturgies used by Eastern Christianity. All three of them can trace their roots to Syria, and all three include dramatic moments when the deacon sings out, invoking "Wisdom". A prayer in the Liturgy of St. Basil the Great reads:

> O Lord Jesus Christ the great God and Saviour of our hope,...Living
> Word, Very God before the worlds, Sophia, Life, Sanctification, Power,
> Very Light...[427]

Invocations to Christ/Sophia appear in other Eastern liturgies. An oblation in the Alexandrian Liturgy of St. Mark reads:

> All things which Thou hast done by Thy Sophia, the true light, Thine
> Only-begotten Son, our Lord and God and Saviour Jesus Christ.[428]

The ancient Liturgy of St. Clement is pre-Constantinian and almost perfectly parallels the Eucharistic text recorded in Rome by St. Justin Martyr (d. 165). It refers to Christ as

> *God the Word, the Only Begotten Son, the living Sophia, the First-born of every creature...*[429]

It also stresses Sophia's presence at creation:

> *For thou didst say to Thine Own Sophia, Let us make man in Our Own Image, and after Our Likeness...*[430]

A very early Christian fresco which actually depicted Christ-Sophia could still be seen in the nineteenth century in a catacomb in Karmouz, near Alexandria. It showed a winged person, above which was the inscription: ΣΟΦΙΑ ΙΣ ΧΣ ("Sophia Jesus Christ").[431] Originally painted in the beginning of the fourth century, it is the earliest example of a Sophia-Christ depiction to have survived almost to the modern era. There was a church of St. Sophia in Alexandria on the island of Pharos at the time of the Arabs took over in 641.[432]

Otherwise, one of the earliest Christian depictions of Sophia still in existence is not meant to represent God at all - though an implicit flattering reference to Divine Sophia was very likely intended. Of all possible people, how interesting that it is a portrait of Princess Anicia Juliana painted in 512 in the above-mentioned manuscript of the *Herbal* of Dioscorides. It depicts her seated on a throne, which is supported by pillars. Flanking her are two other women, the three of whom are identified on the same page as an allegorical group, representing Phrónēsis (Prudence), Sophia (Wisdom), and Magalopsuchía (Magnanimity). Here Anicia Juliana herself is identified in the central role of Sophia.[433]

After this, whenever in history the Byzantine world would attempt to represent "Hagia Sophia" in iconographic art, Christ would sometimes be depicted as a woman, sometimes as an androgynous figure. Usually, these figures were painted with fiery red wings and complexions of the same color. Even though explanations have been attempted, it remains unclear why the face and hands in icons of Hagia Sophia are as fiery red as her seraphic wings. There is an old Byzantine legend which explains the choice of color, but not its symbolism. It relates that Sophia herself personally appeared to the son of one of the architects during the building of Hagia Sophia in Constantinople. In some versions, her face was red; in others, her face was purple.[434] So apparently she's painted this way, because that's the way she looked!

In 1918, just before the Russian Revolution, the highly respected philosopher and writer, Prince Evgenii N. Trubetskoi published an essay entitled "Russia and Her Icons," in which he opined that the red of Sophia's skin was the color of the sunrise. He pointed out that in the earliest Russian Sophia icon, painted in the eleventh century in the St. Sophia Cathedral of Novgorod, Divine Wisdom appears against a dark, starry sky. She is shown this way both because John 1:5 refers to the incarnate Word as "a light that shines in the dark, a light that darkness could not overpower" and because red is an appropriate color for representing the dawn, in the sense that "Sophia is what precedes the days of creation, the power that summons the day out of the darkness of night."[435] In an earlier essay, while commenting on a Sophia icon's "solar nature," Troubetskoi pointed out that an iconographer's associating red with the dawn is prefigured in Homer's well-known references to "rosy-fingered dawn."[436]

The ways Sophia was depicted accurately reflect the dilemma the artists faced. Clearly, they understood "Hagia Sophia" to be a title of the incarnate Christ. It would become even more apparent, when later fuller forms of the name developed - of which there would be several - that the reference was to Christ as the Wisdom or Word of God made flesh. This is confirmed by the fact that, in Constantinople, the patronal feast of Hagia Sophia was celebrated at Christmas.[437] Iconographers also understood Hagia Sophia to be feminine. To depict Hagia Sophia as an angelic being could have been viewed by some as an implicit denial of Christ's Incarnation. Since angels have no bodies, they are obviously not incarnate. This was one reason why, in 692, the Quinisext Council, or Trullan Council,[438] in its canon 82, had explicitly forbidden the use of "symbols" and "shadows" (including, angels, lambs, and fish) to represent the Word of God after his Incarnation.[439] The choice of depicting Sophia as a woman might have been seen to carry with it the inccorrect implication that Christ had been a woman, rather than a man. But at least it implied no denial of the genuineness of Christ's Incarnation, which, as has been noted, was a major issue in the history of Christian dogma. So, for reasons having to do with the demands of Orthodox doctrine, it is likely that many of the icons of Hagia Sophia which writers have described as "angelic" were actually depictions either of women or of androgynes with fiery faces and wings.

Apparently the addition of wings would not have been considered an incontestable proof that an angel was being represented. In every icon of the Old Testament Trinity,[440] all three beings are invariably depicted with wings. These three figures of the "angelic" visitors to the tent of Abraham (in quotes, because Abraham addresses them as "Lord") are always understood to be a foreshadowing of the Divine Trinity. Therefore the figure of one of the three was always considered to be human, rather than angelic foreshadowing. To presume otherwise could have been considered a violation of the restrictions of the Quinisext Council, which explicitly forbade the depicting of the incarnate Second Person of Trinity in the form of an angel.[441] This understanding found its patristic basis in St. Justin the Martyr's *Dialogue with Trypho* 57:2 and in Origen's observations about the Old Testament Trinity in his "Homily on Genesis".

The "problems" which have continued to surface throughout history over the depicting of a feminine Christ spotlight a significant way patriarchal influence has skewed Christian theology. As Elizabeth Johnson has pointed out,

> *The historical particularities of Jesus' person, including his sex, racial characteristics, linguistic heritage, social class, and so on do not signify that God is more appropriately incarnate into these realities than into others. As Rosemary Radford Reuther has tellingly observed, this point has always been clear with regard to Jesus' ethnic and social identity but has been obscured with regard to sexual identity, leading to the prevalent view that the male represents Christ better than the female.*[442]

Wherever Byzantine missionaries brought the Christian faith, they spread devotion to Sophia; for that dedication was given to many of the churches they built. Across the Sea of Marmara from Constantinople was the city of Nicaea, which also had a great church of Hagia Sophia, the site of the Seventh Ecumenical Council (II Nicaea in 787). It had three naves and, since it was built in the fifth century, was older than Justinian's great cathedral.[443] One of Jerusalem's more important churches, dedicated to Hagia Sophia, was built during the Byzantine period at the site in the Praetorium where Jesus was believed to have been flogged.[444] It was one of several churches located on the old Tyropoeon Street, north of Wilson's Arch.[445] Probably razed during the Persian invasion of 614 C.E., it was never rebuilt. The remains of this church appear to be buried beneath a large Crusader structure.[446] The cathedral of Edessa, Syria, also dedicated to Hagia Sophia, was built during the reign of Justinian and the administration of Bishop Amidonius of Edessa. A contemporary Syriac hymn describes it as a square building covered with a windowless dome, probably supported on corner squinches.[447] The main church of Edessa's Greek community, it was destroyed by a flood in 524/5 and rebuilt soon thereafter.[448] By the seventh century, this church housed a famous image of Christ "not made by human hands."[449] According to Eusebius of Caesarea's *Church History* (I 13.1), Jesus himself ordered that this portrait and its accompanying letter be sent to King Abgar of Edessa for the purpose of healing the king. After Christ's Ascension, the Apostle Thomas sent Thaddaeus to bring it to Abgar, who was indeed cured. At first, the image was displayed in a niche over Edessa's city gate, but then it was transferred to Hagia Sophia, where it remained until the church collapsed in an earthquake in 679.[450] The image was then taken to Constantinople. There was also a Hagia Sophia church built in 606, 40 kilometers southeast of Bosra, in the town of Rihab, Jordan.

The brothers, Sts. Cyril (826-69) and Methodius (c.815-85) are considered the Apostles of the Slavs. Given the name Cyril when he became a monk at the end of his life, the younger brother had been baptized Constantine. According to an early account of his childhood, probably written by Methodius, Constantine dreamt of choosing for his wife, from among all the other women in his native Thessalonica, a beautiful woman named Sophia.[451] This was understood to be a pre-figuration of his later life as an apostle whose service to the church would center around the teaching of Divine Wisdom.[452] In the face of an overwhelmingly Christological tenor in Orthodox devotion to Sophia, this eastern account of a saint's mystical marriage to Sophia is remarkably rare.[453] Later in life, Constantine-Cyril even refused a promising marriage, giving as the reason that he was already united to Another. Until the year 863, when the Emperor sent the brothers as missionaries to Moravia, Constantine had been the librarian of Hagia Sophia in Constantinople.

When Prince Boris of Bulgaria embraced Christianity in 865, it was the beginning of a great faith history and an entire tradition of icon painting, which was uniquely Bulgarian. In 1329 Bulgaria changed the name of its capital from Serdica to Sofia, naming it for the ancient church of Sveta Sofia (Holy Wisdom) which was built by Justinian between 532 and 537 and is still in the city's center.[454] This building began as a fourth century burial chapel (*basilica sepulcralis*), adjacent to the acropolis of the old city. The present church dates from the middle of the fifth century.[455] At one time during the fourth century, the Emperor Constantine had used Serdica as his military headquarters. That he also regarded it as his western capital has been suggested by historians who recall that, he once declared, "Serdica is my Rome."[456] Also in the Kingdom of Bulgaria, in the town of Mesembria on the Black Sea coast, was the church of St. Sophia, which prized as a relic the headless body of St. Theodore the Martyr, until it was stolen by the Venetians in 1257.[457]

The great church of Hagia Sophia in Thessaloniki, Greece, was built in the seventh century and was mentioned in a letter written in 795 by St. Theodore the Studite, who was an exile there at the time.[458] The cathedral of Vize (Bizye), on the European side of the Strait of Bosporus, was also dedicated to Holy Wisdom. It was probably built either at the end of the eighth or the beginning of the ninth century.[459] The cathedral of Ochrid, Serbia, called Sveta Sofija, was built by Leo, originally Chartophylax,[460] of Hagia Sophia in Constantinople, who became Archbishop of Ochrid from 1037 to 1057.[461] For several centuries, Armenians ruled over Cilicia, in Asia Minor. In 1196, King Leo I (Levon the Great) of Cilician Armenia was crowned in the church of St. Sophia in Tarsus, home of St. Paul.[462] It was a large building, constructed by the Greeks during the period Cilicia was part of the Byzantine Empire. At Monemvasia in Greece, there rises on a high rocky summit the great church of Hagia Sophia, most spectacularly situated of all Byzantine places of worship, built by Andronicus

II in the late thirteenth century.[463] There was also a famous church of Hagia Sophia built between 1238 and 1263 by Emperor Manuel I in Trebizond, Anatolia, near the Western Armenian border, on the southeast coast of the Black Sea. It was here that scions of the Comnenian branch of the Byzantine imperial family set up a short-lived kingdom after the fall of Constantinople in 1453. The "empire" headquartered at Trebizond lasted seven years before it too fell in 1461, the last place from which Byzantines were ever to rule again.[464] Hagia Sophia in Ypati, Greece, was built in the eleventh century.[465] Hagia Sophia in Mistra, Greece, was built in 1350 by Manuel Cantacuzenos and served as the court church of that city's Palace of the Despots.[466] It was in this church that the last Byzantine Emperor, Constantine XI Paleologus was crowned on January 6, 1449.[467] He died defending the walls of Constantinople on May 29, 1453, the day it fell to the Ottomans.

At the beginning of the fifteenth century, St. Symeon, a monk from Constantinople, was consecrated archbishop of Thessaloniki. This prelate wrote a *Treatise on Prayer* in which he pointed out with no little pride that his own cathedral of Hagia Sophia was the last place on earth where the ancient Greek Cathedral Rite was performed. By that time, in every other cathedral, including Constantinople, the earlier rites had been replaced by the monastic-based Jerusalem liturgical order. In the *Treatise on Prayer*, Symeon reflected on the significance of the "Wisdom" exclamations in the liturgy. Recalling St. Paul's teaching that the Church is the body of Christ, Symeon declares that the Church, having been constituted by Christ, is the dwelling of the living Wisdom of God personified. This derives from Symeon's interpretation of the meaning of *Proverbs* 9:4, which declares that "Wisdom has built herself a house."[468] St. Symeon died in September of 1429. Six months later, Thessaloniki was conquered by the Ottomans and its cathedral turned into a mosque.

Throughout the centuries, in Europe and Asia, dedications to Holy Wisdom continued to appear, extending the devotion to Cyprus, Crete, Italy, Sicily, Sardinia, Gaul, the Iberian Peninsula, as far north west as York, England and as far east as Tokyo, Japan. Sometime after the year 780, Blessed Alcuin, a distinctive person who became head of Charlmagne's palace school at Aachen, wrote a nostalgic poem entitled *The Bishops, Kings, and Saints of York*,[469] in which he recalled that, under the direction of Archbishop Aelberth, he and the future Archbishop Eanbald I of York built a large basilica there with thirty altars, dedicated to Holy Wisdom on October 31, 780. Archaeologists have thus far been able to find no trace of this building. The Greek Orthodox Cathedral of St. Sophia was founded in London in 1877. The city of Harbin, in the extreme north east of China, had a large Russian population, which had the Cathedral of St. Sophia built between 1923 and 1942. They spared no expenses on what became the most beautiful and opulent Byzantine edifice south of Moscow. While there were still 23 Russian Orthodox churches open in Harbin in 1949, today there is only one. St. Sophia, though considered a Class I Protected Building, is currently being used as a furniture warehouse. In 1911, the Jesuits in Tokyo incorporated Sophia University, which opened two years later and still thrives.

Holy Wisdom is seen by thousands of people every day as they gaze at one of the most famous frescoes in the world – the Creation of Adam, painted by Michelangelo Buonarroti on the ceiling of the Sistine Chapel. God the Father is shown embracing Holy Wisdom with his left arm as he extends his right finger to Adam. Divine Wisdom is shown as a lovely woman who appears to be mesmerized by what she sees happening. Michelangelo filled the Sistine frescoes with symbols from Kabbalah -Jewish Mysticism. Having studied Kabbalah with famous teachers in Florence, Michelangelo was well aware that in the daily prayers of traditional Jews, there is a blessing that offers thanksgiving for our life and for the genius of our bodily functions. This prayer expresses gratitude to God *Asher yatzar et Ha-Adam b'Chochmah*, "Who formed Adam (Humankind) with Wisdom.*xxxiv*

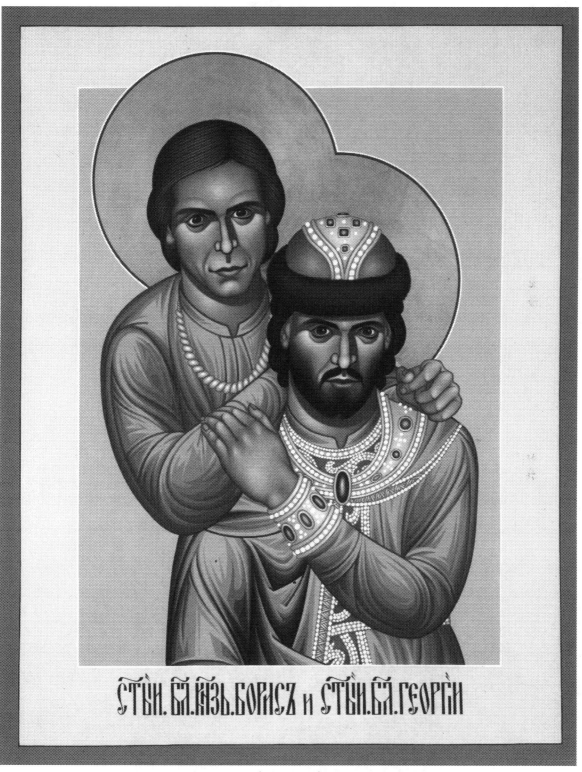

Sts. Boris and George the Hungarian

St. Andrei Rublev

Holy New Martyr Priest-Monk Nestor Savchuck

Chapter XI
How the Sophia Tradition Came to the "Third Rome"
Divine Sophia in the Literature of Westernized Russia
and Sophia in Post-Soviet Russia

The understanding that Hagia Sophia is feminine was brought to Kievan Rus'[470] from the very beginning of its Christian history. Russian Orthodox Church theologians have struggled ever since then with the dogmatic issues which surface when Sophia-Christ is depicted as a woman. Following her baptism in Constantinople in 957, the sainted widow of Prince Igor I of Kiev, Princess Olga (d. 969) had churches built in Kiev, Pskov, and Vitebsk. Her church in Kiev, which eventually would become its cathedral, was consecrated to St. Sophia-Holy Wisdom[471], whom the princess believed to be the Virgin Mary.[472] Indeed, the great mosaic of the Virgin Mary in the apse of St. Sophia in Kiev is still described as a depiction of Sophia.[473] If, during her time in Constantinople, St. Olga saw Christ/Holy Wisdom depicted as a woman, it would be understandable that, in this case, she confused him with his blessed Mother. It is more likely that the huge ninth-century mosaic of the Virgin and Child, an image of astonishing grandeur and tenderness, which she would have seen recently reinstalled in the apse above the sanctuary of Hagia Sophia in Constantinople misled her into believing that she was admiring the patronal image of the cathedral, while she focused on the Mother, rather than her divine Child.[474] It would have been an easy enough mistake to make. When such images of the Christ child enthroned in his seated Mother's lap arrived in the West, they were often called "Seat of Wisdom" figures - Wisdom being Christ and the Seat his Mother.

The cathedral of Kiev was built by Prince Yaroslav the Wise, who succeeded St. Vladimir and ruled from 1016 to 1054. Completed in 1037, it was formally dedicated to Hagia Sophia and still stands today.[475] In 1051, "Yaroslav, after assembling the bishops, appointed Hilarion Metropolitan of Russia in St. Sophia,"[476] thus making him the first non-Greek head of the Eastern Slavic Church and Metropolitan of Kiev. Hilarion was one of the most brilliant and erudite preachers of the Kiev's "Golden Age". His famous "Sermon on Law and Grace" is the oldest Rus' literary-philosophical work and one of the earliest Rus' sermons preserved.[477] Part of its text reads:

> The wisdom of God was not revealed to anyone, but concealed from both angels and men. This wisdom was not shown, but was concealed to be revealed at the end of the age....And so the Divine Grace (of the Son) announced to God, the Father: "It is not yet my time for descending to the earth and to save the world....And so, when the end of the age was nearing, God appeared to the humankind, descended to the earth, and blessed the womb of the Virgin.[477]

Commenting on this passage, Serge Zenkovsky observed that the wisdom of God about which Hilarion speaks is "Holy Sophia".[479]

At about the same time as the Mother of God mosaic was reinstalled in Constantinople's cathedral, there was a similar mosaic installed in the Nicaea's Church of the Dormition (destroyed in 1922). In the Nicaea mosaic, she was standing holding the Christ Child. Likewise a lovely mosaic of a seated Mother and Child can still be seen in the eleventh century in the apse of St. Sophia in Thessaloniki.[480] A remarkable large icon painted c. 1360 for the iconosatsis of St. Sophia in Thessaloniki depicts "Christ the Wisdom of God" as a bearded Christ Pantocrator,[481] which proves that, in that century, Christ continued to be identified with Holy Wisdom. But it may also indicate an incipient discomfort with the traditional feminine/androgynous Sophia/Christ.

Whereas in the mosaics at Nicaea and Thessaloniki, Mary was depicted holding the Christ child, in the majestic apse mosaic at Kiev, there is no Child. She stands alone with her hands raised in the *orans* (intercessory) position. St, Olga may have been responsible for this. She was baptized in Hagia Sophia Cathedral in Constantinople in 958. When she gazed up into the apse of the cathedral, she would have seen the recently restored (in 867) mosaic of Mary the Theotokos, enthroned with her Divine Son, Holy Wisdom, enthroned on her lap. This lovely mosaic is still in the apse. When she gazed at this image, representing Holy Wisdom enthroned, she might well have misunderstood, not realizing that the focus is meant to be on the Child, rather than on the Mother. Then she brought that misunderstanding back with her to Kiev. If St. Olga mistakenly identified Sophia with Mary, then it is understandable that Mary is represented in Kiev without her divine Child. This confusion of Sophia with Mary is also reflected in the Kiev cathedral's iconostasis, whose Sophia icon depicts the Mother of God with the Christ Child on her breast, beneath images of God the Father and a dove, symbolizing the Holy Spirit - the three together constituting a Trinity. In the icon pattern books, the cartoon for a Kiev-type icon, shows Sophia as a winged Mother of God.[483] The feast of Holy Wisdom in Kiev was celebrated on the feast of Mary's Nativity, so the Kievan identification of Sophia with Mary appears there on several levels.[484] Sophia icons of this type could also be found in the hermitage at Optina and in the Zion Cathedral at Tiflis, Georgia.[485]

St. Sophia in Kiev was not the only, and, perhaps, not even the finest monument of its kind. Right next to it was another great church which was destroyed by Batu during the siege of St. Sophia - the so-called *Desyatinnaya* Church (Church of the Tithes), which was also known as the Sophia.[486] The cornerstone of this church was dedicated by St. Vladimir in 989. Known throughout history as the Church of the Assumption of the Virgin, the Desyatinnaya Church is the first and oldest building in Rus'.[487] The original of this church was built of stone and had 25 cupolas.[488] Recalling that St. Olga had a St. Sophia Cathedral constructed in Kiev, there was obviously a building of that name built earlier than the present cathedral. If Grekov is correct in claiming that the Desyatinnaya Church was called Sophia, perhaps he must mean that it had that name until the present St. Sophia Cathedral was built in 1037 by Vladimir's son, Yaroslav the Wise. This would make the present St. Sophia Cathedral the third in Kiev's history.

As Christianity spread, Sophia churches began to spring up all over Rus'.[489] In addition to the St. Sophia Cathedral in Kiev[490], the Cathedral of St. Sophia in Polotsk[491] is mentioned in *The Lay of Igor's Campaign*, which was written on the occasion of Prince Igor's rash campaign against the Kuman nomads in 1185. This Polotsk St. Sophia was built as a replacement for an earlier wooden cathedral of the same name, built at approximately the time of the construction of the present St. Sophia in Kiev.[492] The Kievan school also produced the tale of *Pious Prince Dovmont and His Courage*, which mentions that, in 1267, this prince and his Pskovian and Novgorodian men fought the Germans at Rokover and were victorious, "thanks to the intercession of holy Sophia, the Wisdom of God."[493]

Many of the radiant icons of Saint Sophia-Holy Wisdom which were painted in Novgorod, Moscow, and Jaroslavl can be found in churches and museums to this day. In cities other than Kiev, they represent Christ.

There was a St. Sophia Cathedral in Jaroslavl, which was contemporary with, but slightly smaller than the St. Sophia in Kiev.[494] In Jaroslavl's church of St. John Chrysostomos, Holy Wisdom is depicted as the crucified Savior. Here it is meant to be understood as a symbol of the Church as the Body of Christ.

When the Christian faith arrived in Novgorod, believers built a St. Sophia Cathedral there. The first Novgorod St. Sophia was constructed of oak, had 13 cupolas, and may have been built as early as 989. It was destroyed by fire. Its replacement, constructed between 1045 and 1050, was one of the earliest stone structures in northern Rus'. The oldest Sophia icon in Russia is a fresco above the main altar in this church and also dates from the eleventh century.[495] It is supposed to be a copy of the Divine Sophia icon, which was in Constantinople's Cathedral.[496] In describing it, the early Slavophile writer Ivan Kireyevski (d. 1856) wrote, that, century after century, this icon absorbed the currents of passionate exaltation and the prayers of grieving, unhappy people. "It must have become filled with energy, which became a living organ, a meeting-place of man and Creator."[497]

Fr. Vladimir Ivanov describes St. Sophia in Novgorod as

> *a cathedral surmounted by an angelic being with wings of fire, identified with Sophia-Divine Wisdom...a symbolic point of reference for the city: 'Wherever you find Sophia, there you will also find Novgorod.'*[498]

The icon painters of Rus' were not bound by the complex inheritance of antiquity the way their Byzantine and Greek teachers had been. The roots of the emerging Kievan culture were much less deep. Thus they achieved a remarkably high level and purity of image, which makes Rus' iconography outstanding among many other examples of Orthodox iconography.

> *It was indeed given to Russia to produce that perfection of the pictorial language of the icon, which revealed with such great force the depth of meaning of the liturgic image, its spirituality. It can be said that if Byzantium was pre-eminent in giving the world theology expressed in words, theology expressed in the image was given pre-eminently by Russia.*[499]

Icon painters in Rus' would continue to depict Sophia throughout the centuries. In the Church of the Dormition in Volotovo (Novgorod diocese), there is a fourteenth century fresco of "Sophia Divine Wisdom", who is inspiring St. Matthew. She appears in the form of a woman, of the sort depicted in the allegorical portrait of Anicia Juliana.[500] From the fifteenth century on, Novgorod icons would follow Greek models in resuming the depiction of Sophia in the form of a fiery angel.[501]

Prince Eugene N. Trubetskoi, a respected authority on the history of icon art, refers to Great Novgorod as "the Russian Florence" - the home of Russian religious art in the fourteenth and fifteenth centuries and the place of its highest achievements. He also points out that, in the fourteenth century, the chief representatives of this creative upsurge were the foreigners Isaiah the Greek and Theophanes the Greek. Theophanes, the foremost Novgorod master and teacher of icon painting, included among his pupils St. Andrei Rublev, the founder of the independent school of Russian icon painting. These Greek masters also worked on churches and cathedrals in Novgorod and Moscow. In 1343, they decorated the cathedral of the Assumption in Moscow. Theophanes painted the frescos in the church of the Archangel Michael in 1399; and in 1405, together with Andrei Rublev, frescoes in the cathedral of the Annunciation.[502]

As ecclesiastical head of the studio which was producing most of the best sacred art at the time, Archbishop Gennady (d. 1504) of Novgorod was very interested in theological aspects regarding the veneration of icons and insisted that iconography correspond completely to dogma. Like Constantinople, Novgorod identified Christ with Divine Wisdom and celebrated the feast of Holy Wisdom on Christmas Day. But Gennady tried to bring about "a rapprochement between the images of Sophia-Divine Wisdom and the Virgin by instituting a feast of dedication of St. Sophia Cathedral during the Marian celebration of the Dormition" (also called the Assumption of the Virgin, August 15th).[503] Gennady's attempted "rapprochement" probably only added to the confusion and led even more people into thinking that "Hagia Sophia" must have been a title of the Virgin Mary, rather than of her divine Son.

Representative of the work produced during Gennady's administration is a famous Sophia icon from Novgorod painted around 1500. Here Wisdom is seated on a throne crowned and dressed in imperial garments. The figure holds a scepter as a sign of royal dignity and a scroll representing the content of Wisdom. The face, hands, and wings are fiery-red, and the tunic is of transparent gold. The feet rest on a stone, representing the unshakable foundation of faith. Beneath the throne are seven vertical columns, representing the seven pillars of Wisdom, and the seven gifts of the Spirit mentioned in *Isaiah*.[504] Standing on either side are the Mother of God holding Christ/Emmanuel and St. John the Baptist, both in classic *Deesis* ("entreating") posture - a stance used in icons only when Christ is in the center.

Another presentation of Sophia, in which she is even more clearly represented as a woman, can be found in the icons entitled "Wisdom hath built her house", derived from the passage in Proverbs 9:1-6, which begins, "Wisdom has built herself a house, she has erected her seven pillars..." Examples of this sort of icon exist that date back to the ninth century.[505] A marvelous one can be found in Moscow's Tretyakov Gallery. It was originally painted in the mid-sixteenth century for the Monastery of St. Cyril, near Novgorod.

> *In a large iridescent circle, we see Sophia herself, Divine Wisdom, dressed in white, with a star-shaped halo (in the iconography of Novgorod the figure of Sophia is dressed in red). To the right the Mother of God sits on her throne...*[506]

This is clearly a female Sophia, and not the Virgin Mary

In the mid-seventeenth century, the Novgorod school produced a depiction of "St. Sophia-Divine Wisdom" which shows Sophia as a winged female/androgyne, enthroned and crowned, with a fiery red complexion and similarly colored wings. This is meant to represent Christ, since the Virgin and St. John the Baptist stand on either side, venerating in the Deesis posture. The Virgin is shown holding a disk with the face of the Christ Child/Emmanuel; and above and behind the "Sophia", the upper half of an adult Christ is depicted with his hands extended in blessing. So the image includes the Virgin, St. John, and three aspects of Christ, surrounded by cherubim and seraphim.[507] Apparently, this was as unconfused as it was going to get, despite Archbishop Gennady's efforts.

From the time the metropolitan seat of Moscow was established in 1326, a distinctive civilization began to emerge under its leadership. In 1453, the last Byzantine Emperor, Constantine XI Dragases, died when Constantinople fell to the Ottomans. In 1472, Ivan III, "The Great" of Moscow (d.1505) married Constantine's niece, Sophia, and assumed the imperial title of "Czar (Caesar) of all Russia." His presumption was backed by the military hegemony he achieved during his reign.[508]

Moscow also began to consider itself the "Third Rome", the sole depository of imperial power and the only receptacle of unsullied Orthodoxy. The theory of the Third Rome was first formulated by a monk named Filofei (Philotheus) of Pskov who, in 1510, wrote a famous epistle to Czar Vasili (Basil) III (d. 1533), in which he declared that, with the first Rome fallen to Apollinarianism (a heresy which denied the humanity of Christ) and Constantinople, the Second Rome, fallen to the infidels, a Third Rome had sprung up in the Czar's sovereign kingdom, a Rome which would stand firm and never be followed by a fourth. He declared Vasili III the sole king of all the Christians in the world. This "Third Rome" identity was quickly taken up both by the Czars and by the Russian Orthodox Church.

In the same epistle, Filofei also included a long appeal to the Czar to help in combating a high incidence of genitally expressed same-gender relationships in the monasteries.[509] Vasili III would hardly have been enthused by this exhortation, for he himself seems to have been drawn exclusively to same-gender relationships throughout his life. While it is true that for reasons of state, he married Princess Helena Glinsky, he was only able to carry out his conjugal duties if one of the officers of his guard joined them in bed in the nude.[510] The domestic life of Vasilii and Helena was a hell on earth, which produced two offspring, the mentally challenged Yuri and Ivan IV "The Terrible" (d. 1584). Foreign visitors to Moscow during the reign of Vasili III were both shocked and fascinated at the high incidence of same-gender sexual activity which they observed not only in the Czar and some of the clergy, but at every level of society.[511] In his book *Rerum moscovitarum commentarii*, Sigismund von Herberstein, the ambassador of the Holy Roman Empire to the court of Vasilii III, noted that such relationships were prevalent among all the social classes.[512] "Sermon No. 12" by Metropolitan Daniel, a popular Moscow preacher of the 1530s, is almost totally devoted to denouncing the same-gender activity which he considered rampant.[513] The minor English poet George Turberville reported that he was stunned to have observed the same behavior among Russian peasants during the reign of Ivan the Terrible, whose close spiritual advisor, Father Silvestr, was convinced that all the same-gender sexual activities among the monks was about to bring God's wrath on the Sodom and Gomorrah of the Russian plain.[514]

To the superstitious, the reign of the blood-thirsty, sociopathic, pious Ivan IV was cursed from the beginning. In the year 1547, the year of his coronation, a tremendous fire broke out, which destroyed much of Moscow and many of its churches. Ivan ordered icons brought to his capital from Novgorod, Smolensk, Dimitrov, Zvenigorod, and other cities to replace those destroyed, and he put master icon painters to work, under the supervision of Father Silvestr, who ordered that the icons be painted according to a precise selection of five theological themes, one of which was Sophia-Divine Wisdom.[515] Ivan the Terrible liked his wives, but he was also allegedly attracted to young men in drag. A ruthless man who served on Ivan's Council of Four- whose duty was to superintend the regular operations of Ivan's equally ruthless army – was Fyodor Basmanov. He attained his powerful position because he was reputedly quite attractive, slept with Ivan, and performed seductive dances in female attire for Ivan and his trusted friends, probably at a hunting lodge outside of Moscow, which Ivan used as an exclusively male sort of place[516] Though many hated Basmonov, they learned to keep it to themselves. When Prince Dmitry Ovchina-Obolensky once said to Basmanov, "We serve the Czar with useful labor: you serve him with sodomy," Ivan ordered his dog keepers to strangle Dmitry.[517]

Founded in 1147, the city of Vologda is situated northeast of Moscow. Its importance in the sixteenth century is demonstrated by the great interest Czar Ivan the Terrible took in its development. For the three and a half years, beginning 1567, he was a frequent visitor. He wanted to guarantee that it would remain attached to Moscow, rather than Novgorod. In 1571, the patriarchal see was transferred there from Ust-Vym, near Perm. Its beautiful new cathedral was built at that time. The fact that Vologda cathedral was consecrated to Hagia Sophia, the Wisdom of God, which in itself was highly unusual for the sixteenth century, was undoubtedly meant as a blow to the pride of the Novgorodian church.[518]

The latter half of the sixteenth century saw the emergence of a wealthy boyar family named Stroganov, from whose lavish support an entire school of icon painters developed. The *Icon-Writer's Guide* was produced for use in their studio during that time. The term "patronage" is out of place with regard to the Stroganovs. They not only invested huge sums of money into art but also took personal interest in the work being carried out. They were deeply religious and interested in the theology expressed by the icons as well as the images themselves. The finest example of their work can be seen in the paintings in the Cathedral of the Annunciation (1564), in Sol'vychegodsk (Salt of Vychegda), one of the family's northern properties. Depicted on its iconostasis is an icon probably as unique for its pictorial style as for its iconographic arrangement. It is called "Rebuilding of the Temple of the Resurrection: In Praise of the Mother of God." In its lower portion, there is a depiction of Sophia enthroned between Sts. John the Baptist and John the Evangelist. Here Holy Wisdom is seen to be the link between the Hebrew Testament and the New Testament. In addition, the representation of the two Johns in the presence of Sophia is the fulfillment of the idea that each of these servants had a common charismatic nature founded in Christ, the Wisdom of God.[519] The Stroganov studios continued to produce fine icons for centuries.

Later Wisdom depictions would be the seventeenth century Sophia on the pediment of the Dormition Cathedral, completed in 1479, in the Moscow Kremlin[520] and the seventeenth-century icon of Hagia Sophia in the iconostasis (icon screen) in the Patriarch's Church of the Assembly of the Twelve Apostles - also in the Moscow Kremlin.[521] But none would attain the perfection of the fifteenth-century icons.[522]

There also developed, almost exclusively in Russia, a sort of icon which came to be called "Christ Holy Silence" (*Hagia Hesychia*).[523] The source of this icon can be found in an illumination in the 14th century Codex Crecae 339, preserved at St. Catherine's Monastery on Mt. Sinai. They are very similar to Sophia icons, in that they depict Christ as a royally robed and beardless. But in the Hesychia model, Christ is always a woman with long hair.

On September 17, 1657, a daughter was born to Czar Alexei Mikhailovich of Russia. Because that date was the feast of the legendary St. Sophia the martyr, whose three daughters, Faith, Hope, and Charity were said to be her companions in martyrdom, the baby was given the name Sophia. In 1682, following a dynastic crisis, the twenty-five year old Sophia was appointed Regent to her two younger brothers, the retarded Ivan, and the ten year old Peter the Great. Thus she became the first woman to rule Russia.

In 1689, a Silesian Protestant named Quirinus Kuhlman came to Russia and attempted to introduce a faith which sought to recapture lost links with God by uniting the self with Divine Wisdom. Sophia, in this tradition, was understood to be a physical - sometimes even sexual - force as well as a merely intellectual form of "divine wisdom." The Regent Sophia had Kuhlmann and his followers declared bearers of "schism, heresy, and false prophecy." Six months after his arrival in Russia, she had him, his writings, and his principal collaborator burned in Moscow's Red Square.[524]

Very soon after this, Sophia was ousted by Peter and dispatched to a convent for the rest of her life. During her turbulent life, she made significant contributions to the spreading of devotion to Holy Wisdom. Ever assuming that she was equally under the protection of St. Sophia and Christ-Holy Wisdom, she commissioned many icons of both. In 1685, for example, she commissioned the Armory painter Fyodor Zubov to paint several icons of Holy Wisdom for her rooms, as well as an icon of St. Sophia for the chapel with that dedication in the main Cathedral of the Novodevichy Convent in Moscow.[525]

The Cathedral of Our Lady of Smolensk was right in the center of the Novodevichy Convent. Both had been founded by Czar Vasilii III in 1524 and would serve as Sophia's final home and the place of her burial in 1704. The Czarevna Sophia was conventionally given the epithet "wise" in courtly verses.[526] Her chaplain, Silvestr Mdevedev, eulogized her thus: "For the Divine Wisdom of God has favored her with more wisdom than others and except for her no one else was capable of ruling the Russian state."[527]

In a manner reminiscent of the only extant depiction of the Byzantine princess Anicia Juliana, Sophia too was allegorized in a picture which implicitly compared her to Holy Wisdom. The earliest known pictorial reference to her produced during her regency shows her young brothers Ivan and Peter being blessed by Christ, and above them a maiden with eagle's wings being crowned by heaven. The composition is a variation on the iconographic subject of the Holy Wisdom, Sophia - *premudrost' bozhiia*. In the center of the composition is a columned shrine containing a double-headed eagle with a double heart, illustrating the text 'Wisdom has built herself a house, She has erected her seven pillars'. (*Proverbs* 9:1) The clear implication was that Holy Wisdom influenced and protected the two under aged tsars, just as their Sophia (the de facto ruler) was deemed to do in real life.[528] In August of 1689, Archimandrite Ignaty of the Novospassky Monastery composed an exegesis of the Divine Wisdom icon in which Sophia serves as the central figure of the hierarchy of the Muscovite state.[529]

A century later, between 1782 and 1787, commissioned by Empress Catherine II "the Great" (d. 1796), English architect Charles Cameron built the St. Sophia Cathedral at Tsarskoe Selo, her palace near St. Petersburg.

Despite the efforts of Czar Peter the Great (d. 1725) to Westernize his people at the turn of the eighteenth century, Russia proper remained basically an illiterate and insular country until the nineteenth century.[530] In the year 1800, there were only two bookstores in the entire city of Moscow, and there were more universities in England, France, and Germany than there were university students in all of Russia.[531] (If you include in this statement the half of Ukraine - the Right Bank - which was claimed by Russia to be part of Russian territory at the Treaty of Periaslav in 1654, then the literacy level was a bit higher.)

During the nineteenth century, in many, but not all, respects, Russian intellectual life quickly caught up with the West, to which it continued to look for models and inspiration. Several fine writers emerged, who produced a distinct national literature and philosophical/mystical schools of thought in which Holy Wisdom had a central place.

The most important single influence on the formation of a Russian philosophical tradition was the Silesian mystic, Jacob Boehme (d. 1624). An occult manuscript printed during the relatively liberal reign of Czar Alexander II (1855-81) referred to Sophia as "the auspicious eternal virgin of Divine Wisdom." A. Labzin, Boehme's principal translator and popularizer in Russia, gave himself the pen name Student of Wisdom (*Uchenik Mudrosti*), which he often abbreviated as UM. The most influential philosophic circle to develop late in Alexander's reign called itself Lovers of Wisdom (*Liubomudrye*).[532] Additionally, and most importantly, there was a group who came to be called the sophiologists, whose "father" was philosopher/mystic, Vladimir Soloviev. In the period just before the Russian Revolution attempted to put an end to every aspect of religion in his country, this idealist claimed Divine Sophia as the inspiration of his universal vision.

Born in 1853 and affected by the ideological trends of the sixties, Soloviev was a man preoccupied with religion and aesthetics. His father, Sergius Soloviev, had written a history of Russia, which has never been equaled either in size or in encyclopedic command of sources.[533] The Soloviev household was religiously zealous in atmosphere; and Vladimir started out in life an extremely precocious, devout, and sensitive young man. He had a strong model and teacher in his paternal grandfather, Fr. Mikhail Vassilievich Soloviev, an Archpriest of the Russian Orthodox Church and treasured friend of the saintly, highly-respected Metropolitan Philaret of Moscow. By the age of seven, Vladimir had become so impassioned a reader of the lives of the saints that his parents began to fear that he was overdoing it. From his grandfather, he had heard wonderful stories about the medieval St. Sergius of Radonezh,[534] learning among other things that, under the inspiration of Jesus' Last Supper prayer for the unity of all future generations of believers, St. Sergius had encouraged mutual love among his own followers and found in the Holy Trinity the source, the model, and the goal of such a life. Soloviev was about to find a similar inspiration in the Divine Sophia.

At the age of nine he had the first of his visions of the Eternal Feminine, which would inspire both his poetry and his social theories. This took place while he was attending the Ascension Day liturgy in the chapel of the University of Moscow in May of 1862.[535] As he entered the chapel with his nurse, he was brooding jealously over the fact that a young girl his age, on whom he had a romantic crush was clearly more interested in another boy. Suddenly, during the procession of the Eucharistic gifts, it seemed as though the clergy, the people, and the choir vanished and the boy was alone beneath the vault of heaven, surrounded with an azure veil, shot through with streams of golden radiance. And in the light, at the very heart of his own soul, he first saw the lovely figure of Sophia, whom he came to call his Eternal Friend. All jealousy disappeared, and he was ecstatically happy.

A few years later, while riding a train to Kharkov, he was rescued from nearly falling under the cars by a young woman whom he met during the ride. As they were passing from one car to another, he fainted and would have fallen under the train, if she hadn't saved him. As he gazed at his rescuer, he saw her transfigured into a single image which contained all things, instilling in him an infinite, all-embracing love, through which he felt for the first time the fullness and meaning of life.[536] What he saw was a divine woman, whom he later identified as Sophia. She came to him holding a flower in the midst of shining light. This was an experience typical of the occult mystical tradition which he did much to revive and make respectable in Russia.[537]

From the ages of fourteen to eighteen, he lost his childhood faith and became a passionate and violent atheist, passing through one phase after another of theoretical negation, only to return to faith in his later adolescence.[538]

While preparing for his degree during the academic year 1873-74, Soloviev enrolled as a student in the Theological Academy of St. Sergius's Monastery of the Holy Trinity, which, under the able administration of Metropolitan Philaret, had come to be called the "Oxford of Russia."[539]

He had another vision of Sophia a year later, while he was studying Gnostic texts in London's British Museum, where Karl Marx had earlier in the century been working out his own theories.[540]

In the Museum, as Soloviev was praying to Sophia, her face appeared to him and directed him to go to Egypt, where she would visit him again and give him guidance. He did indeed have a vision in Egypt, in which she instructed him to return to Russia and begin to teach.

He presented his new theories to an eager and welcoming public. The first of his lectures on *Divine Humanity* he read on January 26, 1878 to a packed St. Petersburg audience, which included Leo Tolstoy and Feodor Dostoevsky. As his listeners were able to take in his message, they began to see him as a major philosophical mind who offered a religiously, mystically inspired notion of community which was a viable alternative to socialist notions of it.

Soloviev's conception of renovation was, in many respects, even more revolutionary and utopian than that of the Marxists. It was based on the belief that all things on the planet are in search of a unity, which is bound to be realized in the concrete world through Sophia. The Sophia of his visions combines the feminine principle of Jakob Boehme's theosophy with the Divine Wisdom of the Greek East.

According to Soloviev, by seeking a kind of mystical erotic union with Sophia, we put ourselves in communion with the ideal "all unity" which pervades God's cosmos. He did not advocate a contemplative retreat from the world. He believed rather that the striving for "all unity" impels one into the world of the concrete. God seeks "all unity" through creation, which is an intimate form of God's self-expression. Therefore Soloviev challenged people to seek the same unity and self-expression through art, personal relations, and all other areas of creative experience.

His essay on "The Meaning of Love" is the most remarkable of all that he wrote. Philosopher Nicholas Berdyaev described it as the one and only original message which has been spoken on the subject of love as Eros in the history of Christian thought, declaring Soloviev the first Christian thinker who really acknowledged a personal and not merely a family meaning of love between man and woman.[541]

Soloviev never married and appears to have lived a rather lonely life. Nevertheless he taught that sexual desire is one of the positive impulses through which the sense of division in humanity is gradually being overcome.[542]

He frequently visited the Cathedral of St. Sophia in Novgorod to meditate on its ancient icon called "Sophia, the All-Wisdom of God", to which he was much attracted.[543] There was supposedly some considerable mystery about this icon. Soloviev described it as a depiction of

> *the most exalted, all-encompassing form, the living soul of Nature and cosmos, one with God from all Eternity…an all-encompassing, divinely-human completeness, revealed to us by Christianity…the actual, pure, perfect mankind.*[544]

In his lectures on Divine Humanity, Soloviev affirmed that the sole and exclusive content of Christianity is Christ. He maintained that the uniqueness of Christ is to be found not so much in Jesus' ethical teachings, most of which could be ascribed to other great religious teachers as well. The unique thing about Christ is the concrete, integral fact of his life and mission in overcoming the separation between humankind and God and in bridging the chasm which separates people from each other. And the dynamic which attracts people and draws them into unity is the quality of Sophia in Christ Himself, Sophia being the idea which God has before him as Creator and which God realizes in creation.[545]

According to Soloviev, Sophia is God incarnate in Christ:

> *Sophia is God's body, the matter of Divinity, permeated with the principle of divine unity. Actualizing in Himself, or bearing, this unity, Christ, as the integral divine organism, both universal and individual, is both Logos and Sophia.* [546]

In order to help his contemporaries concretely to find Sophia, Soloviev offered a variety of programs for overcoming conflicts in the late seventies. He began by dividing the royalties from his *Divine Humanity* lectures between the Red Cross and the fund for restoring Hagia Sophia Cathedral in Istanbul. He was involved in many projects to help alleviate human suffering. Concerned about the plight of the Jews in Russia, he condemned the way they were isolated and persecuted.[547]

His teaching also had an important ecological dimension. He wrote:

> *It is time men realized their oneness with Mother Earth and rescued her from lifelessness so they can also save themselves from death. But what oneness can we have with the earth, when we have no such oneness, no such moral relationships among ourselves.* [548]

In the 1880's, he began to proclaim that the reunion of Christendom was a vital component in God's plan for the ultimate unification of humankind. He was determined to do all he could to help unite the Catholic, Protestant, and Orthodox churches. The more he knew about these branches of Christianity, the more he was drawn to Catholicism and saw the Bishop of Rome, the Western Patriarch, as the logical focal point and hub around which Christianity could rebuild unity. The Vatican was the only independent, international ecclesiastical power in the world at the time. Of course, Pope Leo XIII blessed such a plan.[549] And it was supported by leading Western Catholic officials. But, understandably, the notion was not popular among most of the Orthodox clergy.

In 1896, deprived of the sacraments by many of the Orthodox clergy, Soloviev received the Catholic communion from the hands of Father Nikolai Tolstoi, having previously both declared his adhesion to the teachings of the Council of Trent, and reaffirmed his belief that the Orthodox Church was also the single visible Church of Jesus Christ.[550]

During these years, he also urged the Russian people to set aside their political chauvinism, narrowness, and provincialism. In 1881, he reached the sad turning point in his life. He permanently lost the support of many people and was treated with great hostility when he implored Czar Alexander III to forgive the assassins of his father, Alexander II, and to become "the new Charlemagne" who would politically unite Christendom.[551] However, he never lost the support of a significant following, who endorsed most of his projects and his writings. One of his closest friends among them was the novelist, Feodor Dostoevsky (d. 1881).

Soloviev and Dostoevsky knew each other well and significantly influenced each other's thought. Soloviev is the prototype for the character Alyosha Karamazov in *The Brothers Karamazov*.[552] Some years after Dostoevsky's death, his widow wrote the following words in her copy of *The Brothers Karamazov*, in the margin next of the Elder Zossima's farewell conversations, where Alyosha is mentioned: "This was how Dostoyevski regarded his intimate friend, the young philosopher, Vladimir Soloviev."[553]

Holy Wisdom also appears as a character in one of Dostoevsky's novels. In *Crime and Punishment*, the nihilist Raskolnikov, lives up to his name ("schismatic"), cutting himself off from the Russian community, by murdering two women with an axe. But then he finds redemption through the

Christian humility and compassion of Sonia (nickname for "Sophia"),[554] an adolescent girl who works as a prostitute to support her impoverished family. There is an inherent holiness to Sonia because her spirit is not corrupted by the sale of her flesh. Having confessed his crimes to Sonia, Raskolnikov asks her what he should do. With an ecological sensitivity reminiscent of *Genesis 4:10* where God declared to Cain that the blood of his murdered brother Abel cried out from the ground, Sonia says to him,

> 'Go at once, this very minute, stand at the cross-roads, bow down, first
> kiss the earth which you have defiled and then bow down to all the world
> and say to all men aloud, 'I am a murderer!'[555]

In the cosmic web of interconnectedness, an assault on a human being is an assault on Mother Earth herself, a notion which Soloviev would have endorsed wholeheartedly. Raskolnikov and Sonia are a classical example of the contrast between left brain and right brain. He is all mind-thought, severed from the heart and wholeness; while she is a naïve, exploited adolescent, who is nevertheless in touch with heart and emotions.

Soloviev's mystical faith in Divine Wisdom was also one of the main inspirations behind the mysticism in the creative activity of another of his friends, the composer Alexander Scriabin (d. 1915).[556]

There were other Russian composers whose skill and mystical bent served Sophia well before the fall of Czardom. According to Byzantine expert Constantine Cavarnos, "Sacred singing is a means of educating and being educated in Christ's Divine wisdom,"[557] Set to music more frequently than any other in the Orthodox Church, the Liturgy of St. John Chrysostom was set by Pyotr Tchaikovsky[558] in 1878 and by Sergei Rachmaninov in 1910. Interspersed throughout this liturgy are acclamations to Holy Wisdom. In the Greek version of this liturgy, Sophia is evoked in the intercessory prayers, just prior to the reading of the Gospel, and when the doors of the iconostasis are opened prior to the distribution of Holy Communion. The faithful are thereby reminded that they are nurtured on Sophia whenever they receive the Word and the Eucharist. The Russian Orthodox version of this Liturgy is in a strongly Russified form of Old Slavonic. Here, the word for Sophia is *Premudrost'*. *Mudrost* is the word for wisdom. *Premudrost* means Wisdom, with a capital "W."

Vladimir Soloviev died July 28, 1900 in the house of his dear friend and disciple, the philosopher-prince Sergei Nikolayevich Troubetskoi, whose brother, Eugene Nikolayevich, would later include in his book *Icons: Theology in Color* some fine reflections on the significance of the ways Sophia is depicted in Russian icons. By the time of his death, Soloviev had won a significant number of Marxists over to his way of thinking and of unbelievers back to participation in the Church. As a young man, he seems to have had a strong desire to accomplish something equal in significance to his father, Sergius's, achievement as a historian. Vladimir's breadth of vision for humankind's possibilities was remarkable and significant indeed.

His doctrine of Sophia and his verses devoted to it, had an enormous influence upon the symbolist poets of the beginning of the twentieth century, Alexander Blok and Andrei Bely, both of whom believed in Sophia but not in Christ, a fact which constituted an enormous difference between them and Soloviev.[559]

Another contemporary poet who knew Soloviev's work well was Marina Ivanova Tsvetaeva (d. 1941). One of the greatest Russian poets of the 20th century, she was also an innovative prose writer and dramatist. She seems to have used as a model for long 1914 narrative poem, "The Enchanter,"

Soloviev's poem "Three Meetings," in which he described his personal encounters with Divine Wisdom.[560] But her own rapturous poetical tributes to Sophia refer to the first two passionate love affairs of her life, both of whom bore that name. Her 1914-15 cycle "Woman Friend" was inspired by her devotion to lesbian poet Sophia Parnok. Her subsequent devotion to Sonya Holliday inspired "Verses to Sonechka". Her much later prose work, "The Tale of Sonechka" is an encoded rewriting of both of these affairs.[561] In 1932, she wrote "Letter to an Amazon," - part essay and part story – in which she sets forth her ideas about lesbianism, based on her own experiences in this area. She includes in this text a portrait of a lesbian couple whose passion lasted until their deaths. This couple were her friends Polyxena Solovieva (Soloviev's younger sister) and Natalia Manaseina.[562] Christ appears in her poetry in the somewhat mysterious 1917 cycle "St. John," where the love of a man for a younger male companion is likened to the relationship between Christ and the Beloved Disciple.[563]

Like Blok and Bely, the two priests who were Soloviev's disciples in sophiology, Pavel Florensky and Sergei Bulgakov, while they clearly believed in Christ, nevertheless significantly contributed to separating Christ from Sophia.

During the years 1904-1905, a group of close friends from among the Moscow intellectuals founded "The Christian Brotherhood of the Struggle" (*Khristianskoe bratstvo bor'by*), whose aim was radically to renew the social sphere in the spirit of Solovievian theocracy with the voluntary subjugation of the state to the Church.[564] Among them was Pavel Alexandrovich Florensky, who carried Russian sophiological thought into the twentieth century.[565] Florensky was born in Yevlakh, Azerbaijan, in Transcaucasia, on January 9, 1882, the son of a Russian engineer and an Armenian mother. His secondary studies were done in Tiflis, where he showed exceptional skill in mathematics. He matriculated in the Physics and Mathematics Faculty of Moscow University, graduating in 1904, after which he enrolled for religious studies and seminary training in the Moscow Theological Academy. He married Anna Mikhailovna Giatsintova in 1910, was ordained a priest in 1911, and, in 1914, defended his masters thesis, *Of Spiritual Truth*. With modifications and amplifications, this would eventually become his most famous work, *The Pillar and Foundation of Truth*. When the Revolution came, he refused either to participate in politics or to emigrate. Rather, he attempted to serve as a priest, wearing beard, pectoral cross, and cassock, while assuming high responsibilities in major research institutions of the new atheistic state. His appearance in clerical garb at a celebration of the Society of Physics in 1926 was tolerated, but not forgotten. Stalin's purge of nonconformist academicians led to Florensky's being deprived of all his professional capacities and imprisoned in 1933, after which he was sent to a labor camp in Siberia, where he is said to have died on December 15, 1943.

For Florensky, Sophia was many things, but not the Son of God. In writing about Russian Sophia icons (of the Novgorod type), he said:

> *This sublime, royal and feminine nature, who is not God or the eternal Son, nor an Angel, nor one of the saints...is she not the true synthesis of all humanity, the higher and more complete form (of the world), the living soul of nature and the universe?*[566]

While denying that Sophia is identical with the Word of God, he said that Holy Sophia cannot be thought to be in abstraction from the Word of God, the Logos, and is, indeed His eternal Spouse.[567] which Florensky described as "a fourth hypostatic element" in the Holy Trinity."[568] He avoided dividing the Trinity into four equal persons by writing that, while Sophia intimately participates in the inner life of the Trinity, partaking in Divine Love, Sophia is created and therefore not a consubstantial Person.[569] He also characterized Sophia as a monad or personal unity in which the Creator encompasses all of creation. For him, Holy Sophia is the living link between the Creator and creation. [570] To support his claims, he frequently invoked St. Athanasius the Great, according to whom Sophia impressed her image in space and time, thus preceding the universe as the pre-existent whole of all ideas and prototypes of creation.[571] However, unlike Florensky, Athanasius was unquestionably referring to Uncreated, Divine Sophia, which he identified with Christ, the Second Person of the Trinity.

From his study of other sorts of Rus' Sophia icons, Florensky determined that Sophia also sometimes represented the Church (as in Yaroslavl) and sometimes the Mother of God (as in Kiev). He saw three fundamental developmental stages in the theological understanding of Divine Wisdom. The first, the patristic, Byzantine, Justinianic stage, in which Sophia was identical with Christ; the second, the early Slavic stage in which the focus shifted to the Mother of God; the third, more or less characteristic of the contemporary era, in which interest is focusing on the cosmological dimension of Holy Wisdom.[572]

Florensky made an important liturgical discovery related to Sophia. Considering the time-honored principle, *lex orandi lex credendi*,[573] he found it highly significant that there existed a special Divine Office to Sophia, the Wisdom of God in Old Church Slavonic, about which most people were unaware. He unearthed it at the parish church of Holy Sophia near Moscow's Lubyansky Square. Desiring to make this service more widely known, as editor of the *Theological Messenger*, in 1912, Florensky published a manuscript copy of it. Rubrical indications make it clear that it was originally composed for the annual celebration in the Church of Holy Sophia in Novgorod on August 15, the Feast of the Dormition of the Mother of God.[574] Recalling that centuries earlier, Archbishop Gennady of Novgorod had tried to reconcile the two conflicting tendencies to identify Sophia both with Christ and with his Mother by celebrating Novgorod Cathedral's patronal feast on the Feast of the Dormition, we can see that this decision only helped further to propagate the confusion, even down to the present. The *Office of Holy Sophia* which Florensky published variously identifies Sophia as the Mother of God, the Word of God, and a creative power.[575]

The point of departure and the point of arrival for Florensky's sophiology is the experience of love.

> *In the sophianic vision, God's infinite love is grasped to be the true, creative*
> *cause of the ordered beauty of the cosmos....Love is, indeed, the spark that*
> *initiates creation, and also the energy force that sustains it.*[576]

Finally, Florensky declared that the three grand ideas of Sophia, Truth, and Friendship were intimately connected and that only in friendship can people be said to abide in truth and truly to know Sophia.[577]

A sophiological writer who regarded Florensky as his mentor was Father Sergei Bulgakov (d. 1944). Early in his career, he had been a professor of Political Economy at Kiev and was later elected as a member of the Second Duma (the parliamentary body set up in Russia after 1905). At that time, he courageously pointed out the many "strange ways in which the ardent orations of the atheistic left" echoed "the Orthodox outlook."[578] And he championed Sophia in an obvious attempt to revitalize Orthodoxy and to re-establish the spirit of the Divine Feminine, so that the Church would not remain off-balanced by its Christocentric view."[579] He taught that a Sophianic understanding of the world and the human struggle to love the world out of love for the world was the only hope of the planet and its inhabitants.

As a result of the October Revolution, Bulgakov decided to become a priest. He was ordained in 1918 in the presence of his friends, Pavel Florensky, the philosopher Nicholas Berdayev and Soloviev's dear friend E. N. Trubetskoi.[580]

His theories came under investigation by the Russian Orthodox Church in 1922 when he was accused of promulgating the doctrine of an androgynous Christ and a Sophiology which regarded God as androgynous and characterized God equally as "Father" and "Mother."[581] Undaunted by this, Bulgakov continued to write about Sophia and a mature theology which attempted to loosen the constraints of patriarchal philosophy while striving to remain within the boundaries of Orthodoxy.[582]

In trying to make a clear statement which would cut through the Russian confusion between Christ-Sophia and Theotokos-Sophia, Bulgakov oversimplified the matter. He claimed that it was really the Byzantines who had been confused and he ignored all but one of the nuances traditionally ascribed to the various sorts of Russian Sophia icons and dedications. He wrote that Byzantine theology did not really answer the question of Sophia and that the theological significance of the Sophia churches remained hidden for a long time. He said that Sophia churches, which were understood Christologically in Byzantium, are understood Mariologically in Russia, where Sophia devotion took on a Marian character. Thus Christosophia and Theotokosophia complement each other.[583]

An expulsion of Russia's intelligensia in 1922 included Bulgakov and Berdyayev. Bulgakov travelled to Istanbul and Prague and then finally settled in Paris, where he was a professor of Dogmatics at the Orthodox Institute of St. Sergius until his death in 1944.

The philosopher Nicolai Berdyaev (d. 1948) and Bulgakov were friends and part of the same intellectual circle prior to the Russian Revolution. In 1913, when Berdyaev published an article challenging the Holy Governing Synod of the Russian Orthodox Church for its identification with the czarist state, he was arrested and charged with blasphemy - an offence that carried an obligatory sentence of exile for life in Siberia. He only escaped the sentence because of the outbreak of World War I and the chaos that followed. He was exiled in 1922 because he was as critical of the Bolsheviks as he had been of the czarist government. He eventually turned his criticism to Bulgakov's sophiology, declaring that, while Bulgakov was opposed to identifying Sophia with the Logos, he variously identified Sophia with the Trinity and with each of the Divine Persons, as well as the cosmos, humanity, and the Mother of God, thereby creating a muddle of semi-divine mediaries.[584]

Berdyaev could not agree with all this confusion and declared, "I do not myself share the views of the sophiological school."[585] He criticized the sophiologists for placing too great a belief in the possibility of arriving at the knowledge of God through the intellect.[586] He also criticized the "sophiological determinism" of a system which, while being optimistic about the future, had no solution to the question of the role of human freedom.[587] "The fundamental idea is not that of freedom, but the idea of Sophia."[588] Though he was a devout Christian, with an Orthodox understanding of Holy Wisdom, he saw that the sophiologists had painted themselves into such a corner that their ideas would not readily prompt people to assume responsibility for their own freedom. Whereas Soloviev had dreamed of the Russian Church and government eventually assuming a sort of ideal world leadership, Florensky and Bulgakov let go of that notion, and Berdyaev saw that their ideas too were heading for a sort of eschatological dead end. After parting with the sophiologists, Berdyaev said this about himself:

> *It is not without grounds that I have been called the philosopher of freedom. The subject of man and creativity is linked with the subject of freedom....I have been called a modernist and this is true in the sense that I have believed and I believe in the possibility of a new era in Christianity, an era of the Spirit, and that this will also be a creative era.*[589]

The first appearance of Sophia in the Bible was as the Creator's associate in bringing creation into being. In the twentieth century, just as television was completing the work of photography in helping image to replace word as a primary means of communication, Russian Sophia began to diminish as a theme of philosophical importance and reappeared in painting. Berdyaev's exact contemporary, the Russian artist and philosopher Nicholas Roerich (d.1947) was both an ambassador of Sophia and an example of the kind of creativity Berdyaev included as a component of the new era. For his efforts to preserve cultural institutions and monuments in times of war, Roerich was awarded the Nobel Peace Prize in 1929. He wrote:

> *Verily, the hour of the affirming of beauty in life is come! It came in the travail of the spirits of the people...Each living rational being, may receive... the living raiment of beauty, and cast away from him that ridiculous fear which whispers: "This is not for you"...All is for you if you manifest the wish from a pure source.*[590]

Holy Wisdom is that pure source. Roerich is known for having designed a banner of peace, which consisted of three red spheres in a red circle on a white field. The design has been interpreted as symbolizing religion, art, and science, encompassed by the circle of culture, or as the past, present, and future achievements of humanity in the circle of eternity.[591] He also painted two canvases of Sophia, one of which he called *Mother of the World*[592] and the other, *Madonna Oriflamma*. The latter depicts an enthroned, veiled woman, who displays the peace banner, in the way St. Veronica is often depicted showing the face of Christ on a veil. The purple gown of Roerich's Madonna associates her with Sophia. And the Greek XP monogram (the first two letters of the Greek word for Christ), which Roerich placed on the front of both arms of his Madonna's throne, associates her with Sophia-Christ.[593]

During the period when the Soviet Russian government forbade the practice of religion and oppressed the churches and synagogues, Russian mystical life continued an underground existence, with several distinct features. It continued to value the blend of Christian and pre-Christian belief which characterized Russian Christianity from its beginning. It also blended a sense of national distinctiveness and universalist claims with a strong social orientation and connected Russian history with an eschatological sense of national and universal destiny. Finally, it included the worship of Sophia as the feminine spiritual essence of the universe.[594]

Because they only began to appear in print in 1989, the writings of Daniil Andreev (d. 1959) are only now becoming known in the West. He was a dreamer and visionary who earned his living as the editor of a factory newspaper in Moscow. He wrote poetry and novels privately at home and discussed them only with his wife and a small circle of intellectuals. In 1947, he and his wife were arrested when, on the basis of a novel he was writing at the time, they were accused of a terrorist plot against Joseph Stalin (d. 1953). They were released after ten years. Andreev died two years later, desolate that a Russian Orthodox priest refused him Holy Communion before death because he had confessed to believing in reincarnation.

Andreev wrote his great mystical work, *Roza mira* (The Rose of the World), while in prison. While considering himself a Christian, he disputed the doctrine of the Trinity. He identified the Father with the Holy Spirit, thus leaving a vacancy for a third Person. In his interpretation, the Trinity is composed of Father, Mother, and Son, with the second feminine person representing virginity, maternity, spirit, and Holy Wisdom.[595] Thus by accepting the Kievan identification of Divine Sophia with the Mother of God, and then putting her in the place of the Holy Spirit, he upheld the divinity of Holy Wisdom while undermining the Holy Trinity.

In 1988, during the millennium of Rus's conversion to Christianity, a friend of the author's visited the Soviet Union with several travel agents as part of a deal offered to promote tourism. One morning, as they were standing in the plaza before St. Sophia Cathedral in Kiev, a boy approached and asked if they would like to see some lacquer boxes, decorated by his mother with pictures in traditional Russian style. When they expressed interest, the boy brought them to the stall where his mother displayed her work. Since they were in a cathedral square, the friend asked the woman if she had any religious images. After an unsettling pause, during which she gazed into his eyes, apparently wondering whether he could be trusted, she rummaged through her bag until she found a small icon of the Savior, the size of a brooch, which he purchased.

Just then, the bells of St. Sophia began to ring. The apparent effect on the city was astonishing. Traffic stopped, and the city dramatically quieted down. Most people had tears in their eyes. It was later explained to the amazed tourists that this was the first time the bells had rung in nearly seventy years.

The Soviet government's allowing church bells to ring again was one of many concessions made by the government in that year, which marked the millennium of Rus's conversion to Christianity, as part of a futile attempt to hold the Soviet Union together. Nevertheless, all the old legislation forbidding church activities remained in force until 1990, and control of the church by local authorities was hardly eased, especially in the provinces.[596]

In 1990, the Soviet Union started to fall apart. People began more publicly to support the church, to demand that churches be reopened, and publicly to raise funds to repair the few churches which had been allowed to remain in use. To this end, people set up booths at the entryways of historical monuments and attractions, from which they sold religious items. Writer Nathaniel Davis and his wife were touring Leningrad (renamed St. Petersburg in 1991) in 1990, when they met a man outside the Pavlovsk Palace, who was selling attractive Easter cards to raise funds for the repair of St. Sophia church in the suburb of Pushkin.[597] Such sales, still made furtively in 1988, were now made without fear. By 1991, all the former Soviet republics had become independent.

This remarkably speedy shift towards religious and national freedom is a primary characteristic of people acting under the prompting of Holy Wisdom. How deliciously ironic! Leonard Shlain has pointed out that, when Communism first came into power in Russia, two of the earliest objects of execration were the worship of Sophia and the veneration of religious images.[598]

Given that this is so, it shouldn't be too surprising that the collapse of the Soviet Union was accompanied by the martyrdoms of two men – one of whom died protecting icons and the other of whom died for boldly proclaiming Sophia as a challenge to totalitarian government.

Fortunately, several icons survived the Revolution's wanton destruction. For example, half millennium earlier, the great Andrei Rublev had painted a tier of icons for a church in Zvenigorod. In 1918, icon restorer Vasili Kirikov came upon all that remained of the set. As he was entering a barn near Zvenigorod's Cathedral of the Dormition, he accidentally turned over one of the steps. What it revealed stunned him. Staring up at him was a severely damaged icon which still bore Rublev's face of the Savior. Nearby he found the icons of Rublev's Archangel Michael and St. Paul.[599]

Unfortunately, the end of the Communistic system did nothing to diminish another threat to the surviving ancient icons. Their popularity in the West has made them a prime target for an icon-stealing ring connected with the Russian mafia. One church whose art they coveted was in the isolated village of Zharky. Its pastor, Father Nestor Savchuk, was born in the province of Crimea, southern Russia, in 1960. As a youth he excelled in boxing, wrestling, the martial arts, and painting. In his twenties, he began to work as an apprentice painting religious murals in Odessa. The subjects he painted so inspired him that he joined the monastery of Pochaev. After ordination, he was advised by his spiritual guide to go to the parish church at Zharky, which had ancient and remarkable icons. He became so devoted to these icons and determined to protect them that it was his custom to stay up during the night to guard the church. On December 31, 1993, he was found murdered outside his rectory.[600] He is now honored with the title of Holy New Martyr and has been depicted in an icon by William Hart McNichols.[601]

Nestor Savchuk was not only a protector of icons. He was a man whose faith and dedication made his life, as it unfolded, a living image of Holy Wisdom. In 1958, Russian theologian Paul Evdokimov wrote:

> ...the Wisdom of God is pre-existent to the formation of mankind, and every man carries within him 'a guiding image', his own Sophia or Wisdom, he is thus God's living project. He must decode this image, in the process decoding himself, freely conquering his own intelligence, and making his own destiny.[602]

Another who found and followed this "guiding image" was Alexander Men. He was born in Moscow in 1935, by which time the public existence of the Russian Orthodox Church had virtually come to an end. All the monasteries and seminaries, and more than 95 per cent of the churches were closed. Countless numbers of Christians were either dead or interned in the Gulag camps. All the outstanding living Christian thinkers were in exile. Alexander managed to obtain a theological education anyway and was ordained a priest in 1960. He turned out to be one of the most remarkable priests to come out of the modern Russian Orthodox Church. His influence as a parish priest, spiritual guide, and theologian was enormous. Opposed to any fundamentalist trends, he was open to the world and tolerant towards other faiths.

On April 29, 1988, Mikhail Gorbachev received Patriarch Pimen and other hierarchs of the Church in the Kremlin, thus putting an end to seventy years of persecution. On 11 May Fr. Alexander made the first of what were to be many public addresses on the subject of Christianity. Indeed, that summer brought a renewal of religious life.[603] Fr. Men conveyed a sense of urgency in his writings and public addresses; for, as he said, "Notice that no one, not even the bishops they produce on television, is preaching Jesus Christ, or God; they don't speak of the essentials of what we believe."[604]

On September 9, 1990, a week after he celebrated his thirtieth anniversary of ordination, Alexander Men was murdered by two men, who struck him in the back of the head with an axe. No one has been charged with his death.

At the beginning of a series of interviews, entitled *About Christ and the Church*, in characterizing the life of the early Christians, he said "They lived in faith, hope, and love, and let us not forget "'sophia' – wisdom."[605] and added that "the fullness of the Church is manifest in brotherly unity, in that which existed from the beginning: Faith, Hope, Love, and Sophia.[606] One of his many articles was entitled "Religion, the 'Cult of Personality' and the Secular State."[607] In a section entitled "Christ and Caesar", he proclaimed Holy Wisdom a challenge to totalitarianism, when he wrote:

> *Although there were times when Christ could be severe - even frightening - he always respected human freedom. He sought children, not slaves. There are no 'knock-down' arguments in the Gospels designed to paralyze the will, whether in the form of irrefutable miraculous phenomena or incontestable logic. St. Paul expressed this clearly when he said: "For Jews demand signs, and Greeks seek wisdom, but we preach Christ crucified, a stumbling block to Jews and folly to Gentiles, but to those who are called, both Jews and Greeks, Christ is the power of God and the wisdom of God."[608]*

Fr. Men once expressed sorrow at the memory of the wanton destruction of Moscow's Cathedral of Christ the Savior.[609] In 1931, Stalin had it dynamited and replaced with a public swimming pool. Had he lived only five more years, Men would have seen the beginning of glorious reconstruction of the Cathedral. Under the supervision of the Patriarch Alexis II, Mayor Yuri Luzhkov of Moscow, and a public supervisory council, the building was completed with the voluntary work and donations of the Russian people and dedicated in 1999. The first Christmas liturgy was celebrated there January 7, 2000. Worshippers entering through the north façade can look up and seen a large marble medallion honoring St. Sergius the Martyr. and on the top tier in the center of the iconostasis they can see an icon of St. Sophia/Holy Wisdom.

The collapse which occurred in Eastern Europe and Russia at the close of the twentieth century would warmly have been endorsed by the sophiologists. In 1912, Pavel Florensky wrote that

> *the idea of Holy Sophia, indeed, 'determines Russian religious consciousness in its very sources, and in it is precisely the deepest foundation of its originality.' He even goes so far as to state elsewhere...that "Russia" and "Russian" without Sophia are contradictions in terms. In the same connection, he further remarks that to his mind all contemporary philosophical and theological problems both flow from and return to the problem of Sophia.[610]*

Even down to the present, the writings of the sophiologists has continued to influence contemporary Russian theologians. In a 1996 publication, John Meyendorff, described sophiology as

> *a significant event in the history of Orthodox thought (which) still fascinates those involved in the renascent religious thought among Russian intellectual dissidents today.[611]*

At the end of a turbulent twentieth century, Sophia blessed Russia with the long-desired gift of freedom. Among those who benefited were distinctive people, who were persecuted during the Soviet Era, just as they had been during the Iconoclastic Era, and, indeed, during the Czarist period.

In the winter of 1989-90, just as the churches were beginning to experience freedom, the activism of Russia's distinctive people also found its voice when a group of folks working for rights for sexual minorities, the Libertarian Party, decided to form the Moscow Association of Sexual Minorities.[612] During most of the Soviet era, gays had been treated as criminals and lesbians as mentally ill.

> *Soviet Stonewall[613] occurred in July and August of 1991 and brought together about seventy persons from the United States and tens of thousands persons from the Soviet Union. In Moscow, Stonewall was a combination of seminars conducted by the Americans on subjects ranging from AIDS to coming out, a gay/lesbian film festival, and press events – such as a "kiss-in" in front of the Bolshoi Theater. In St. Petersburg, both the seminars and the film festival took place, albeit with far fewer numbers.[614]*

In 1993, a group of distinctive people was able to register in Tomsk, and the city of Omsk managed to hold Siberian Gay Festivals in 1992 and 1993. On April 29, 1993, President Yeltsin signed a bill that eliminated the law against consensual sex between adult men.

Nevertheless, even though homosexuality is no longer illegal in Russia, the social costs of being openly distinctive are still very high. A recent poll found that nearly half the population of the country still believes that distinctive people should either be killed or at least isolated from the rest of society.[615] After over seventy years of being officially labeled either criminal or sick, it is understandable that many distinctive people in Russia have difficulty overcoming internalized homophobia. This is especially so because many Russian distinctive folks have a stronger sense of national identity than they do gender identity in any exclusive category. The result is that they would rather feel that they can privately remain free to relate sexually with folks of whichever gender if they please and many are not very interested in liberation movements.

Be that as it may, a singular event was reported in international news on September 5, 2003. A column entitled "Church Defrocks Priest Over Gay Wedding" reported that Russia has now seen its first distinctive church wedding, which was conducted by a priest named Father Vladimir in a church in the city of Nishny Novgorod, east of Moscow. Denis Gogolev and Misha Morozov were joined in a traditionally Orthodox ceremony which included taking vows, exchanging rings, and wearing crowns. Diocesan officials said that, because he officially witnessed this "blasphemous act," Father Vladimir has been defrocked. Meanwhile, the gay couple, who said that their ceremony should highlight how "gays can and should live in Russia, and quite openly," stood for the Russian Parliament in December of 2003 in a bid to take gay rights through the country's legal system. [616]

As the world entered the twenty-first century, Sophia continued to be an object of lively interest among Slavic scholars. From November 9th to 12th, 2000, the 32nd National Convention of the American Association for the Advancement of Slavic Studies took place in Denver, Colorado. The theme of the convention was "Visions of Sophia in Medieval and Early Modern Russia and Ukraine."

CONCLUSION

The Living Circle was incorporated on October 22, 1993. When it opened its first chapel in February of 1994, over a hundred people attended the dedication ceremony. A couple of them were transgendered folks who claimed that TLC was the first spirituality group explicitly to include them among those invited to participate. There was one painting that particularly caught their attention. Done by Robert Lentz and quite different from his more renowned icons, it reproduces a mural on the wall of a kiva – a semi-underground sacred prayer room – at Pottery Mound, New Mexico. Painted by a shaman of the ancient Anasazis, it depicts a person dressed in the costume of the Zuni *berdache* kachina, Kolhamana. The *berdache* kachina is considered an incarnation of the Native American "two spirited" one. Half dressed as a male and half as a female, this spirit was believed to manifest itself in every lesbian, gay, bisexual, or trans-gendered person, who, earlier in history, were considered especially selected by and sacred to the deities to be the mediators between this world and the Otherworld and between men and women hoping to resolve conflict. Most conspicuously manifesting both male and female characteristics, such folks were thought to constitute a sort of middle "third gender" – people who were just as much a part of the divine plan as anyone else. Lentz gathered mud and actual pigment fragments left behind by the ancient shamans and used them to paint his reproduction. The transgendered viewers were deeply touched that there had been a spiritual system which took into account and highly valued gender minorities.

On another wall, they found a different picture, which fascinated them. It was a copy of one of Lentz's icons of Christ-Holy Wisdom. When I explained who it was, they both burst into tears. Raised as devout Catholics, they had become embittered by the sense that their Church had no room for them and that many fellow-Catholics considered them freaks. But this icon revealed to them a whole authentic Catholic tradition which chooses to depict Christ either as a woman or as an androgyne and is based on an ancient Christology which goes back to St. Paul himself! They had found that the faith in which they had been raised actually embraced a traditional way of relating to Christ with which they could totally identify. The icon reached out to them, reconnected them with their own tradition, and embraced them in what they considered a joyous homecoming. Now Christ-Sophia, who has long been a great sign of hope for some feminist theologians, has also become an anchor for many who find themselves part of a minority within the minority of gender identity or inclination. And, for the past several years now, transgendered members of TLC have considered it a special honor to carry the Christ-Sophia icon in Chicago's annual gay pride parade.

In June of 1994, two events happened of critical importance to the revival of interest in Sts. Sergius and Bacchus. John Boswell's *Same-Sex Marriage in Premodern Europe* revealed that they have been the primary saints invoked in the blessings of same-gender relationships throughout history. Boswell included in his text a translation of the earliest account of their passion and martyrdom. Simultaneously, Robert Lentz's icon of Sts. Sergius and Bacchus was completed. The original was carried in Chicago's Gay Pride Parade for the first time, and prints of it were made available for public purchase. The company which, at the time, had the right to sell reproductions of Lentz's icons later revealed that, out of well over a hundred of his images available for purchase from their catalogue, the print of Sts. Sergius and Bacchus was the most popular in 1995. By now, prints of the Sts. Sergius and Bacchus icon can be seen hanging on walls in many places throughout the world. Even though the Roman Church dropped their feast from the liturgical calendar in 1969, at the time of this writing, the Vatican is still releasing relics of the two martyrs for the veneration of the faithful. There is no more tangible contradiction to the notion that saints may never actually have existed than that the Church continues to allow the veneration of fragments of their bones. Portions of their relics are honored in TLC's chapel.

Same-Sex Unions in PreModern Europe also included a discussion of Polyeuct and Nearchus.[617] Because of the controversial nature of the book's subject, the story of these two friends has now been brought to the attention of an enormous number of people. Having read Boswell's book, several Greek Orthodox priests approached this book's author at an AIDS memorial service in 1995 and asked whether TLC had commissioned an icon of St. Polyeuct. When they received an affirmative response, they said that they looked forward to its completion with great relish.

The icon was painted in by Robert Lentz in1998. Whereas, until recently, traces of this martyr's once widespread cult had nearly been erased by the vicissitudes of history, Lentz's depiction of Polyeuct and Nearchus together in an icon for the first time in history reintroduces them to the faith community which first preserved their story over seventeen hundred years ago. Considering the role the muses took in carrying their story through the centuries, it is worth noting that it was the late composer, Alan Hovhaness, and his wife, soprano Hinako Fujihara, whose request led to the Armenian text painted on the icon being provided by Armenian Church authorities and that poet, novelist, librettist Ursula Vaughan Williams, widow of composer Ralph Vaughan Williams, has helped to edit this text.

The icon was formally unveiled during a welcoming ceremony on October 22, 1998,[618] in Chicago's Episcopal Cathedral of St. James, with Robert Lentz as the guest speaker. The ancient narration of Polyeuct's martyrdom was once again read in public, and there was a live performance of music from all the major works composed on the Polyeuct theme.

Poor St. Polyeuct! In 1991, a Russian Orthodox priest friend of the author wrote to his patriarch-ate, requesting a relic of the martyr for The Living Circle chapel. He received, instead, a long-distance phone call from denominational headquarters, inquiring why he was interested in such a "shady saint." When he reminded them what an inveterate relic-collector he was, the relic was sent.

Anyone in agreement with an Orthodox bureaucrat's scornful remark about of Polyeuct would do well to take to heart the motto of the British Order of the Garter:

> *"Honi soit qui mal y pense."*

(Shamed be the one who thinks ill of it.)

This is precisely the judgment rendered by the wise old Egyptian monk introduced in the Prologue of this journey through history.

Over a ten year period, the re-emergence and veneration of St. Polyeuct among distinctive people has already led to a remarkable reversal in some branches of the Eastern Christianity. When they attended church on the first Sunday of the twenty-first century, January 7, 2001, 50,000 of the faith-ful in 300 parishes throughout the English-speaking world[619] brought home bulletins on the cover of which was a color representation of an icon of the martyrdom of St. Polyeuct, with the caption "Icon of Saint Polyeucte - January 9th." The accompanying story, entitled "Relationships of Love," is a return to the original version of the story in that it is all about Polyeuct and Nearchus. In a revisionistic reversal, there is now no mention of Polyeuct's father-in-law, wife, or children. This extraordinary version of the story even declares that Polyeuct and Nearchus were martyred together![620] These are the beginning and ending paragraphs:

In Sacred Scripture our Lord tells us that "there is no greater love than this: to lay down one's life for one's friend." (John 15:13) The feast of Saint Polyeucte, which is celebrated on January 9th,is the tale of such friendship....

The story of Saint Polyeucte and his friend reminds us that, in Christ, all of our relationships must be characterized by love. Sometimes we may think that there are certain circumstances where we may deal with other human beings without love, but no such circumstances ever exist.[621]

Moved by the story of Polyeuct and Nearchus as it was told in the first edition of this book, a French writer named Robert Dartois turned the story into a libretto, which was then set to music by the Swiss composer Thierry Châtelain. The world premiere of the oratorio *Polyeucte et Nearchus* was performed in the great church of Saint-Eustache in Paris on March 24, 2009. It was well received by the critics and by those who attended. By setting the text as an oratorio to be performed in church, rather than an opera to be performed on stage, this artistic collaboration has returned the original narration to the Church, which was its original home for well over a millennium. In the composer's web-site, when the section entitled *Polyeucte et Nearchus* opens, above the text is The Living Circle's icon of the two inseparable companions..

The stories about the saints which you have been reading are among those told at The Living Circle. Our mission is to supplement the good work already being done for and with distinctive folks by some of their own faith traditions and to help mend wounded spirits and spirits who feel cut adrift from their faith communities by bigotry and misunderstanding. We do this primarily through the combination of words and images. We are grateful for everyone who helps to spread the message of our work, because it brings good news to so many people who hunger for words of hope, encouragement, and connectedness. We are a spirituality center, and spirituality is concerned with finding connections and making connections.

In this regard, we must acknowledge the pioneering work of the late Professor John E. Boswell of Yale University, who first brought the story of Sergius and Bacchus to the reading public through his published translation of the earliest account of their passion and martyrdom.[622] We thank him also for accepting the research we had done on Polyeuct and Nearchus and for incorporating it into his book, thereby first bringing it to the attention of a wide public. It is an interesting thing that even though a number of critics attacked the main thesis of *Same-Sex Unions in Premodern Europe*, no critic questioned the veracity of the saints' stories. Two others who cannot be thanked enough are Robert Lentz and William Hart McNichols. Inspired by these stories, they have represented the saints in splendid icons, copies of which are now available to everyone. The images continue to encourage viewers to inquire about the stories. Even those who never hear the stories are already uplifted by the art. Pictures continue to be worth at least a thousand words; and these particular pictures are a feast to those who are spiritually hungry and a threatening development to those who are spiritually blind and have not yet learned the language of the heart.

On March 21, 2001, an interviewer asked playwright Arthur Miller what he thought of the Taliban government's recent destruction of some famous ancient Buddhist sculptures. At the conclusion of his response, he said, "Art is the one reassurance that I have about the continuity of the human race."[623]

Sts. Brigid and Darlughdach of Kildare

Sts. Perpetua and Felicity

Appendix A
Meanwhile, in Ireland: Northern Sophia: Sts. Brigid and Darlughdach of Kildare – How Brigid Became a Bishop

Brigid of Kildare (d.525) was the exact contemporary of the Byzantine Princess Anicia Juliana (d. 527). Even though she built no great churches and gave away anything she ever possessed, Brigid's impact in the world was ultimately greater. There are several aspects of her story which provide valuable data for current discussion on the role of women and men in the Church. Additionally, St. Brigid was heiress to a tradition which probably considered her a personal incarnation of divine wisdom, as it had been understood and reverenced by the ancient Celts. She was the most revered of all the holy women in the early Christian history of Ireland. Among her many titles are "Queen of the South", "Mary of the Gael", "Prophetess of Christ", and even "Foster-Mother of Christ". The bards and the early Christian writers have recorded so many tales about this holy, hospitable, beautiful woman that it is sometimes difficult to separate the mythic from the factual. To further obfuscate historical precision in a treatment of her life, she was named after the most beloved Celtic goddess and epitomized most of her traits.[624] Celtic scholar Shirley Toulson identifies St. Brigid with Eastern Christianity's Sophia, describing her spirit as that of an androgynous divinity, who preserved and enhanced life, who fed the people with earthly food and with the milk of loving kindness and who could grant the gift of immortality.[625]

The goddess Brigid had been a pan-Celtic deity – special protectress of Leinster as well as the rest of Ireland, the eponymous goddess of the Brigantes - a great tribe who lived both in north central England in and around Yorkshire, as well as in Wexford. From her name are derived the words Brigantia, the Hebrides, and the word "bride". Other continental derivations are the cities of Bregenz, Bragança, and Briançon, Corunna (originally called Brigantia), and ancient Nemetobriga, in northern Spain. The Lake of Constanz (Bodensee) was called by the Romans *Lacus Brigantinus* (Brigid's Lake). Even a peak in the Himilayas and an island off the coast of Japan were named for her.[626] The name Brigid means "the bright or exalted one," but the ancient source of the name also appears in the stem word for "bear,"[627] making it likely that the goddess Brigid was a lineal descendant of the ancient mother-bear goddess of prehistoric Europe.

The bear mother is humankind's oldest identifiable deity.[628] Artemis (from "Arctos," Greek for Bear) was one of her progeny. Artemis began as a solar/mother goddess; but, under the influence of patriarchal religion, was demoted to being a lunar/virgin goddess, with her supposed twin brother Apollo assuming her solar role. Patriarchal pressure never effected Brigid in this way. In her own solar aspect, Brigid was mother goddess of the fertility of the fields and of mothers, of sheep, and of cattle. In her lunar aspect, she was also maiden goddess of the coming of Spring. As queen of the Underworld, Brigid had also been goddess of springs and wells, which were considered connecting channels between this world and the Otherworld. If the custom followed by the Kildare nuns in the Christian era originated earlier in history, the goddess Brigid had a perpetual fire kept burning in her honor at Kildare ("church by the oak"), which was her principal shrine in Ireland. This fire represented inspiration, poetry, bardic skill, healing, therapy, and creativity - especially metallurgy. Of all these things, Brigid was goddess. She appears to have had a priesthood of 19 fire-attending virgins, similar to the Vestals in Rome. Some archaeologists have offered the likely hypothesis that her high priestess was always named after her, being considered her incarnation. As an incarnation of the divine Brigid, this high priestess would also have been considered a pre-Christian version of divine wisdom incarnate.

As the Celtic goddess of wisdom, Brigid was northern Sophia. Perpetual fire is northern Sophia's symbol.[629] In Celtic tradition, there are many rituals concerning the making and keeping of fires; and all of them invoke Brigid. Giraldus Cambrensis,(d. 1223), in his *Itinerary of Ireland* (1185) described the sacred fire which was kept at Kildare and had not been extinguished since the saint's time. It was surrounded by a thorn hedge, which men were not allowed to penetrate. The fire was tended by nineteen nuns; and on the twentieth night the nun on the previous shift would say, 'Brigid, guard your fire. This is your night.' Brigid was then considered responsible for keeping the fire enclosed and alight. The continuous occupation of the site by a strong abbess who was believed to be mystically attuned to the Goddess-Saint lasted until 1132, when Abbess MacFaelain of Kildare was raped by one of the soldiers of King Dermot MacMorrough of Leinster during an assault on Kildare which also caused the death of 107 of the town's citizens.[630] Since Dermot wanted one of his own kinswomen to become Brigid's successor, the rape was perpetrated in order to disqualify the reigning abbess. This sacrilege, which shocked the Celtic world, marked the beginning of the end of the Abbess of Kildare's unusual power.[631] Thus the assault on an individual abbess ended up damaging the respect presumed due to her office itself. Kildare's perpetual fire was extinguished around 1540 by order of Archbishop George Browne of Dublin as part of King Henry VIII's Dissolution of the Monasteries.

What was the reason for the special power accorded the abbesses of Kildare? Their authority derived from their being successors to Brigid. According to the *Rennes Dinnsenchus*, collections of sacred stories, written down in verse and prose from1160 onwards,[632] Brigid was a *ban-drui*, a female Druid, before she converted to Christianity.[633] She was born about 451 at Faughart, County Louth, the daughter of a Leinster chieftain named Dubhtach and of Brocca, a slave. She was raised in fosterage in the home of a Druid. Fosterage was the Celtic method of education, in which children were given over to households other than their own for rearing and for tightening the bonds between affiliated families. After her conversion to Christianity, Brigid and some of her friends felt such an interior call radically to follow in the footsteps of Christ that they decided to request veiling as Christian nuns. This happened in 468.

Irish writer, J. F. Kenney, the archaeologist R. A. Stewart MacAlister, and others have shown it to be quite plausible that, prior to her baptism, St. Brigid may have been the last high priestess of the goddess.[634] Among other things, this would help to explain why she and her successor abbesses of Kildare were given such enormous power - something unusual, even in a culture where men and women were already treated with more equality than in most parts of Europe. It appears that whereas, in pre-Christian Celtic faith, an individual priestess became identified mythically with the goddess herself, having adopted Christianity, the priestess herself became the focus of devotion rather than the more abstract deity.[635]

The shift from high priestess to Christian nun seems to have been easy enough for a woman who was already known for her deep faith, graciousness, hospitality, humility, and generosity. But the people would not quickly forget the high position she had held. Perhaps this is why her friend, St. Mél, Bishop of Ardagh (d. 490), is said to have ordained her a bishop. According to an anonymous ninth-century *Life of Brigid*, as Brigid knelt to receive the nun's veil, Bishop Mel 'being intoxicated with the grace of God there did not recognize what he was reciting from his book, for he consecrated Brigid with the orders of bishop.' This virgin alone in Ireland,' said Mél, 'will hold the episcopal ordination.'[636] Later versions of this story, however, while never denying that it happened, attempted to discredit or dismiss this incident by arguing that it clearly had been a mistake: St. Mél must have consecrated Brigid while he was drunk, thus making it invalid![637]

This episode is first mentioned in an ancient Commentary on the *Hymn of Brigid*, written at the beginning of the seventh century by St. Broccán (Brogan) Cloen (d. 653).[638] Since the first *Life of St. Brigid the Virgin* was written by the Kildare cleric, Cogitosus ua hÁeda, in 650, Broccán's hymn might contain the earliest recorded details about her life.[639] The Commentary on Broccán's hymn says:

> *...the orders were read over her, and it came to pass that Bishop Mél conferred on Brigit the episcopal order, though it was only the order of penitents that she herself desired....And hence Brigit's successor is always entitled to have episcopal orders and the honors due to a bishop.*[640]

According to the *Life of Brigid*, which was recorded in the fifteenth century *Book of Lismore*:

> *It came to pass then, through the grace of the Holy Ghost, that the form of ordaining a bishop was read over Brigid. Mac-caille ("son of the veil", a nickname for Mél himself) said that a bishop's order should not be conferred on a woman. Bishop Mél said: "No power have I in this matter. The dignity has been given by God unto Brigid, beyond every other woman." Whereupon the men of Ireland from that time to this give episcopal honor to Brigid's successor.*[641]

In 1152, with the support of Archbishop Theobald of Canterbury, Cardinal John Paparo, the Papal legate charged with reorganizing the Irish Church, assembled a Synod at Kells. It was the first instance in history of this kind of intrusion into the jurisdictional authority of the Irish Church. During this synod, the precedence the abbess of Kildare had always exercised over the other Irish bishops in synodal assemblies was abolished. The bishops had formerly sat at her feet.[642] This took place just twenty years after Abbess MacFaelain was raped in a deliberate attempt to diminish her authority. One other Brigidine abbess retained her special authority for a few more centuries. Until the Reformation, the abbess of St. Brigid's convent at Douglas, on the Isle of Man, had the authority to hold her own courts, having the title and authority of baron and being considered a peer of the realm.[643]

After founding religious establishments at Croghan Hill and elsewhere in Meath, St. Brigid set up her main foundation at Kildare in 470. Kildare was the earliest known Celtic double monastery, with houses both for women and for men. The women were experts in weaving wool and the men at metalwork, consistent with the goddess Brigid's former patronage over sheep and metalurgy. Brigid appointed St. Conleth (d. 519) to be the men's spiritual guide and, eventually, Bishop of Kildare. She founded a school of art whose illuminated manuscripts became famous, notably the lost Book of Kildare. She was one of the most remarkable women of her age, well known for her prayerfulness, patience, inclusivity, and, most of all, her compassion.

Many early Irish lives of the saints mention the affection and friendship which existed between women and men saints. St. Brigid cultivated a wide network of friends. According to legend, she maintained close ties with the sainted bishops Erc of Slane, Mél of Ardagh, and Ailbe of Emly. Some stories even maintain that she was close to St. Patrick, though this is less likely, since he may have died before she was born. She was also described as a friend of Sts. Brendan, Finian of Clonard and

Ibar of Beg-Eri. These churchmen provided her with advice and material and spiritual assistance at various times. St. Gildas the Wise was said to have made a bell, which he sent to St. Brigid.[644]

Remarkably advanced for her time in history, she held love to be the vital component of marriage and was once even willing to play Cupid when she thought the occasion warranted it. According to her "Life" in the *Book of Leinster*, she provided a man with a love potion when he sought her help, because his wife would neither eat nor sleep with him and was about to leave him. She solved the problem by blessing some water and telling him to pour it over their house and their beds and into their food and drink. When this was done, his wife began to love him so exceedingly that he couldn't stand ever to be anywhere but at his side.[645]

Brigid was one of many Celtic saints who taught that it was essential for each person to have an *anam cara* ("soul friend"), someone with whom she or he could share all of life's experiences, so as to discover, often in the telling, that the seemingly insignificant events are really the most important of all, the times when and places where God speaks. Once, when she intuited that a visiting cleric's soul friend had died in another part of Ireland, she told him quickly to find another, for 'anyone without a soul friend is like a body without a head.'[646] While the role of *anam cara* might well have been a Druidic practice, pre-dating Christianity's coming to the Celtic world, this kind of spiritual bonding was warmly endorsed by St. John Cassian,[647] whose *Conferences* were significant in the development of Celtic monasticism. Cassian declared the bond between friends to be indissoluble, since friendship is "what is broken by no chances, what no interval of time or space can sever or destroy, and what even death itself cannot part."[648]

Brigid's own deep compassion qualified her to be an extraordinary soul friend, and she had a treasured companion in Darlughdach ("Daughter of Lugh"—the sun god), a younger nun in her community. There are only a few stories recorded about Darlughdach; but, the following gives a picture of the affection she and Brigid had for each other. One of the early lives of St. Brigid records that, being very dear to her, Darlughdach slept in the same bed with Brigid (*in lectulo cum S. Brigida*).[649] On one occasion, Darlughdach saw and fell in love with a man, who also became enamored of her, their ardent glances revealing their mutual passion. They decided to elope on a certain night. On the designated evening, she lay in the bosom of the sleeping abbess with beating heart, troubled by the conflict between duty and passion. Finally, she rose, and in an agony of uncertainty, cast herself on her knees, begged God to give her strength to master her love. Then, in the vehemence of her resolve, she thrust her naked feet into the red hot coals that glowed on the hearth, and held them there till she felt the pain had conquered passion. After that, she gently stole back into bed, cuddling into Brigid's bosom. When morning broke, Brigid rose and looked at the blistered and scorched soles. Touching them, she said gently, 'I slept not, dear child, but was awake, and saw your struggle. And now, because you have fought valiantly and hast conquered, the flame of lust shall no longer harm you.' Then Brigid healed her feet, exercising a skill that would have been part of the training of a former fire priestess.[650]

Authors Peter Cherici and, quoting him, Peter Berresford Ellis, retell a variation on the same story in which Brigid imposed the hot coals on Darlughdach, both as a punishment and a purification, and then took her back to bed when she had suffered enough. According to Cherici, the story has heretofore overlooked lesbian implications.[651] Ellis agrees with him by declaring that 'we seem to be left in little doubt that Brigid had a lesbian relationship with another member of her community... Darlughdacha.'[652] While this might be so, neither author alludes to the possibility that these two dear friends slept together not only out of affection but simply for warmth - something that has been routinely done in many places throughout history, down to the modern era. St. Joan of Arc (d.1431) also slept with women when she was out with her troops, and there is no record that even her worst slanderers thought anything of it. Considering the importance she and everyone else placed on her being a virgin, she couldn't very well have slept with the men![653] To return to Brigid and Darlughdach, when we consider rigorous ascetical practices of most of the Celtic saints, it is apparent that they were not terribly concerned with comfort. So maybe these two saints slept together simply because they enjoyed sleeping with each other.

The *Chronicon Pictorum* tells the story of Darlughdach's having been sent to Scotland as Brigid's delegate to accept from a grateful Pictish King Nechtan a donation of the land upon which St. Bride's Cathedral in Abernethy was eventually built. Apparently Brigid had once given him shelter at Kildare when his life was in peril from the antagonism of his predecessor, King Talarg.[654] That Abernethy had been a center where previously the goddess Brigid had been honored is demonstrated in place-names to be found there. They prove that two classes of officials in the ancient Celtic civil and religious system, whose occupations came under the protection of Brigid, dwelt there. The place-names Balvaird and Balgonie mean "town of the bard" and "town of the smith."[655]

Towards the end of her life, Brigid told Darlughdach that she would be dying soon. Darlughdach implored her to let her die with her, but Brigid promised that she would follow on the anniversary of her departure, after the passing of a year.[656] Brigid died in February 1, 525, and Darlughdach, after having succeeded her as abbess, died a year later on the same date. This date, which became their common feast day, is also the date of Imbolc (or Oimelc), the pre-Christian festival of the goddess Brigid, when she reappears as the Bride of Spring, in a role similar to the Greek Persephone and the Roman Proserpina.

While St. Brigid was sometimes referred to as the "Mary of the Gael," she was more often referred to as the "Foster Mother of Christ." In the Celtic system, the role of foster mother was considered more honorable and more intimate even than that of birth mother. At the age of seven, the children of elite families were sent to other friendly households for a fosterage which could extend to adulthood. In early Ireland, the woman who gave birth to a child was her or his mother (*mathair*) but never the child's mommy. *Muimme*, the intimate and affective form, is the Old Irish word for foster mother; no such term exists in the language for birth mothers.[657]

How could a sixth century saint have been foster mother to Christ? Such a question would never bothered the Celts. They knew that St. Brigid had synthesized a goddess who was worshiped long before the birth of Christ; and they drew no clear distinction between history and myth anyway. [658]

The claim that St. Brigid was Christ's foster mother was a way of saying symbolically that the old faith welcomed Christ and nurtured and protected the young Christian faith, by declaring the goddess of wisdom his protectress and the guarantor that He would thrive. This notion is expressed in several old tales about Brigid.

One story links her with Winter Solstice and the way the Swedes celebrate St. Lucia, whose feast of December 13th originally fell on Winter Solstice, until the Gregorian calendar reform of 1582. It is said that, when Mary and the Christ child were fleeing into Egypt, they found the road blocked by a party of soldiers. Brigid arrived on the scene and offered to deflect the attention of the soldiers from the fugitives. She did this by donning a garish head-dress with lighted candles. The distraction worked, and Mary and Jesus escaped.[659]

There is another, even more extraordinary version of this story, which links Brigid with Ursa Major, the great Mother-Bear constellation - sometimes also called The Plow, or The Harrow. In it, the saint/goddess Brigid reaches back to her ancestress, the oldest goddess in history, the Bear-Mother, to use one of her symbols for the protection of the Christ Child, whose incarnation is the fulfillment of the yearnings of the entire history of faith. In this version, instead of distracting pursuers with a candle head-dress, Brigid distracted them with a harrow. When she raised it up over her head, the pins gave out flames like candles. The flaming pins represent the stars of Ursa Major, the Great Bear[660] So, in this simple story, St. Brigid's entire spiritual genealogy is traced right back to the bear goddess.

There is no record of any Brigidine convents from the sixteenth to the nineteenth centuries. Then, during the time when Catholicism was still banned in Ireland, on February 1, 1807, Bishop Daniel Delaney of Kildare and Leighlin restored the sisterhood to Ireland by reviving Brigid's ancient order. The first sisters in the restored order lived as lay catechists in Tullow, Co. Carlow. In 1992, something rather remarkable happened. Having discerned that it was high time for the Brigidines to return to Kildare, two sisters, Mary Minehan and Phil O'Shea, moved there and established a center for Celtic spirituality, which they named *Solas Bhríde* (Brigid's Light). Brigid's fire was relit on her feast day in 1993 by Mary Teresa Cullen, the superior general of the Brigidine sisters, in the Market Square of Kildare, during a peace and justice conference. This perpetual fire is kept at *Solas Bhríde* and is used to rekindle the brazier in the Market Square annually on February 1st, always in the setting of a peace and justice conference.[661] The site of Brigid's ancient fire temple, located next to St. Brigid's Church of Ireland Cathedral in Kildare, was excavated in 1988. The Brigidine sisters are welcome to rekindle St. Brigid's fire in the temple site during the annual Imbolc festival and conference.

On February 1, 2000, four members of The Living Circle were present there when the fire was lit.[662] For the occasion, they brought with them to the fire temple Robert Lentz's recently completed icon of Sts. Brigid and Darlughdach. For the first time in history, they are depicted together with arms linked and Celtic tonsures, dressed in the white gowns worn both by Druid priestesses and by Celtic nuns. Since fire is the symbol of Northern Sophia, the mandala on their breast contains in a flame a face of Christ evocative of the Book of Kells. This represents Christ/Holy Wisdom, whose divine Love inflames, them, consumes them, is the bond between them and the gift they bestow. The three flames above them are also a reminder that the pre-Christian Brigid was a triple goddess whose blaze represented the spiritual fires of poetry, healing, and smithcraft. Thus it is appropriate that parts of the icon are painted with copper, silver, and three different carats of gold.

There are very few representations of pre-Christian Brigid in the world, and these few were sculpted under Roman influence. The ancient Celts rarely depicted their deities. Like the ancient Jews, they believed that divinity was so vast that it was ridiculous, insulting, and impossible to attempt to delineate it in an image. They often resorted to symbols instead. The main Celtic wisdom symbols are of great significance to distinctive people, because they reveal the link between distinctive people and Wisdom-Christ.

As queen of the Underworld, Brigid was also goddess of springs and wells, which were considered connecting channels between this world and the Otherworld. Not only did the Celts consider all wells and springs sacred places of power and healing, but they were also, just as much as fire, symbols of Northern Sophia and and primary sources of wisdom because the mythical salmon and eels of wisdom dwelt in them.

> *According to Celtic mythology, a sacred salmon dwelled in the Otherworld*
> *in the Well of Segais, the model of all surface sacred springs....How does*

the Christian share in this salmonoid symbolism? As far back as the second century, the fish has been used in Christian iconography as a symbol of Christ's being. A specific iconography was used to convey this symbolism that incorporated the Greek letters ΙΧΘΥΣ, *which form the word for "fish". The letters of the word also stand for Jesus Christ, God's Son, Savior....The image of the fish proceeded to take on the symbolism of Christ himself....There is one more important factor peculiar to the salmon, the eel, and Jesus that is decisive in providing the possibility of a syncretism between Celt and Christian. Let us begin with a symbolic examination of the salmon. What is distinctive about the salmon in relationship to other fish is that it lives in the sea but leaves the sea and enters a freshwater river to mate. In other words, the salmon is a boundary crosser, which by crossing the boundary is able to bring about transformation and new life. Further, the boundary crossed is from salt to fresh water, symbolically from the feminine to the masculine, from earth to sky. It is also important to note that the river to which the salmon returns is the place of its birth. The eel is also a crosser of boundaries. It, too, moves from salt to fresh water and back again, but the process is in the reverse order to the salmon. Thus the eel spends most of its time in fresh water, then at night crawls on its belly across the land to the Bermuda Islands where it breeds. The origin of the eel is in the sea, the salmon in the rivers. The salmon in accordance with its place of origin is masculine, the eel feminine, and together they form the totality of the gods. Both eel and salmon are mercurial figures, bringers of transformation, wisdom, and life.*[663]

Through his Incarnation, death, apocryphal visit to the Underworld, and Resurrection, Christ is the ultimate eternal Boundary Crosser. So the Celtic syncretism of Holy Wisdom-Christ with the salmon and the eel make perfect sense in that world view.

Since lesbian, gay, bisexual, and transgendered people are also constantly crossing over boundaries set by the heterosexual majority, not only in what they do but in who they are, the Christ-salmon-eel-wisdom syncretism can actually have a fifth component, consisting of distinctive people.

The association of the salmon (Wisdom) with Christ is a recurring theme in Celtic Christian stone carvings (e.g. the fish and cross symbol on a tombstone at Fuert, in Roscommon, Ireland and the crucified Savior with the head of Christ and the body of a fish in Riskbuie, Argyll, Scotland) and in illuminated manuscripts, among them the Book of Kells. "The fish is common in the Book of Kells, n ormally accompanying the face or name of Christ as a suprascript abbreviation bar. The species is like a salmon."[664] The name of Jesus is frequently embellished and abbreviated in illuminated manuscripts. The Kells abbreviation consists of the first three Greek letters of the name Jesus, ΙΗΣ, with a salmon above the second and third letter

Appendix B
Sts. Epipodius and Alexander, Sts. Perpetua and Felicity

The period of the Christian persecution by the Roman government has bequeathed to posterity a rich legacy of inscriptions, many of them to be found in the Roman Catacombs. They are often quite touching. Among them is an inscription in the Catacomb of St. Callixtus, which bears witness to a close friendship between two men. So attached was Januarius to Severinus that he wanted them to remain physically close to each other even after death. Their tombstone inscription proclaims their affection: "Januarius wanted to be buried together with his friend Severinus."[665]

During the persecution of the Church under Emperor Marcus Aurelius, in the summer of 177, many Christians died for their faith in the city of Lyons, Gaul. The names of forty-eight of them have come down to us. Among them were the ninety-year-old bishop, St. Pothinus, and St. Blandina, who was a slave-girl. The persecution claimed at least thirty-six more citizens of Lyons the following year - among them two young men named Epipodius and Alexander. Epipodius was a native of the city, and Alexander was a Greek by birth; but they had known each other from childhood, had gone to school together, and were bosom friends.

St. Eucherius, Bishop of Lyons (d.449), wrote a homily in their honor. In 858, St. Ado, a Benedictine Archbishop of Vienne,[666] published a Martyrology, which is a compilation of a Roman Martyrology he found at Ravenna with other more local source material. In it, he wrote about Epipodius and Alexander, describing one of them as being *carissimo* (most dear) to the other. Guerin records that they had a "tight friendship"[667] and Butler declares that they were "linked by the bands of the strictest friendship, which grew up with them, and was strengthened and spiritualized by their mutual profession of Christianity."[668] At the time the persecution broke out, they were both in the prime of their lives, with good positions, and unmarried.

One of their servants betrayed them for being Christians. They had been friends of Pothinus and Blandina, so they knew what cruelty they could expect if they were apprehended. They fled to a neighboring town and hid themselves in the house of a poor widow. Eventually they were arrested anyway.

Even though they had done all they could to save their lives, after three days in prison, they began to show exemplary courage. When they boldly professed their faith before the governor, the two were separated. Since Epipodius was the younger man, it was presumed he would be the weaker and would more easily give in. After promises of reward and sensuous pleasures failed to persuade him, he was stretched on a rack, while his sides were torn with iron claws. Since the crowd was clamoring for his death, the governor ordered him beheaded.

Two days later, when Alexander was again brought before the judge, he publicly reaffirmed his faith, praised God for the glorious examples of courage he had been given by Epipodius and the other martyrs, and "expressed his desire of joining his dear Epipodius."[669] He too was racked and survived scourging by three executioners. They decided to crucify him, but he died as soon as his limbs were fastened to the cross. These deaths took place in April of 178.

At first, the Christians buried them privately on a hill outside the city. By the time St. Eucherius wrote his homily in the fifth century, their tomb was inside the city. According to St. Gregory of Tours, by the sixth century, they had become such revered martyrs that they were re-buried, one on either side of the great Church father, St. Irenaeus, who succeeded Pothinus as bishop, in the crypt of the church of St. John (later renamed for St. Irenaeus) in Lyons.[670] Gregory would have been in a position to know this personally, for he completed his studies in Vienne, under its bishop, St. Avitus. And one of Gregory's own ancestors, St. Vettius Epagatus, had been one of those beheaded in Lyons in 177.[671] Epagatus was known as the "Advocate of the Christians", because he had bravely but futilely undertaken their defense.[672] Sts. Epipodius and Alexander's bones were still buried in St. Irenaeus Church in 1410, but they are gone now.

Twenty-five years after the deaths of Epipodias and Alexander, two North African women who were dear friends were likewise martyred. Sts. Perpetua and Felicity died for their Christian faith in the amphitheater at Carthage on March 7, 203. We know precise details of their imprisonment because Vibia Perpetua, a twenty-two year old of a distinguished noble family, kept a journal - the first known written document by a woman in Christian history, with a concluding narrative by an eye-witness.

Perpetua mentions that those arrested with her were a slave named Felicity and three men, Saturninus, Secundulus, and Revocatus. She details the misery of their cell, the efforts her father made to persuade her to recant, the naming of her family members, everyone who helped the martyrs, and those who condemned them. One person conspicuous in not being mentioned was her husband. As a noblewoman, she would have been married; but, for whatever reason, he was not there for her when one would think he would have been most needed. The person there for her was Felicity, who was expecting to give birth at any time.

Perpetua's greatest concern was that she have her baby son with her as long as she lived. Felicity was worried that she might not be allowed to die with her companions because of her pregnancy. In answer to prayer, she gave birth to a girl. The pain of the delivery was compounded by the mockery of the jailer; but she was assisted and comforted by Perpetua. On the day of their death, they alone refused to wear the required pagan costumes - insisting on maintaining the dignity of their female-ness,[673] even while they were dying. According to the narration:

> First the heifer tossed Perpetua and she fell on her back. Then sitting up she pulled the tunic along the side so that it covered her thighs, thinking more of her modesty than her pain. Next she asked for a pin to fasten her untidy hair: for it was not right that a martyr should die with her hair in disorder, lest she might seem to be mourning in her hour of triumph.[674]

They gave each other the kiss of peace, held on to each other as they were further attacked by wild animals, and were finally beheaded.

The companionship of these women inspired subsequent ages. They were buried in the Basilica Maiorum, on a high plateau south of the city of Carthage, in a place visible for a good distance to the many faithful who made it an object of pilgrimage. By the year 313, when Emperor Constantine's Edict of Milan put an end to the persecution of Christians, the anniversary of their martyrdom already appeared in the official calendar of the Roman Church.[675] Even though the stone commemorating the martyrs in their shrine listed the two women last, their commemorative feast has always been called by their two names alone.

The persecuted Christian communities of the third century for whom Perpetua recorded her dreams were different from the fourth century communities, who were guided to salvation by their bishops. Perpetua's text was explained and modified by churchmen who wanted to reshape the vision.[676] Perpetua's journal became such a beloved text in North Africa that St. Augustine of Hippo felt he had to warn people not to give it a reverence due only to Scripture. In an attempt to reconcile the fact that these strong young women were so venerated in his socially conservative diocese, Augustine co-opted the power of Perpetua's text by turning it into a subject of sermons,[677] in which he repeatedly toned down both Perpetua's and Felicity's achievements by framing them within the context of his understanding of the Fall of Eve. In the mid-fifth century, Bishop Quodvultdeus of Carthage reiterated these same ideas.[678] Many acts of the martyrs were rewritten during this period to make them more consistent with the prevailing doctrines. One fourth-century redactor rewrote (and shortened) Perpetua's account, making it clear that gender issues were in his mind by asking questions about Felicity's husband, creating a husband for Perpetua, and claiming he joined her family at her trial.[679] Despite these efforts to modify the powerful grip these two women had in the minds and hearts of North African Christians, Perpetua's full account was given a public reading during the annual celebration of their feast until the Vandals took over the Basilica Maiorum. After the Arab conquest of Carthage in the seventh century, their relics in Africa were lost.[680]

Appendix C
St. Boris and George the Hungarian

One of the earliest extant works from the literature of Medieval Rus' is "The Legend of Boris and Gleb," which forms a portion of *The Primary Chronicle*, structurally a very complicated document compiled by various writers from about 1040 to 1118.[681] It is possible that the author of "The Legend of Boris and Gleb" was Iakov, a monk of Kiev's Pechera Monastery, who wrote "In Memory and Praise of St. Vladimir."[682] This was done under the direction of Nestor, one of the authors of *The Primary Chronicle* and the most outstanding literary figure in the monastery at that time.[683]

With its blend of history, hagiography, and poetry, "The Legend of Boris and Gleb" enjoyed a remarkably wide circulation in subsequent centuries. It concerns a tragedy, occurring in 1015, of which the death of St. Olga's grandson, St. Vladimir, was the catalyst. This extraordinary prince had founded the state of Rus' and compelled his people into mass conversions to Christianity. Shortly after his death, two of his sons, the Kievan princes Boris and Gleb, were assassinated for dynastic purposes by minions of their half-brother Sviatopolk, called "the Accursed" because of the deed. Professor Simon Karlinsky,[684] who has made a complete translation and analysis of "The Legend," points out that the description of the murder of Prince Boris gives a noble place to his beloved servant,

> *"Hungarian by birth, George by name" (Hungarians and Kievan Russians had a common border at the time). Boris had a magnificent golden necklace made for George the Hungarian, for "he was loved by Boris beyond reckoning." When the four assailants stabbed Boris with their swords, George flung himself on the body of his prince, exclaiming: "I will not be left behind, my precious lord! Ere the beauty of thy body begins to wilt, let it be granted that my life may end." The assailants tore Boris out of George's embrace, stabbed George and flung him out of the tent, bleeding and dying. After Boris died, first having forgiven his assassins, his retinue was massacred. The murderers were unable to undo the clasp of George's golden necklace. So, rather than damage the necklace, they cut off George's head, flinging it far away, so that, the narrator adds indignantly, his head and body could not later be reunited for decent Christian burial. Not only was the author of this story clearly sympathetic to the mutual love of Boris and George but he also seemed to realize that "the gratuitous murder of George resulted from his open admission of the nature of this love."*[685]

George's brother Moses, later canonized by the Russian Orthodox Church as St. Moses the Hungarian,[686] was the only member of Boris's retinue to have escaped the massacre. His subsequent fate is revealed in "The Life of St. Moses the Hungarian," included in the compilation of the lives of early Russian saints known as the *Kievan Paterikon*. Moses was captured by the troops of Svyatopolk and sold as a slave to a Polish noblewoman who became enamored of his beauty and his powerful physique. He spent the next year resisting the woman's efforts to woo him, preferring the company of his fellow-prisoners. At the end of the year, exasperated by his refusals and taunts, she ordered that he be given one hundred lashes and that his sex organs be removed, saying: "I will not spare his beauty, so that others may not enjoy it either."[687] Eventually, Moses escaped and found his way to the Kievan Lavra Monastery, where he lived as a monk for ten more years. By then, he had become a great misogynist, constantly warning the monks about the wickedness of women. The monk who recorded the story of Moses described his powerful body and beautiful face with such great relish and so much emphasis, it is clear that he delighted in male beauty and that he expected his readers to have a similar appreciation. Otherwise, the text is permeated with the misogyny and the fear of all sexuality which is typical of medieval monastic tradition in Rus'.[688]

Meanwhile, after he had disposed of Vladimir's favorite son Boris, Svyatopolk now went after Boris's young brother, Gleb - safe at the time in Murom and believing that all his family were still alive. The young prince was lured from security by couriers, who brought the message that his father was very ill and calling for him. Meanwhile, Gleb's brother Yaroslav sent him a messenger to inform him of the murder of Boris and to warn him to stay away from Kiev. The messenger caught up with him at Smolyensk, just as he was boarding the boat which would take him down the Dnieper to Kiev. Gleb had been extremely attached to his older brother and, without him, felt lost in the world. Tearfully he prayed to him to beg God that they might dwell together in heaven.'[689] At that very moment, Svyatopolk's assailants, led by a man called Goryaser, rode down to the shore. They seized the boat by its rope and drew their swords, but no one dared to strike the first blow at a son of Vladimir. So Goryaser ordered Gleb's cook, Torchin, either to do the deed or face a fearful death himself. Torchin caught Gleb by the hair, threw him to his knees, and cut his throat.

Boris and Gleb were the first saints canonized by the Russian Orthodox Church. There is something paradoxical in this canonization. Neither brother was killed because of his attachment to the Christian faith, and neither showed any desire for death in the manner of some of the ancient martyrs. Actually, until the moment when the tragedy occurred, during their short lives, neither had manifested any lofty principles of holiness at all.[690]

Except in the case of martyrs for the faith, the canonization of members of the laity was a rare occurrence in the Greek Church. Even though many miracles were attributed to the intercession of the murdered princes, the Greek Metropolitan had doubts about the holiness of these new wonder-workers.[691] So the Russian Church had to find way of explaining just why the nation considered them "holy" and precisely what was the nature of their special Christian achievement.

The solution was a novel view of the Christian way to salvation. Boris and Gleb were "kenotic," that is "imitators of Christ in his *kenosis*, his self-humiliation and his voluntary, sacrificial death." Because of their voluntary suffering, the brothers were given the title of "Passion Bearers" at their canonization.

Their cult developed so quickly and extensively, Boris and Gleb became the chief rivals of St. Sophia as objects of devotion in Rus. Sadko, a rich Novgorod merchant,[692] erected, at his own expense, an imposing church in Novgorod in honor of the two brothers. With the consent of the Novgorod veche and the bishop, he selected a site in the Kremlin where at one time the first wooden Sophia church stood, just opposite the new Sophia, to which it seemed almost a challenge. At various times seven more churches were built in Novgorod in honor of Boris and Gleb.[693]

Since the Greek Metropolitan had his seat in Kiev, it was more difficult to promote their cult in such a grand way there. But a church bearing their names was built in 1072 at Vichgorod, the favorite country residence of the Kievan princes. And the relics of Russia's first saints were transferred there with unusual solemnity. A feast was instituted to commemorate the event, and this church quickly became the most honored of Kiev's sanctuaries.[694] A chapel was erected on the banks of the Alta River, at the spot where Boris met his death. There were also churches dedicated to them in Pereyaslavl Russky, in Rostov, Chernigov, Ryazan, Pskov, Grodno, and Polotsk. Their feast is celebrated by the Russian Orthodox Church six times a year - an exceptional practice.[695] A few years after their canonization, their cult spread to Bohemia where a chapel was built in their honor in the Sozava Monastery. The same thing happened in Armenia, as well as in Constantinople, where about 1200, an icon of them presented by the Archbishop of Novgorod was installed in Hagia Sophia.[696] Boris and Gleb became the patron saints of Russia, and Boris came to be regarded as the special protector of Moscow. Their cult was confirmed by the Roman Catholic Church in 1724, with a feast on July 24.

Considering the special efforts that went into explaining the holiness of Boris and Gleb, it seems rather unfair that similar efforts were not extended to George the Hungarian, who is not honored as a saint. Just as Nearchus desired to be with Polyeuct for eternity, and Sergius with Bacchus, so George yearned to be with Boris. Just as Polyeuct was canonized and Nearchus was not, so Boris was canonized and George was not. The difference is that George and Boris both were companions in death as well as in life, as were Sergius and Bacchus. Perhaps George's heroism was an embarrassment because of his outspoken affection for Boris. Canonizing him might remind people that Boris had been equally outspoken and public in demonstrating his affection for George. The fact that Zenkovsky's anthology, *Medieval Russia's Epics, Chronicles, and Tales*, omits the more homoerotic words in the dialogue between Boris and George is proof that their relationship has continued to be treated as an embarrassment even until recently.[697]

An account of one of the miracles which led to the canonization of the royal brothers makes it clear that, at least in the popular mind, George was a saint as well. After the remains of Boris and Gleb were deposited in St. Basil's church in Vladimir, a lame boy, the servant of one of the town's senior officials, came to visit the graves and remained there, praying day and night. One night, he had a vision of the sainted brothers, who healed his leg. The boy also saw and bore witness to the fact that they were accompanied by George the Hungarian.[698]

Some iconographers found a way of honoring George's place in Boris's life. It was sometimes customary to frame an icon's primary depiction of a saint by surrounding it with smaller images, showing scenes from the life of the saint. Some icons of Sts. Boris and Gleb were painted in this manner. There was a fine icon of them painted in the fourteenth century for the Church of Sts. Boris and Gleb at Kolomna. It can now be viewed at the Tretyakov Gallery in Moscow. It depicts St. Boris and George the Hungarian together in four separate scenes: Boris confides his fears of death to George; Boris prays in his tent with George; George observes Boris dreaming of a wild beast - symbol of his forthcoming death; Boris and George are murdered in the tent.[699] Finally, in the year 2000, Robert Lentz has properly honored Boris and George by painting together as the subject of an icon.

Appendix D
St. Andrei Rublev and Daniel Cherny

It was for the St. Sergius-Holy Trinity Monastery (*Troitse-Sergeyeva Lavra*) that one of the most famous icons in the world was produced - a perfect iconographic expression of the harmony, serenity, peace, love, joy, and light which is at the heart of God and which, according to Sergius of Radonezh (d. 1392), should be the goal of every spiritual journey and every relationship. St. Sergius was inspired by the prayer of Christ and his disciples, "That they may be one even as we are one." (John 17:22) His ideal was the transfiguration of the world in the image of the Holy Trinity, that is, the inner union of all beings in God.[700] "The Trinity of the Old Testament" is the masterpiece of St. Andrei Rublev, one of the most famous disciples of St. Sergius, and a man who, through his craft and in his friendship with Daniel Cherny, would experience a taste of the bliss at the heart of the Trinity.

Andrei Rublev, who was canonized by the Russian Orthodox Church in 1988, merits being considered the greatest of Russian artists.[701] Although his name appears several times in contemporary records, nothing is known about his origin, his early life, or his earliest artistic schooling. Even though the Soviet Government celebrated the six-hundredth anniversary of his birth in 1960, many scholars place it as much as ten years later. It seems certain that he was already a monk at Holy Trinity Lavra while St. Sergius was still its abbot.[702]

St. Sergius was a close friend of Grand Duke Dmitri Donskoy and his family. He was godfather of Prince Yuri of Zvenigorod. So it was likely St. Sergius who urged Dmitri's elder son Vasili and Yuri himself to offer Andrei some important commissions. He was apparently working for Prince Yuri in the 1390's. By 1400, by the order of the Metropolitan Alexis, and with the blessing of St. Nikon, successor to St. Sergius, Andrei had become a monk at the Andronikov Monastery (now the Rublev Museum in Moscow). He was no longer connected with Holy Trinity Lavra by 1405, when he was given work at Vladimir. By 1408, he had returned to the Andronikov Monastery, founded some 40 years before by St. Sergius's beloved disciple, St. Andronik. Though Rublev may have gone back to Holy Trinity while he was painting icons for its new cathedral, basically he remained attached to Andronikov until his death.

Earlier in his career, Rublev's name was connected with fellow-artist Prokhor Gorodetsky, but contemporary records later associate him with Daniel Cherny (or Chorny, i.e. "the Black"), whom he first met as a fellow monk at Andronikov Monastery. Andrei took Daniel as his teacher. Cherny is not mentioned until 1408, but from then on, he and Rublev were colleagues in painting and lifelong friends.[703] Having distinguished himself in 1405 by working with Prokhor and with his teacher, Theophanes the Greek, in painting Moscow's Annunciation Cathedral, Rublev was sent with Daniel in 1408 to paint murals in Vladimir's Dormition Cathedral.

> *It was probably at Vladimir that the spiritual and creative union between the two - which even death would not alter - was born. The impact of a spiritual communion of this nature is felt in the icons of the apostles Peter and Paul, of the "anargiri" ("moneyless ones", since these physicians served the poor for no charge) Cosmos and Damian, and in those of the holy princes Boris and Gleb.[704]*

By about 1409-10, having become Medieval Russia's foremost Iconographers, they were both painting in the Lavra's Holy Trinity Cathedral. They had been commissioned to do so by St. Nikon.

> *Since they were such good friends and worked so closely together, it is nearly impossible to separate the lives of Daniel and Andrei; the historical documents nearly always speak of them together.*[705]

Nowhere is the theme of dedicated service and Sergius' theological vision of the Trinity expressed more clearly than in the icon of the Old Testament Trinity, which Rublev painted in honor of his teacher, Sergius. This icon, Rublev's masterpiece, once occupied the niche to the right of the royal gates. According to the monastery's records, this icon was given to it by Ivan the Terrible. This means that, contrary to general belief, the icon did not originate at Holy Trinity-St. Sergius Monastery.[706] One special feature of this remarkable image is that the central angel is clothed in a dark-red robe, trimmed with gold, and a blue cloak, which were ordinarily the colors of Christ's robes in the icon tradition. So the central androgynous, angelic figure would have been easily recognized as representing Christ to the medieval viewer.[707] As the original of this icon is now at the Tretyakov Gallery of Art, a copy is displayed in the iconostasis.[708] Other icons attributed to Rublev are those in the same iconostasis of the Apostles, St. Peter and St. Paul and also the Archangel Gabriel. Daniel Cherny is considered the painter of the figures of the Savior Enthroned, Archangel Michael, and David.

All the short descriptions of the life of St. Andrei call Daniel his friend and fellow-faster. They are described in the *Life of St. Nikon* as men made perfect in the virtues and as virtuous elders and painters, ever maintaining a spiritual brotherhood and great love for each other. And thus they departed to God in the sight of each other, in spiritual union, even as they had lived here on earth.[709]

In his *Responses*, St. Joseph of Volokolamsk (d. 1515),[710] the first to write about their legendary friendship, declared that only death could separate them, physically, but not spiritually. Andrei, the younger of the two, died on January 29, 1430;[711] but then, shortly afterwards in the same year

> *Daniel fell ill, and during his last moments, saw his companion Andrei in a great and glorious light. Andrei called Daniel to come join him in eternal and infinite happiness.*[712]

This vision is also reported in *The Life and Works of St. Nikon of Radonezh*, contained in the chronicle written by Pacomius the Logothete:

> *As soon as Daniel arrived at the moment of leaving this material world, he saw his beloved friend who called him to come join him in a life of great happiness. When Daniel perceived Andrei expressing his desire, he was filled with joy and told the vision of his friend to the other monks present. Then he died.*[713]

This happened in the Andronikov Monastery, where they were buried. The narration of Daniel's vision of his departed companion is notably similar to the vision Sergius had of his beloved Bacchus centuries earlier. In the *Life of St. Nikon*, it is recorded that Andrei Rublev reposed in "venerable and honorable old age", which means that he was at least 70 years old at the time of his death. Before they died, they had contributed to the construction and decoration of the monastery's principal church, which was dedicated to the Transfiguration. Since the memory of these two icon painters was an object of great veneration throughout the 16th and 17th centuries and revived again in the 20th, Orthodox writers have pointed out that

> *It is not out of place to wonder why the Russian Church did not also*
> *glorify Daniel at the canonization of Andrei Rublev in 1988.*[714]

Fr. Steven Bigham has pointed out that, there are at least two historical references to "St." Daniel. The first is found in the notice of St. Sergius of Radonezh: "In 1422, the relics of St. Serge were transported…to the new church decorated with the admirable frescoes painted by Sts. Daniel the Black (Chorny) and Andrei Rublev."[715] The other comes the contemporary writing of Leonid Ouspensky, who declares that, during the 14th and the 15th centuries, "St. Andrew (Rublev)…worked with his friend and teacher, St. Daniel (the Black).[716]

The Russian Orthodox Church observes St. Andrei Rublev's feast on July 4th.

ENDNOTES

ii. Rocca, Rev. Peter D.,C.S.C., *The Order of Prayer in the Liturgy of the Hours and Celebration of the Eucharist 2009 – Archdiocese of Chicago, Dioceses of Joliet and Rockford* (Matwah, New Jersey: Paulist Press Ordo, 2008) p. 239,

v Lasarev, Vikor Nikitich, *The Double-faced Tablets from the St. Sophia Cathedral in Novgorod* (Moscow: Iskusstvo Art Publishers, 1983) reverse side of Plate I.

vi. Rolland, Romain, *Some Musicians of Former Days* (New York: Henry Holt & Company, 1915) p. 118, n.1.

viii. (ibid.) p. 101.

ix (ibid.) p. 243.

x http://andrejkoymanski.com/liv/mar/mar14.html

xiii. Segal, J. B., *Edessa: 'The Blessed City'* (Piscataway, NJ: Gorgias Press, 2001) pp. 183-84.

xiv. Baumer, Christoph, *The Church of the East* (London & New York: I. B. Tauris, 2006) p. 19.

xv. (ibid.) p. 103.

xvi. (ibid.) p. 62.

xix. *Excavati on Campaign 1998 at Nitl and Umm al-Rasas* (Madaba, Jordan, Franciscan Archaeological Institue, 1998).

xx. Piccirillo, Michele, *The Church of St. Sergius at Nitl, Jordan* (London: *Minerva*, International Review of Ancient Art and Archaeology, Vol. 16, N. 6, November/December, 2005, p. 42.

xxii. Baumer, Christoph, (*op. cit.*) p. 195.

xxv. Bray, Alan, *The Friend* (Chicago: University of Chicago Press, 2003) p. 126.

xxvi. (ibid.) p. 126-7.

xxvii. (ibid.) p. 62

xxviii. Simson, Otto G. von *Sacred Fortress: Byzantine Art and Statecraft in Ravenna* (Chicago: University of Chicago Press, reprint, 1976) p. 70

xxix. Holweck, *op. cit.*, p.32.

xxx. Bustacchini, Gianfranco, *Ravenna, Mosaics, monuments and environment* (Ravenna: Cartolibreria Salbaroli, 1984) p. 77.

xxxi. *Excavations at the Deserted Medieval Village of Vöhingen: Archaeology in Baden-Württemberg* http://home.bawue.de/-wmwerner/hoehing/e_kirch.html

xxxii. http://andrejkoymansky.com/liv/mar/mar22.html

xxxiv. Blech, Benjamin, and Doliner, Roy, The Sistine Secrets: Michelangelo's *Forbidden Messages in the Heart of the Vatican* (New York: HarperCollins, 2008) pp. 197-99.

1. Shlain, Leonard, *The Alphabet Versus the Goddess: The Conflict Between Word and Image* (New York: Viking, 1998) p. 21.

2. (ibid.) p. 23.

3. (ibid.) p. 23.

4. (ibid.) p. 24.

5. (ibid.) p. 25.

6. (ibid.) p. 43.

7. Roscoe, Will, *The Zuni Man-Woman* (Albuquerque, NM: University of New Mexico Press, 1991) p. 5.

8.Waddell, Helen, tr.,"The Desert Fathers," from *The Sayings of the Fathers*, translated from the Greek by Pelagius the Deacon and John the Subdeacon (New York: Sheed & Ward, 1942) pp. 109-110. Translators Pelagius and John became Pope Pelagius I (d. 561) and his successor, Pope John III (d. 574) . The quote is an excerpt from a chapter entitled "On Fornication."

9. Vööbus, Arthur, *History of Asceticism in the Syrian Orient* (Louvain: Secretariat Du Corpus SCO, 1960) pp. 137-8) describes an heretical group called the Messalians (or Massalians), who had a following in Syria and Asia Minor. One of their characteristics was an attitude of indifference to the sacraments of the Church. He specifically calls attention to the pertinent piece of dialogue in the account of Polyeuct's martyrdom when he adds that "It is interesting to observe that indifference toward the sacraments appears in some circles which were located in the vicinity of Militene". (p. 137, f. 69). The Messalians first appeared in the latter part of the fourth century as a Manichaean type of Christian Gnosticism, with men and women in leadership roles. They believed that a period of strict self-denial was necessary for them to reach a purified state, at which point sin was no longer possible. Once in this state, believers no longer required self-denial and could engage in any sex without sin. Obolensky, Dmitri, *The Bogomils* (Cambridge: Cambridge University Press, 1948) p. 50)."The Messalian doctrines were the extreme expression of the longing to comprehend mystical revelation through sensual experience." Loos, Milan, *Dualist Heresy in the Middle Ages* (The Hague, Martinus Nijhoff, 1974) p. 72).

10. It might be argued that their martyrdom alone is the reason for which they were honored as saints, since martyrdom is a "baptism of blood", which brings with it total forgiveness for anything in one's past. This argument loses its impact, when we consider that the Roman Catholic Church was willing to dishonor two genuine, historic martyrs for the faith, Sergius and Bacchus, by striking them from the calendar - most likely because they had lived as each others' lovers.

11. Benedictine Monks of St. Augustine's Abbey, Ramsgate, *The Book of Saints* (Harrisburg, PA: Morehouse Publishing, 1993) p. 505.

12. Greif, Martin, *The Gay Book of Days* (New York: Lyle Stuart, 1989) recalls that Graves, born in London in 1895, had a gay youth and wrote an early play about homosexuality entitled, "But It Still Goes On" p. 128.

13. e.g. Boswell, John, *Christianity, Social Tolerance, and Homosexuality* (Chicago: University of Chicago Press, 1980); Comstock, Gary David, *Gay Theology Without Apology* (Cleveland: The Pilgrim Press, 1993); Glaser, Chris, *Come Home!* (San Francisco: Harper & Row, Publishers, 1990); Horner, Tom, *David Loved Jonathan* (Philadelphia: The Westminster Press, 1978); and McNeill, John J., *The Church and the Homosexual* (Boston: Beacon Press, 1988).

14. Tutu, Desmond, "South Africa's Blacks: Aliens in Their Own Land," published November 26, 1984, in "Christianity and Crisis," reprinted in *Ethics in the Present Tense: Readings from Christianity and Crisis 1966-1991* edited by Howell, Leon, & Lindermayer, Vivian (New York: Friendship Press, 1991) p. 131.

15 An international news brief in *Bondings*: Volume 24, Number 3 (Mt Rainier, MD: a Publication of New Ways Ministries, Spring, 2004) p. 6.

16. "Distinctive people" is a term preferable to "homosexuals" both because the latter word was created by people who considered homosexuality a clinical disorder and because, being half Greek and half Latin, "homo-sexual" is a word poorly fashioned from the beginning.

17. Moretti, Girolamo, *The Saints Through Their Handwriting* (New York: The Macmillan Company, 1964) p. 152.

18. (ibid.) p. 158.

19. *The Jerusalem Bible* (Garden City, NY: Doubleday & Company, Inc., 1966) p. 943.

20. Wainwright, Arthur W. *The Trinity in the New Testament* (London: S.P.C.K., 1962) p. 135.

21. Aldredge-Clanton, Jann, *In Search of Christ-Sophia* (Mystic, CT: Twenty-Third Publications, 1995) p. 9.

22. Schüssler Fiorenza, Elisabeth, *Jesus: Miriam's Child, Sophia's Prophet* (New York: Continuum, 1995) p. 136.

23. (ibid.) pp. 137-38.

24. (ibid.) p. 138.

25. (ibid.) p. 141.

26. (ibid.) p. 142.

27. Stuhlmueller, Carroll, C.P., *Thirsting for the Lord: Essays in Biblical Spirituality* (Garden City, NY: Image Books, 1979) pp. 200&203.

28 Haughton, Rosemary, *The Catholic Thing* (Springfield, IL: Templegate Publishers, 1979) p. 10.

29 Official Catholic teaching takes issue with what it claims distinctive people **do** and condemns it, the same teaching claims to accept distinctive people **as they are**.

30 Haughton, Rosemary, (op. cit.) p. 9.

31. Schüssler Fiorenza, Elisabeth, *Searching the Scriptures: A Feminist Commentary* (New York: Crossroad, 1994) pp. 699-700.

32. Quasten, Johannes, *Patrology*: Vol. I (op. cit.) p. 123.

33. Davies, Stevan L., *The Gospel of Thomas and Christian Wisdom* (New York: The Seabury Press, 1983) p. 17.

34. (ibid.) p. 146.

35. (ibid.) p. 61.

36. (ibid.) pp. 44-45.

37. (ibid.) p. 55.

38. Funk, Robert W., Hoover, Roy W., and the Jesus Seminar, *The Five Gospels* (New York: Macmillan Publishing Company, 1993) p. 515.

39. Davies, Stevan L., (op. cit.) p. 87.

40. Funk, Robert W., Hoover, Roy W., and the Jesus Seminar, (op. cit.) p. 529.

41. Davies, Stevan L., (op. cit.) p. 93.

42. Funk, Robert W., and Hoover, Roy W., (op. cit.) p. 494.

43. Funk and Hoover, (ibid.) p. 486.

44. Quoted in Schüssler Fiorenza, Elisabeth, *Searching the Scriptures: A Feminist Commentary* (op. cit.) p. 700.

45. Aldredge-Clanton, Jann, (op. cit.) pp. 23-24.

46. Theophilus of Antioch, *Discourse with Autolycus* 2:10

47. Irenaeus of Lyons, *Against the Heresies* 4:20

48. Ruether, Rosemary Radford, *Womanguides: Readings Toward a Feminist Theology* (Boston: Beacon Press, 1996) p. 24.

49. (ibid.) pp. 22-24.

50. McCullough, W. Stewart, (op. cit.) p. 33.

51. Ruether, Rosemary Radford, (op. cit.) p. 24.

52. Quasten, Johannes, *Patrology*: Vol. I (Utrecht-Antwerp: Spectrum Publishers, 1966) p. 162.

53. Quasten, Johannes, (ibid.) p. 275.

54. Prestige, G. L., D.D., *God in Patristic Thought* (London: S.P.C.K., 1969) p. 91.

55. Evdokimov, Paul, *The Art of the Icon: a Theology of Beauty* (Redondo Beach, CA: Oakwood Publications, 1990) pp. 348-49.

56. Kelly, J. N. D., *Early Christian Doctrines* (New York: Harper & Row Publishers, 1960) p. 95.

57. *Patrologia Graeca, Vol. 6, col. 464.*

58. (ibid.) col. 381.

59. Cavarnos, Constantine, *Byzantine Thought and Art* (Belmont, MA: Institute for Byzantine and Modern Greek Studies, 1974) pp. 16-17.

60. Aldredge-Clanton, Jann, (op. cit.) p. 31. Justin Martyr, "The Works of S. Justin the Martyr" (Oxford: J.H. and Jas.Parker, 1861) p. 150.

61. Athenagoras, *A Plea For Christians* XXIV, in *The Ante-Nicene Fathers*, Vol. II, ed. Roberts, Rev Alexander, D.D., and Donaldson, James, LL.D., (Grand Rapids, MI: Wm. B. Eerdmans Publishing Company, 1971) p. 141.

62. Clement of Alexandria, *On Spiritual Perfection: Miscellanies*, Book VII.2.7 , in *Alexandrian Christianity* ed. Chadwick, Henry, (Philadelphia: The Westminster Press, 1954) p. 97.

63. Quasten, Johannes, *Patrology* Vol. II, (Westminster, MD: The Newman Press, 1964) p. 37.

64. Aldredge-Clanton, Jann (op. cit..) p. 31. Origen, *Commentary on John, The Ante-Nicene Fathers: The Writings of the Fathers down to A.D. 325*, ed. Allan Menzies, vol. 9 (New York: Christian Literature Company, 1896) pp. 317-18.

65. Smith, John Clark, *The Ancient Wisdom of Origen* (Cranbury, NJ: Associated University Presses, Inc., 1992) p. 176. The quote is from Origen's *Commentary on the Gospel of John I.*^{34} (43.^{24}ff.), tr. Menzies, A., *The Ante-Nicene Fathers* X, 317B, Books I-X only.

66. Menzies, Albert, D.D., *The Ante-Nicene Fathers, Vol. X* (Grand Rapids, MI: Wm. B. Eerdmans Publishing Company, 1969) *Commentary on Matthew* XII:25, p. 464; *Commentary on Matthew* XIV:6, p. 498; *Commentary on John* I:22, p. 307; *Commentary on John* I: 39, p. 317, *Commentary on John* II:12, p. 318; *Commentayr on John* IV:18, pp. 334&336.

67. Quoted in McGinn, Bernard, *The Foundations of Mysticism* Vol. I (New York: Crossroad, 1992) p. 122.

68. St. Gregory of Nyssa, "Vita Gregorii," *PG, Vol. XLVI, col. 912*. The English translation comes from Lebreton, Jules, S.J., and Jacques Zeiller, *The Triumph of Christianity* (New York: Collier Books, 1947) p. 148.

69. Pelikan, Jaroslav, *The Emergence of the Catholic Traditon (100-600)* (Chicago and London: University of Chicago Press, 1975) p. 186.

70. Pelikan, Jaroslav, (op. cit.) pp. 186-93.

71. Vawter, Bruce, C.M., *The Path of Wisdom: Biblical Investigations* (Wilmington, Delaware: Michael Galzier, 1986) pp. 164-65.

72. Schaff, Philip, D.D., LL.D., and Wace, Henry, *Nicene and Post-Nicene Fathers*, Vol. 2, Socrates, Sozomenus: *Church Histories* (Hendrickson Publishers, 1994) p. 4. from Socrates, *Ecclesiastical History* I:6.

73. See *Athanasius* tr. Gregg, Robert C., (New York: Paulist Press, 1980) in "Epistle I:19 *to* Bishop Serapion Concerning the Holy Spirit," and in "Epistle II-III;2 to Bishop Serapion Concerning the Holy Spirit". Athanasius wrote that St. Anthony the Great taught the same thing ("*The Life of Anthony 69*") p. 82, and "Letter to Marcellinus on the Interpretation of Psalms 5" p. 104.

74. Eusebius of Caesarea, *Life of Constantine* IV:24, quoted in *A New Eusebius*, ed. Stevenson, J. (London: S.P.C.K., 1957) p. 390.

75. Eusebius of Caesarea, *Oration on the Tricennalia of Constantine 2:1-5* (A.D.^{336}), quoted in *A New Eusebius* (ibid.) p. 391:

> *He who is the pre-existent Word, the Savior of all things, imparts to His followers the seeds of true wisdom and salvation, makes them at the same time truly wise, and understanding the kingdom of their Father.*

76. "Concerning the Holy Spirit 19 & 21", in *The Letters of St. Athanasius Concerning the Holy Spirit* (op. cit.) p. 112, n. 22.

77. "Commentary on I Corinthians I:22ff"., in Cyril of Alexandria, St., Vol. VII, *PG Vol. 74*, pp. 861-2:D and 863-4:B.

78. "Discourse on the Resurrection I", in Methodius of Olympus, St., ed., Roberts, the Rev. Alexander, D.D., and Donaldson, James, LL.D., *The Ante-Nicene Fathers, Volume VI* (Grand Rapids, MI: Wm. B. Eerdmans Publishing Company, 1971) p. 369.

79. Fragment from a "Commentary on Proverbs IX:1" "Wisdom hath builded her house," in Roberts, the Rev. Alexander, D.D., and Donaldson, James, LL.D., ed., *The Ante-Nicene Fathers*, Vol. V., Hippolytus, Cyprian, Caius, Novatian, Appendix," (Grand Rapids, MI: Wm. B. Eerdmans Publishing Company, 1978) p. 175.

80. *PG 42*, p. 296.

81. *PG 87*, p. 388A.

82. "The Four Centuries of Charity III:22&24", in *PG 42*, p. 296, in St. Maximus the Confessor, *The Ascetic Life and The Four Centuries of Charity* tr. Sherwood, Polycarp, O.S.B., S.T.D., (Westminster, MD: The Newman Press, 1955) pp. 176-77, and n.152 on p. 259.

83. *Philocalia* (Athens, 1893) Vol. 1, p. 111. quoted by Cavarnos, Constantine, (op. cit.) pp. 17-18:

> *Many of the Greeks and not a few of the Jews undertook to philosophize; but only Christ's disciples strove after the true wisdom, for they alone had Wisdom itself as their teacher*

84. among his "Select Demonstrations," "On Pastors X:8," in Aphrahat, ed. Schaff, Philip, D.D., LL.D., and Wace, Henry, D.D., *A Select Library of Nicene and Post-Nicene Fathers of the Christian Church*, Vol. XIII (Grand Rapids, MI: Wm. B. Eerdmans Publishing Company , 1969) p. 386.

85. "On the Orthodox Faith, Book I:8," in John of Damascus, St., Schaaf, Philip, D.D., LL.D., and Wace, Henry, D.D., *A Select Library of Nicene and Post-Nicene Fathers of the Christian Church Vol. IX* (Grand Rapids, MI: Wm. B. Eerdmans Publishing Company, 1973) pp. 6&80.

86. "Against Eunomius I:23, II:17", in Fedwick, Paul Jonathan, *Basil of Caesarea: Christian, Humanist, Ascetic* (Toronto: Pontifical Institute of Mediaeval Studies, 1981) Part I, pp. 89&100, "On the Holy Spirit 6:15, 8:17, 19 & 20," in St. Basil the Great, tr. Anderson, David, *On the Holy Spirit* (Crestwood, NY: St. Vladimir's Seminary Press, 1980) pp. 30, 35, 39, &40.

87. "On Virginity 20" and "On Perfection," in St. Gregory of Nyssa, tr. Callahan, Virginia Woods, *Ascetical Works* (Washington D.C., The Catholic University of America Press, 1967) Vol. 58 of *The Fathers of the Church*, pp. 64&101. "Against Eunomius: Book III:2" and "The Great Catechism I," in Schaff, Philip, D.D., LL.D, and Wace, Henry, D.D., *A Select Library of Nicene and Post-Nicene Fathers of the Christian Church*, Vol. V (Grand Rapids, MI: Wm. B. Eerdmans Publishing Company, 1969) pp. 140&476.

88. "Oration 29:17 On the Son" and "Oration 30:2 On the Son," in Norris, Frederick W., intro. & comm., Wickham, Lionel, and Williams, Frederick, tr.,*Faith Gives Fullness to Reasoning: The Five Theological Orations of Gregory Nazianzen* (Leiden: New York: E.J. Brill, 1991) pp. 255&262.

89. *Oration 31:7 On the Holy Spirit* See Aldredge-Clanton, Jann, (op. cit.) p. 27.

90 Schug-Wille, Christa, *Art of the Byzantine World* (New York: Harry N. Abrams, Inc.: 1969) pp.18-19.

91 (ibid.) pp. 53-54.

92 (ibid.) pp. 44-51.

93 Eisen, Gustavus A., *The Great Chalice of Antioch* (New York: Fahim Kouchakji, 1933) p.

94 DuBourgute, Pierre, S.J., *The Art of the Copts* (New York: Crown Publishers, Inc.: 1967) p. 83.

95 Dalton, O. M., *Byzantine Art and Archaeology* (New York: Dover Publications, 1961) p. 282.

96. Also Polyeuctos, Polyeuktos, Polyeuctes, or Polyeucte - a Greek name meaning "much beloved"

97. Also Nearchos, Nearchon, or Nearque - a Greek name meaning "new leader"

98. Now called Malatya

99. Génier, Fr. Raymond, *Vie de Saint Eutheme Le Grand* (Paris: Librairie Victor Lecoffre, J. Gabalda & Cie, 1909) pp. 54-55.

100. Kostof, Spiro, *Caves of God: Cappadocia and Its Churches* (New York: Oxford University Press, 1989) p. 6.

101. Antreassian, Assadour, *Jerusalem and the Armenians* (Jerusalem: St. James Press, 1969) pp. 37-38.

102. Der Nersessian, Sirapie, *Armenia and the Byzantine Empire* (Cambridge, MA: Harvard University Press, 1945) pp. 29-30.

103. (ibid.) pp. 54-55.

104. (ibid.) p. 56. It is obvious from Basil's "Epistle 181" that he and Otreius were both friends and correspondents.

105. "Un Nouveau Ménologe Grec De Janvier Dans Un Manuscrit De Glasgow", in *Analecta Bollandiana* (Bruxelles: Société Des Bollandistes, 1957) Vol. 75, pp. 68-70.

106. Conybeare, F.C., M.A., *The Apology and Acts of Apollonius And Other Monuments of Early Christianity* (New York: Macmillan & Co., 1894) p. 123.

107. Aubé, B., *Polyeuct Dans L'Histoire: Étude Sur Le Martyre De Polyeucte, D'Après Des Documénts Inédits* (Paris: Librairie De Firmin-Didot Et Cie., 1882).

108. The text was translated into English by F.C. Conybeare and published in 1894.

109. Conybeare, (op. cit.) pp. 129-30.

110. (ibid.) p. 131.

111. (ibid.) p. 131.

112. (ibid.) p. 131.

113. (ibid.) p. 132.

114. (ibid.) pp. 132-33. There is an irony and an element of rhetorical flourish to this statement, since it will shortly become apparent that Polyeuct does indeed have a child, from whom he is willing to be separated by death for love of Nearchus and of his newfound Christ. And Nearchus would surely have known about this child's existence.

115. (ibid.) p. 137.

116. (ibid.) p. 139.

117. (ibid.) p. 142.

118. (ibid.) pp. 144-5.

119. Boswell, John, *Same-Sex Unions In Premodern Europe* (New York: Villard Books, 1994) p. 144.

120. Aubé B. (op. cit.) p. 13.

121. (ibid.) p. 11.

122. Milne, J. Grafton, M. A., *A History of Egypt Under Roman Rule* (London: Methuen & Co. Ltd., 1913) pp. 169-71.

123. De Blois, Lukas, *The Policy of the Emperor Gallienus* (Leiden: E. J. Brill, 1976) p. 177.

124. Bowman, Alan K., *Egypt after the Pharaohs (California University Press, 1989) p. 44.*

125. (ibid.) pp. 9-10.

126. Genier, Fr. Raymond, (op. cit.) p. 56.

127. See the first two chapters of I Samuel.

128. Cyril of Scythopolis, *Lives of the Monks of Palestine* tr. R.M. Price, introduction and notes by John Binns, in the *Life of St. Euthymius* 13:15-20 (Kalamazoo, MI: Cistercian Publications, 1991) p. 9.

129. Genier, Fr. Raymond, (op. cit.) p. 68.

130. Cyril of Scythopolis, (op. cit.), *Life of St. Euthymius* 14:21- 24", p. 10.

131. Genier, Fr. Raymond, (op. cit.) p. 86.

132. (ibid.), pp. 82&90.

133. Narkiss, Bezalal, *Armenian Art Treasures of Jerusalem* (New Rochelle, NY: Caratzas Brothers, Publishers, 1979) p. 21.

134. Antreassian, Assadour, (op. cit.) p. 39.

135. (ibid.) p. 28. Many thanks to Fr. Razmig Boghossian, Chief Dragoman of the Armenian Patriarchate of Jerusalem, for the information he provided on the Musrara Mosaic.

136. (ibid.) p. 5.

137. Since it is a Christian belief that, even after death, those who are now participating in the communion of saints are still aware of and concerned about those who have not yet died on earth, Christians throughout history have developed different means of trying to nurture relationship with the saints.

Meditating on icons is one method. By gazing into the eyes of an icon, it is believed that a person can be drawn into a deeper communion with whichever holy one is depicted. This was such a commonly held belief that even the followers of Mohammed (d. 632), who were opposed to the use of images in worship, had a superstitious fear of icons. They generally either destroyed or covered over any Christian images they found. When time did not permit total removal, they often gouged out the eyes of the images.

Another means of communion with the saints was the veneration of relics. In his book *Furta Sacra* (Princeton, NJ: Princeton University Press, 1990) p. 36, Patrick J. Geary points out that, actually, "in the East, the cult of relics developed prior to the cult of images...a transition from cult of physical object to cult of visual representation took place in Byzantium." It was believed that the saints' physical remains still retained something of their spirit and their holiness. So from early in Christian history, possession of the bones of the saints was considered so highly desirable that people would sometimes even steal them, when they could obtain them by no legitimate means. It was as though by possessing a relic, one actually possessed the saint. By the Middle Ages, this was taken so literally that, in some places, Geary says (p. 34), the Eucharist itself came to be considered a relic, differing only in its being the body and blood of Christ, rather than the body and blood of one of his saints.

138. Lagrange, P. Marie-Joseph, *Saint-Étienne et Son Sanctuaire à Jérusalem* (Paris: Alphonse Picard et Fils, 1894) Not only was she baptized in the Church of St. Stephen in Constantinople, but she built the basilica of St. Stephen in Jerusalem. And there she was buried. p. 71.

139. Procopius of Caesarea wrote that St. Lawrence was one of the churches built along the Golden Horn. Cameron, Averil, *Procopius* (London: Duckworth Press, 1985) p. 101.

140. Moorehead, John, *Justinian*, (New York: Longman Publishing, 1994) pp. 42-43.

62. Holweck, The Rt. Rev. F.G., *A Biographical Dictionary of the Saints* (St. Louis, MO: B. Herder Book Co., 1924) p. 321.

142. Gibson, Margaret. ed., *Boethius* (Oxford: Basil Blackwell, 1981) p. 34.

143. Moorehead, John, (op. cit.) p. 49.

144. Harrison, Martin, *A Temple For Byzantium* (Austin: University of Texas Press, 1989) pp. 36&40.

145. Moorehead, John, (op. cit.) p. 50.

146. Thomas, John Philip, *Private Religious Foundations in the Byzantine Empire* (Washington D.C.: Dumbarton Oaks Research Library and Collection, 1987) p. 23.

147. Thomas, John Philip, (op. cit.) pp. 23-24.

148. Mango, Cyril, *Byzantium: Empire of the New Rome* (New York: Charles Scribners Sons, 1980) p. 262.

149. (ibid.) p. 51.

150. Harrison, Martin, *A Temple for Byzantium* (op. cit.) p. 142 refers to the source: Ciggaar, K. N., "Une description de Constantinuple traduite par un pèlerin anglais", *Revue des Études Byzantines* 34 (1976) pp. 211-267.

151 *Bibliotheca Sanctorum* (Vatican City: Pontificia Università Lateranse, 1968) Vol. X, p. 998.

152. (ibid.) p. 143. He quotes from de Khitrowo, B., *Itinéraires russes en Orient* (Geneve, 1889) pp. 104, 137, 162, 203; cf. Janin, R., *Les églises et les monastères* (Paris, 1953) pp. 419-420.

153. Harrison, R. Martin, and Firatli, Nezih, "Excavations at Saraçhane in Istanbul: Fourth Preliminary Report" (Washington D.C.: Center for Byzantine Studies, 1967) Dumbarton Oaks Papers, Vol. 21, p. 275, n. 8.

154. Gilles, Pierre, tr. Ball, John, *The Antiquities of Constantinople* (New York: Italica Press, 1988).

155. In a letter to the author dated March 4, 1992, Martin Harrison wrote, "St. Polyeuktos is in the middle of Istanbul, whereas the text has it about two miles away in the area of S. Sophia and the Hioopdrome, so I'm afraid that I can't make a link with the Sigma."

156. Jacoff, Michael, *The Horses of San Marco and the Quadriga of the Lord* (Princeton, NJ: Princeton University Press, 1993) p. 4.

157. Nichol, Donald M., *Byzantium and Venice* (Cambridge: Cambridge University Press, 1992) p. 183.

158. Matthews, Thomas F., *The Early Churches of Constantinople* (University Park, PA: Pennsylvania State University Press, 1980) p. 52).

159. Holweck, F.G., (op. cit.) p. 876.

160. Cyril of Scythopolis, (op. cit.) from *The Life of Our Pious Father Sabas* 145:7, p. 154.

161. It is likely that Sabas was concerned with the temptation occasioned by presence of eunuchs and young boys in communities of vowed celibates. Apparently, the temptation was sometimes irresistible. That this was also a problem in Egyptian communities of monks is apparent from some of the *Sayings of the Desert Fathers* translated by Benedicta Ward, SLG (Kalamazoo, MI: Cistercian Publications, 1975). (In the sayings of) Isaac, Priest of the Cells (395): "He also said to the brethren, "Do not bring young boys here. Four churches in Scetis have been deserted because of boys." (p. 84). On the other hand, there are remarkable examples of tolerance of human foibles to be found in the anecdotes passed on from these same desert fathers. (From the sayings of John the Persian): "A demoniac boy came one day to be healed, and some brothers from an Egyptian monastery arrived. As one old man was coming out to meet them he saw a brother sinning with the boy, but did not accuse him; he said, 'If God who has made them sees them and does not burn them, who am I to blame them?'" (p. 91).

162. Cyril of Scythopolis, (op. cit.) *The Life of Our Pious Father Sabas* 171:6 (pp. 180-81). This is St. Theodosius Coenobiarch ("Preceptor of the Desert"), who died at the age of 105 on January 11. 529.

163. Harrison, Martin, (op. cit.)p. 40.

164. Gregory of Tours, St., ed. and trans. by Van Dam, Raymond, *Glory of the Martyrs* (Liverpool: Liverpool University Press, 1988) p. 125.

165. (ibid.) p. 126.

166. Mango, Cyril, and Ševç enko, Ihor, "Remains of the Church of St. Polyeuktos at Constantinople" (Washington D.C.: Dumbarton Oaks Research Library and Collection, 1961) Dumbarton Oaks Papers, Number 15, p. 246.

167 Polyceut was honored thus in Ravenna and in Gaul too, but not in Rome. Solemn vows made publicly in Rome were always sworn in the church of the martyr San Pancrazio (St. Pancras).

168. Gregory of Tours, St., tr. Lewis Thorpe, *The History of the Franks* (New York: Penguin Books, 1986) p. 391.

169. "L'Hagiographie Ancienne de Ravenne" in the *Analecta Bollandiana* (Bruxelles: Société Des Bollandistes, 1929) Vol. 47, p. 14.

170. Delahaye, Hippolyte, *Les Origines Du Culte Des Martyrs* (Bruxelles: Société Des Bollandistes, 1933) p. 323.

171. "Le Manuscrit 377 de Berne" in the *Analecta Bollandiana* (Bruxelles:Société Des Bollandistes, 1974) Vol. 92, p. 78.

172. Kelley, Fr. Christopher P., *An Iconographer's Patternbook: TheStroganov Tradition* (Torrance, CA: Oakwood Publications, 1992) p. 180.

173. Hetherington, Paul (tr.), *The 'Painter's Manual' of Dionysius of Fourna* (Torrance, CA: Oakwoods Publications, 1989)) pp. 57&75.

174. Buckton, David, with Entwistle, Christopher, and Prior, Rowena, ed., *The Treasury of San Marco Venice* (Milan: Olivetti, 1984) pp. 141-7.

175. Lasarev, Viktor Nikitich, *The Double-faced Tablets from the St. Sophia Cathedral in Novgorod* (Moscow: Iskusstvo Art Publishers, 1983) reverse side of Plate I.

176. (ibid.) p. 44.

177. Holweck, F.G. (op. cit.) p. 918.

178. Mango, Cyril, *Byzantium: The Empire of New Rome* (op. cit.) pp. 250-51.

179. Constantinople's Patriarch Nicholas IV Muzalon (d.1151)ordered the destruction of a *Life of St. Paraskeve the Younger* on the grounds that it had been written 'by some peasant' in ordinary language.

180. quoted in Boswell, John, *Same-Sex Unions in Premodern Europe* (op. cit.) pp. 141-2.

181. (ibid.) p. 145.

182. Corneille, Pierre, ed. Braunholtz, E.G.W., M.A., Ph.D., *Polyeucte* (Cambridge: University Press, 1907) p. xi.

183. Armenian Church Calendar (Jerusalem: Jerusalem Patriarchate, 1996) p. 20.

184. Boswell, John, *Same-Sex Unions in Premodern Europe* (op. cit.) pp. 154-55.

185. There is a St. Nearchus listed among the martyrs in the Greek calendar , whose feast is April 21, but this is not the companion of St. Polyeuct. While Nearchus is not generally mentioned in the liturgical calendars, there is a Greek hagiographical fragment from either the 8th or 9th century in the Royal Library of Brussels which mentions the martyrdom of Sts. Polyeuct and Nearchus under a separate reference to the martyrdom of St. Barbara. The placing of the two commemorations in this sequence can thus far be found nowhere else. "Fragments Hagiographiques Grecs Dans Le Palimpseste Bruxelles, Bibl. Roy. IV.^{459}" mentioned both in *Analecta Bollandiana* (Société Des Bollandistes) Vol. 90 (1972) and Vol. 95 (1977).

186. In writing about this same St. Pelagia/Pelagius, the famous Jesuit Bollandist expert in what is actual and what is mythical in the lives of the saints, Fr. Hippolyte Delehaye, pointed out that the names Pelagia and Marina - as well as Aigaia, Epipontie, Thalassaia, Pontia, and Euploia - are all titles of the love goddess Aphrodite, in her aspect as divinity of the sea, who was supposedly born in Cyprus. He also wrote that the divinity of Amathus in Cyprus "could be regarded at will as Aprhodite or Aphroditos, and...wore the dress of a woman and the beard of a man. In the sacrifices offered at this shrine the men were dressed as women and the women as men. It was the worship of the Hermaphrodite. The legend of Pelagia, it is suggested, has retained the imprint of this; but the cultus continues formally within the Church; the bearded woman has been raised to the altars. In Rome it is St. Galla; in Spain, St. Paula; and in other places SS. Liberata, Wilgefortis, Kümmernis, Ontkommer, etc." in *The Legends of the Saints* (Notre Dame: University of Notre Dame Press, 1961) pp. 204&206.

187. Talbot, Alice-Mary, ed., *Holy Women of Byzantium: Ten Saints' Lives in English Translation* (Washington D.C.:Dumbarton Oaks Research Library and Collection, 1996, from Cyril Mango's Introduction on p. 14.

188. (ibid.) p. 13.

189. Topping, Eva Catafygiotu, *Saints and Sisterhood* (Minneapolis, Minnesota: Light and Life Publishing Company, 1 990)p. 58.

190. Holweck, (op. cit.) p. 141

191. Cavallo, Guglielmo, ed., *The Byzantines* (Chicago and London: The University of Chicago Press, 1997) p. 267.

192. Talbot, Alice-Mary, (op. cit.) p. 30, n. 54, says "This establishment does not appear to be recorded elsewhere. Another St. Hilaria (called Hilara in the *Vita*), martyred in the 3rd century, was also a woman monk: cf. A.J. Wensinck, *Legends of Eastern Saints. II. The Legend of Hilaria* (Leiden. 1913) 9-89."

193. Topping, Eva Catafygiotu, (op. cit.) p. 56.

194. Talbot, Alice-Mary, (op. cit)p. 63. "And after she had returned from Beirut, and he had ordained her overseer of souls, so to speak, and had given her authority for the laying of hands on others (to receive them), he did not give her woolen girdles and veils, such as women are accustomed to use, but wide, dark leather men's girdles and white men's cloaks, which they wear constantly. Through the benevolence and love of mankind of our Lord Jesus Christ this same order has been followed unto the present day in her monastery, preserved by those who have succeeded her."

195. St. Matrona's Irish contemporary, St. Brigid of Kildare, is an example of a woman who was ordained a bishop by a bishop, St. Mel of Ardagh.

196. How ironic, then, that some Western clerics would condemn St. Jeanne d'Arc to be burned at the stake on May 31, 1431, ultimately because she chose to resume the wearing of men's clothing.

197. Talbot, Alice-Mary, (op. cit.) p. 48.

198. Topping, Eva Catafygiotu, (op.cit.)p. 56.

199. Cavallo, Guglielmo, (op. cit.) p. 267.

200. Topping, Eva Catafygiotu, (op. cit.) p. 58.

201. Talbot, Alice-Mary, (op. cit.) p. 16.

202. *Cassell's Encyclopedia of Queer Myth, Symbol and Spirit* (op. cit.) cites the case of Vasil Popovici (1815-1905), a monk of Romania's Tzibucani Monastery from about 1880 until he died. Revered as a compassionate, contemplative mystic, he stunned everyone when it was discovered after his death that he was anatomically a female. So the spirit of Matrona survived to the twentieth century. p. 270.

203. Mango, Cyril, "The Church of Saints Sergius and Bacchus at Constantinople and the Alleged Tradition of Octagonal Palatine Churches", in *Jahrbuch der österreichischen Byzantinistik* (Wien: Osterreichische Akademie Der Wissenschaften Institut fur Byzantinistik Der Universitat Wien, 1972) p. 190.

204. Diehl, Charles, *Theodora: Empress of Byzantium* (New York: Frederick Ungar Publishing Co., 1972) p. 30.

205. (ibid.) from flyleaf of book's cover.

206. Downey, Glanville, *Constantinople in the Age of Justinian* (Norman: University of Oklahoma Press, 1960) p. 33.

207. Elected patriarch of Antioch in 512, he was deposed by Justin in 518, and died either in 539 or 542. He is listed among the saints in Holweck, F.G., (op. cit.) p. 906.

208. Conway, Msgr. J. D., *Times of Decision* (Notre Dame, IN: Fides Publishers Association, 1962) p. 63.

209. St. Leontius was the patron saint of Syria before Sts. Sergius and Bacchus were martyred. He had been a Greek and a General in the Roman army, who refused to sacrifice to the genius of the Empire. For this he was condemned to death and died under torture at Tripoli in Phoenicia, probably in the year 135. His companions were the two soldiers who arrested him and then were converted by him - the tribune Hypatius and the soldier Theodulus. Both suffered along with Leontius and were beheaded for their new-found Christian faith. Leontius is the principal martyr of Phoenicia and was formerly venerated as patron of Syria. In 507, a church was dedicated to him at Antioch (Daphne). His feast in the Roman calendar is June 18. He is an important saint in the Greek, Melchite, Syrian, and Coptic Churches. St. Severus of Antioch preached a homily in his honor. Holweck, (op. cit.) p. 605.

210. Haag, Michael, *Cadogan Guides: Syria & Lebanon* (Old Saybrook, CT: The Globe Pequot Press, 1995) p. 125.

211. Crowfoot, J.W., C.B.E., M.A., "Churches at Bosra and Samaria - Sebaste" found in the *Supplementary Paper 4*, p. 3.

212. Der Nersessian, Sirarpie, (op. cit.) pp. 37-38. Because the Armenians *were bitterly opposed to the Nestorians, and the latter had greeted the Calcedonian profession of faith as a personal victory.. .the Armenian clergy.. consequently voted to reject the acts of the council of Chalcedon. Because of this rejection the Armenians have been considered as Monophysites both by the Orthodox and the Catholic churches. They are Monophysites, if the term "one nature" is to be understood as it was used by St. Cyril (of Alexandria); but they are not Monophysites if a Eutychian interpretation is attached to it. The Armenian formula "one nature united" is based on that of St. Cyril. The Armenian church recognized the divine and the human natures of Christ, a complete humanity animated by a rational soul. She violently rejected the mingling or confusion of the natures, taught by Eutyches, and anathematized Eutyches together with the heretics Arius, Macedonius, and Nestorius, The Armenians maintained, however, that to speak of two natures after the union, as did the Chalcedonians, was t o revert to the Nestorian heresy.*

213. Narkiss, Bezalel, (op. cit) p. 11.

214. Mango, Cyril, "The Church of Saints Sergius and Bacchus at Constantinople and the Alleged Tradition of Octagonal Palatine Churches" (op. cit.) pp. 191-2.

215. Mango, Cyril, "The Church of Sts. Sergius and Bacchus Once Again", in *Byzantinische Zeitschrift* (München: C.H. Beck'sche Verlagsbuchhandlung, 1975) p. 386.

216. Downey, Glanville (op. cit.) p. 141.

217. Boswell, John, *Same-Sex Unions in Premodern Europe* (op. cit.) p. 147, n. 172.

218 Theodoret of Cyr: Patrologia Graeca LXXXIII, col. 1033.

219. (ibid.) p. 147, n. 172.

220. This account is translated into English for the first time by John E. Boswell, in *Same-Sex Unions in Premodern Europe* (ibid.) pp. 375-390.

221. (ibid.) p. 150.

222. (ibid.), p. 154.

223. (ibid.) p. 155.

224. Haag, Michael, *Cadogan Guide: Syria & Lebanon* (op. cit.) p. 262.

225. Hastings, Arthur F., *In His Honor* (Muskego, WI: H. H. P. Publishing, Incorporated, 1994) p. 138.

226. (ibid.) p. 139.

227. Vööbus, Arthur, *History of Aseticism in the Syrian Orient III* (Louvain: E. Peeters, 1988) p. 233.

228. Vööbus, Arthur, *History of Asceticism in the Syrian Orient* (Louvain: Secretariat Du Corpus SCO, 1960). Tomus 17, Vol. 197, p. 65.

229. (ibid.) p. 351, f. 47.

230. The Benedictines of Paris, *Vie Des Saints et Des Bienhereux selon l'Ordre du* Calandrier *avec L'historique des Fêtes* (Paris, Éditions Letouzey et Ané, 1952) Vol. X, p. 194.

231. Fowden, Elizabeth Key, *The Barbarian Plain: Saint Sergius Between Rome and Iran* (Berkeley: University of California Press, 1999) Map 2).

232. Butler, Howard Crosby, *Early Churches in Syria* (Princeton, NJ: University Press, 1929) p. 47.

233. Delehaye, Hippolyte, (op. cit.) p. 210.

234 Peña, Ignacio, *The Christian Art of Byzantine Syria* (Garnet Publishing Ltd., 1996) p. 56.

235 (ibid.) p. 101.

236 Gabra, Gawdat, ed., *Be Thou There: The Holy Family's Journey in Egypt* (Cairo, New York: American Universityh in Cairo Press, 2001) p. 15. See also Mulock, Cawthra, and Langdon, Martin Telles, *The Icons of Yuhanna and Ibrahim the Scribe* (London: Nicholson and Watson, 1946) p. 10.

237 Gabra, Gawdat, (ibid.) p. 17.

238. Dalton, O. M., *Byzantine Art and Archaeology* (New York: Dover Publications, Inc., 1961) pp. 282-283.

239. Delahaye, Hippolyte, (op. cit.) p. 211.

240 Evans, Helen C., editor, *Byzantium: Faith and Power (1261-1557)*, Metropolitan Museum of Art, New York (New Haven and London: Yale University Press, 2004) p. 197.

241. It was originally brought from Mt. Sinai to Kiev, along with several other icons dating from before the iconoclastic period, by the Russian Bishop Porphyrius Uspenski, who placed them in the Ecclesiastical Academy of Kiev.

242. Treadgold, Warren, *The Byzantine Revival 780-842* (Stanford, CA: Stanford Universtiy Press, 1988) p. 50.

243. Stuart, Elizabeth, *Spitting at Dragons* (London: Mowbray, 1996) p. 6, where she quotes Lawrence Cunningham, *The Meaning of Saints* (San Francisco: Harper and Row, 1980) p. 5.

244. Shlain, Leonard, (op. cit.) pp. 79-80.

245. (ibid.) p. 276.

246. Ovtchinnikov, Adolphe Nikolaevich, "Icons, a Reflection of Faith," in *Divine Harmony* (Paris:Opus 111, 1998) pp. 20&23.

247. Threadgold, Warren, (op. cit.) p. 50.

248. It was in this monastery that the original of the most venerated icon type in Constantinople, the Virgin, called the Hodegetria, had been kept and honored. The original, lost in the sack of Constantinople in 1453, depicted a standing Virgin holding the Christ Child in her left arm. See Weitzmann, Kurt, *The Icon: Holy Images - Sixth to Fourteenth Century* (New York: George Braziller, 1978) p. 62.

249. Boswell, John, *Same-Sex Unions in Premodern Europe, op. cit.*, p. 241. Boswell points out that this can be read in Theodore's *Epistola* 10 (99:941) and says that the same ruling is quoted verbatim in the ninth-century rule (*Typicon*) for the Lavra of St. Athanasios on Mt. Athos.

250. Threadgold, Waren, (op. cit.) p. 208-209.

251. Mango, Cyril, *Byzantium: the Empire of New Rome* (op. cit.) p. 26.

252. Grosvenor, Edwin *Constantinople* (Boston: Little, Brown and Company, 1900), in two volumes, from Vol. I, p. 410.

253. Diehl, Charles (op. cit.) p. 175.

254. Procopius of Caesarea, *Buildings* I.8.5.

255. Cameron, Averil, *Procopius* (London: Duckworth, 1985) p. 104, n. 151.

256. Matthews, Thomas F., (op. cit.) p. 43.

257. Bréhier, Louis, *Le Monde Byzantin *** La Civilisation Byzantine* (Paris: Éditions Albin Michel, 1950), Vol. 3, p. 263.

258. Young, George, *Constantinople* (New York: Barnes and Noble, 1992) pp. 36-7.

259. Taylor, Jane, *Imperial Istanbul* (London: Weidenfeld and Nicolson, 1989). p. 44.

260. Ecumenical Patriarchate of Constantinople Web Site, (op. cit) p. 4 of 5.

261. Taylor, Jane, (op. cit.) p. 45.

262. Mango, Cyril, "The Church of Sts. Sergius and Bacchus Once Again" (op. cit.) pp. 385-6.

263. Moorhead, John, (op. cit.) p. 127.

264. (ibid.) p. 127.

265. (ibid.) p. 133.

266. It has already been pointed out the way Emperor Leo III's *Ecloga* would eventually intensify the harassment of gays which had its legal beginning with Justinian's law. But it should also be noted that, on August 6. 390, Emperor Theodosius I issued a law which read: "All persons who have the shameful custom of condemning a man's body, acting the part of a woman's to the sufferance of an alien sex, for they do not appear different from women, shall expiate a crime of this kind in avenging flames in the sight of the people." (Codex

Theod. 9.7.6). However, his law seems have had as its primary focus men who dressed as women and duped other men into having sex with them, regardless of weather or not the "victims" had actually been fooled. So this law seems to have had as its primary object the condemning to death by fire of convicted sexually active cross-dressers, rather than sexually active gays. Ide, Arthur Frederick, *Gomorrah and the Rise of Homophobia* (Las Colinas, TX: Liberal Press, 1985) p. 76.

267. Edwards, George R., *Gay/Lesbian Liberation: A Biblical Perspective* (New York: The Pilgrim Press, 1984) p. 25, quotes Justinian's 77th Novella, promulgated in 538 C.E., which asserts:

> *Since certain men, seized by diabolical incitement, practice among themselves the most disgraceful lusts, and act contrary to nature: we enjoin them to take to heart the fear of God and the judgement to come, and to abstain from suchlike diabolical and unlawful lusts, so that they may not be visited by the just wrath of God on account of these impious acts, with the result that cities perish with all their inhabitants. For we are taught by the Holy Scriptures that because of like impious conduct cities have indeed perished, together with the men in them.*

In footnote 2 on p. 25, Edwards also points out that John Boswell agreed with Edward Gibbon that Justinian's law on homosexual acts was merely a guise for charging those "to whom no crime could be imputed."

268. Boswell, John *Christianity, Social Tolerance, and Homosexuality* (Chicago: University of Chicago Press, 1980) p. 171.

269. Boswell, John, *Rediscovering Gay History: Archetypes of Gay Love in Christian History* (London: Gay Christian Movement, 1985) pp. 6-7.

270. Bury, John, *History of the Later Roman Empire* (London: Macmillan, 1923) Vol. 2, p. 412, n. 5.

271. Mann, Rt. Rev. Msgr. Horace K., D.D., *The Lives of the Popes in the Early Middle Ages* (London: Kegan Paul, French, Trubner, & Co. Ltd., 1902) Vol. I, pp. 16-17. Mann agrees with De Rossi from his research on inscriptions that it is the opinion of the learned that Gregory the Great belonged to the patrician family of the Anicii. While many early writers agree that Gregory was a member of an important Roman senatorial family, it is a later tradition that he was one of the Anicii. There is also some dispute whether he was the great-grandson of Felix II or Felix III. Gregory himself only mentions his *atavus* (third or fourth grandfather) Felix. There is no doubt that Felix II (483-492) had been a married man with three children. But Gregory the Great's late and not always reliable biographer, John the Deacon, who wrote the *Vita Gregorii* at the request of Pope John VIII (872-882), claims that Gregory the Great's papal ancestor was Pope Felix III (526-530), who was reigning in Rome the very year Juliana completed the building of St. Polyeuctos and Justinian began the building of Sts. Sergius and Bacchus. The majority of writers opine that Gregory's great-grandfather was Pope Felix II.

272. Holweck, F.G., (op. cit.) p. 446.

273. Gibson, Margaret, ed., *Boethius* (Oxford: Basil Blackwell, 1981) p. 19.

274. Chadwick, N.K., *Poetry and Letters in Early Christian Gaul* (London: Bowes & Bowes, 1955) p. 64.

275. Anicius Manlius Torquatus Severinus Boethius was a famous statesman and philosopher who also wrote theological works on the Trinity and the Incarnation, he held an eminent position in the court of the Ostrogothic Emperor Theodoric the Great. In 525, he fell into disfavor and was accused of treason when he defended in court a senator and an ex-consul named Albinus, who had been wrongly charged with plotting with emperor Justin I against Theodoric. Because he defended them, Boethius was accused both of treason and of sacrilege, imprisoned, and eventually executed at Pavia. During his time in prison he wrote his most famous work on the *Consolation of Philosophy*. He was considered a martyr for justice. His remains are venerated in the Cathedral of Pavia, in which diocese he is considered a saint. He is also venerated in several Roman churches. His ancient cult was confirmed by Pope Leo XIII, who canonized him in 1883 with a feast day on October 23.

276. Holweck, F.G. (op. cit.) p. 146.

277. Mann, Rt. Rev. Msgr. Horace K., D.D., (op. cit.) Vol. XIII, p. 415.

278. Bardill, Jonathan, *The Church of Sts. Sergius and Bacchus in Constantinople and the Monophysite Refugees* (Wahington D.C.: Dumbarton Oaks Papers, No. 54, 2000) p. 5.

279. Mango, Cyril, "The Church of Saints Sergius and Bacchus at Constantinople and the Alleged Tradition of Octagonal Palatine Churches" (op. cit.) p. 191, n. 7.

280. Cameron, Averil, (op. cit.) p. 124.

281. Vööbus, Arthur, *History of Asceticism in the Syrian Orient III* (op. cit.) pp. 219&237.

282. (ibid.), pp. 236-237.

283. Haag, Michael, *Cadogan Guides: Syria & Lebanon* (op. cit.) p. 260.

284. Fowden, Elizabeth Key, *op. cit.*, p. 178-179

285. Whitby, Michael, *The Emperor Maurice and His Historian Theophylact Simocatta on Persian and Balkan Warfare* (Oxford: Clarendon Press, 1988) pp. 116-17.

286. Vööbus, Arthur, *History of Asceticism in the Syrian Orient III* (op. cit.) p. 252.

287. (ibid.) p. 252.

288. Whitby, Michael and Mary, *The 'History' of Theophylact Simocatta* (Oxford: Clarendon Press, 1988) p. 133.

289. Brown, Peter, *The World of Late Antiquity* (London: Thames and Hudson, 1971) p. 169.

290. "Histoire Des Saintes de De La Sainteté Chrétienne" Vol. II (edit. 1988) p. 283.

291. Whitby, Michael and Mary, (op. cit) p. 151.

292. Vööbus, Arthur, (op. cit.) p. 256, f. 13.

293.McCullough, W. Stewart, *A Short History of Syriac Christianity to the Rise of Islam* (Chico, CA: Scholars Press, 1982) p. 158.

294. (ibid.) p. 159.

295. (ibid.) p. 159.

296 Labidge, Michael, editor, *Archbishop Theodore* (Cambridge: Cambridge University Press, 1995) pp. 176-77.

297. Fowden, Elizabeth Key, *op. cit*, pp. 90, 120-121, 134.)

298 Peña, Ignacio, (op. cit.) p. 243.

299. Vööbus, Arthur, (op. cit.) p. 257.

300. (ibid.), p. 259.

301. Whitlow, Mark, *The Making of Byzantium 600-1025* (Berkeley & Los Angeles: University of California Press, 1996) p. 65.

302 Kondoleon, Christine, *Antioch: the Lost Ancient City* (Princeton, NJ: Princeton University Press, 2001) p. 211.

303. McCullough, W. Stewart, (op. cit.) p. 187.

304.Delehaye, Hippolyte, (op. cit.) p. 211.

305. Vööbus, Arthur, (op. cit.) pp. 228, 238, 351-52.

306. (ibid.) p. 352.

307. Delehaye, Hippolyte, (op. cit) p. 186.

308. (ibid.) p. 211.

309. Choricius of Gaza, *Laudatio Marciani* I, 17ff., quoted in Mango, Cyril, *The Art of the Byzantine Empire 312-1453* (Toronto: University of Toronto Press, 1986) p. 60.

310. (ibid.) pp. 55&62.

311. Ruggieri, Vincenzo, S.J., *Byzantine Religious Architecture (582-867): Its History and Structural Elements* (Roma: Pont. Institutum Studiorum Orientalium, 1991) p. 247.

312. Boswell, John, *Same-Sex Unions in Premodern Europe, op. cit.* p. 230. He cites as his reference: Venice, 1884; reprint, Leipzig, 1973, in *Subsidia Byzantina lucis ope iterata*, VIII) 134, p. 481

313. Palmer, Andrew, *Monk and Mason on the Tigris Frontier: the Early History of Tur-Abdin* (New York: Cambridge University Press, 1990) pp. (30) and p. 217.

314. Der Nersessian, Sirarpie, *Miniature Painting in the Armenian Kingdom of Cilicia from the Twelfth to the Fourteenth Century* Vol. I, (Washington, D.C., Dumbarton Oaks Research Library and Collection, 1993) p. 89.

315. Gervers, Michael, ed., *The Second Crusade and the Cistercians* (New York: St. Martin's Press, 1992) p. 199.

316. Atiya, Aziz S., *History of Eastern Christianity* (Notre Dame, IN: University of Notre Dame Press, 1968) p. 263

317. Fowden, Elizabeth Key, *op. cit.*, p. 4.

318.Kostof, Spiro, (op. cit.) pp. 134-135.

319. Boswell, John, *Same-Sex Unions in Premodern Europe* (op. cit.) part of the text accompanying Figure 5, among the pictures between pp. 192 and 193 of the text.

320.Paliouras, Athanasios, *The Monastery of St. Catherine on Mt. Sinai* (Glyka Nera Attikis, Greece: E. Tzaferi A.E., 1985) p. 26.

321.Cormack, Robin, *Writing in Gold: Byzantine Society and Its Icons* (London: George Philip, 1985) p. 83 & p. 93.

322. Hetherington, Paul, *Byzantine and Medieval Greece* (London: Paul Murray, 1991) p. 140.

323.Chatzidakis, Manolis, *The Cretan Painter Theophanis* (Mt. Athos: Published by the Holy Monastery of Stavronikita, 1986) p. 56, and pl;ates 139 &140.

324. Gregory, Timothy E., Caraher, William, Jones Hall, Linda, and Moore, R. Scott, *Archaeology and History in Roman, Medieval, and Post-medieval Greece* (Ashgate, 2008) p. 269.

325. Dale, Thomas E. A., *Relics, Prayer, and Politics in Medieval Venetia* (Princeton, NJ: Princeton University Press, 1997) p. 34.

326. Morris, Jan, *Trieste and the Meaning of Nowhere* (New York: Simon and Schuster, 2001) pp.171-72.

327. Simson, Otto G. von, *Sacred Fortress: Byzantine Art and Statecraft in Ravenna* (Chicago: University of Chicago Press, 1976.

328. Wolfram, Herwig, *History of the Goths* (Berkeley. Los Angeles. London: University of California Press, 1990) p. 326.

329. Ecumenical Patriarchate of Constantinople Web Site, *The Byzantine Monuments: The Monastery of the Sts. Sergius and Bacchus*, 10/6/98, p. 3 of 5.

330. Mango, Cyril, *Byzantine Architecture* (New York: Rizzoli, 1985) p. 76.

331. Harrison, Martin, (op. cit.) p. 141.

332. Franzoni, Lanfranco, *Verona* (Venice: Edizioni Storti Venezia, 1978) pp. 16-17.

333. On December 22, 1997, Paola Marini, the Directress of the Castelvecchio Museum wrote to the author, "Per quanto riguarda la provenienza del sarcofago, non ci sisulta che in origine fosse collocato in una chiesa dedicata ai Santi Sergio e Bacco."

3234. Demus, Otto, *The Church of San Marco In Venice* (Washington D.C.: Dumbarton Oaks Research Library and Collection, 1960) p. 3.

335. (ibid.) pp. 4-5.

336. (ibid.) p. 5.

337. (ibid.) p. 4, n. 2.

338. (ibid.) pp. 16-17.

339. Krautheimer, Richard, *Rome: Profile of a City, 312-1308* (Princeton, NJ: Princeton University Press, 1980) p. 75.

340. Benedict, Canon of St. Peter's, *The Marvels of Rome* (New York: Italica Press, 1886) p. 95.

341. Davis, Raymond, tr., intro., and comm., *The Lives of the Eighth-Century Popes (Liber Pontificalis)* (Liverpool: Liverpool University Press, 1992) Chapter 97:90, p. 169.

342. Artaud de Montor, The Chevalier, *The Lives and Times of the Popes* (New York: The Catholic Publication Society of America, 1911) in X Volumes, Vol. I., p. 179.

343. Krautheimer, Richard (op. cit.) p. 203.

344. Benedictines of Paris, *Vie Des Saints et Des Bienhereux Selon l'Ordre du Calendrier avec l'Historique des Fêtes*, (op. cit.) p.^{195}.

345. Sayers, Jane, *Innocent III* (Harlow, Essex: Longman, 1994) pp. 33-34. These towers are mentioned by a canon of St. Peter's named Benedict in his book, *The Marvels of Rome*, written around 1143. *The Marvels of Rome (Mirabilia Urbis Romae)* edit. and trans. Nichols, Francis Morgan, (New York: Italica Press, 1986) p. 54.

346. (ibid.) p. 36.

347. Hibbert, Christopher, *Rome - The Biography of a City* (Middlesex, England: Penguin Books, 1985) p. 341.

348. Davis, Raymond, (op. cit) p. 25, footnote 40.

349. (ibid.) Chapter 92:13, p.25, footnote 40 (Though it is not known when this oratory was introduced in St. Peter's, it may have existed prior to the building of the first Roman church dedicated to Sergius and Bacchus. Pope Gregory the Great (d. 604), who, while he was Papal Envoy to Constantinople, presided from the church of Sts. Sergius and Bacchus for seven years prior to being elected Supreme Pontiff is a possible candidate for the person who introduced devotion to these martyrs at St. Peter's.).

350. (ibid.) p. 211.

351. (ibid.) p. 214, footnote 149.

352. (ibid.) pp. 215-16.

353. Krautheimer, Richard, (op. cit.) p. 74.

354. Davis, Raymond, (op. cit) p. 214, footnote 149.

355. Krautheimer, Richard, (op. cit.) p. 74.

356. (ibid.) pp. 89-90.

357. Ashley, Kathleen, and Sheingorn, Pamela, ed. *Inerpreting Cultural Symbols: Saint Anne in Late Medieval Society* (Athens and London: The University of Georgia Press, 1990) p. 11.

358 *Histoire Des Saintes et De La Sainteté Chrétienne* (edit. 1988) Tome IV, p. 50.

359. Jones, Charles W., *Saint Nicholas of Myra, Bari, and Manhattan* (Chicago: University of Chicago Press, 1978), p. 3. This early glimmer of Western devotion to the man who would become one of the most beloved of saints would eventually lead to greedy merchants from Bari stealing his body from Myra and translating it to Bari in the year 1087.

360. *Histoire Des Saintes et De La Sainteté Chrétienne*, (op. cit.) p. 50.

361. Nichols, John A. and Shank, Lillian Thomas, ed., *Distant Echoes: Medieval Religious Women* Vol. I, (Kalamazoo, MI: Cistercian Publications Inc., 1984) p. 37.

362. (ibid.) pp. 31-32.

363. Kitzinger, Ernst, *The Mosaics of St. Mary's of the Admiral in Palermo* (Washington, D.C.: Dumbarton Oaks Research Library and Collection, 1990) in the Forward and Preface, and photos as well.

364. Cobham, Claude Delaval, *Excerpta Cypria* (New York: Kraus Reprint Co., 1969) Turner, William, Esq., excerpt from the year 1815. P. 438.

365. Papageorgiou, Athanasius, *Icons of Cyprus* (New York: Cowles Book Company, Inc., 1970) p. 122.

366. Galatariotou, Catia, *The Making of a Saint: The Life, Times and Sanctification of Neophytos the Recluse* (Cambridge: Cambridge University Press, 1991) p. 58, n.83.

367. Gaul is the Roman name for a territory, most of which is now France.

368 Peña, Ignacio, (op. cit.) p. 233.

369. Benedictines of Paris, *Vie Des Saints et Des Bienheureux selon l'Ordre du Calendrier avec l'Historique des Fêtes (op. cit.) p. 196.*

370. (Ibid.) p. 196.

371. Gregory of Tours, *The History of the Franks* (op. cit.) pp. 413-14.

372. (ibid.) p. 602.

373. McNeill, John, *Blue Guide to the Loire Valley* (New York: W. W. Horton, 1995) p. 229

374. Eastern military martyrs seem to have been in vogue in Gaul at the time. The cults of Sts. Theodore and George were introduced during this period, and they will both appear among the beautiful sculptures in the medieval Cathedral of Chartres. In an extract from the *Histoire des Saints et de la Sainteté Chrétienne*, Tome IV, (edit. 1988) entitled "Le Culte des Saints Orientaux en Occident", p. 50, it is pointed out that the queen of Clovis II, St. Bathilde, dedicated one of the altars at at Chelles to St. George. In *Forgetful of Their Sex* (Chicago and London: University of Chicago Press, 1998) p. 356, Jane Tibbetts Schulenburg points out that:

> *The vita of the queen-saint Bathild is also informative in regard to female friendship within the monastic community. The author of Bathild's Life notes the queen's special fondness for Bertilla of Chelles. Bathild had specifically chosen Bertilla to become abbess of her newly refounded house*

at Chelles. And according to her vita, "the abbess always welcomed the requests of her royal companion, for they were, like the apostles, one in heart and soul and they loved each other tenderly in Christ."

375. Midner, Roy, *English Medieval Monasteries: 1066-1540* (Athens, Georgia: University of Georgia Press, 1979) pp. 311&314.

376. Benedictines of Paris, *Vie des Saints et Des Bienheureux selon l'Ordre du Calendrier avec l'Historique des Fêtes,(op. cit.) p. 196.*

377. Daniel-Rops, Henri, *Cathedral and Crusade* (Garden City, NY: Image Books, 1963) Vol. II, p. 147.

378. Epiphanius the Wise, *Life of the Saint and God-bearer, Abbot Sergius the Wonder-Worker*, translated and quoted in *Contemplating the Mystery: Saint Sergius and Rublev*, edited and translated by Anne Marie Swift (Slough, England: St. Paul MultiMedia Productions, 1996) p. 19.

379. Demshuk, Vladimir, *Russian Sainthood and Canonization* (Minneapolis, MN: Light and Life Publishing Company, 1978), p. 52.

380. Kelley, Fr. Christopher P. (op. cit) p. 37.

381. Hetherington, Paul, (op. cit.) pp. 57&73.

382 Collins, Rev. Raphael, B.A., translator, *The Roman Martyrology* (Westminster, MD: The Newman Press, 1952).

383 *The Roman Calendar: Text and Commentary* (Washington DC: United States Catholic Conference, 1976) p. 94.

384 Webb, Matilda, *The Churches and Catacombs of Early Christian Rome* (Brighton and Portland: Sussex Academic Press, 2001) p. 120.

385 Kelly, Sean, and Rogers, Rosemary, *The Birthday Book of Saints* ((New York: Villard, 2001) p. 291.

386. Venantius Fortunatus, ed. *PL Vol. 88* Under "Et in Jesum Christum", he wrote, "Unicum Filium ideo...de sapientia sapiens". This is found in Venantii Hon. Clem., Fortunati Operum Pars I, Miscellanea. - Lib., XI, p. 548.

387. McNamara, Jo Ann, & Halborg, John E., with Whatley, G. Gordon, *Sainted Women of the Dark Ages* (Durham and London: Duke University Press, 1992) p. 61.

388. Gregory of Tours, *The History of the Franks X:15*, tr. Lewis Thorpe (op. cit.) p. 570.

389. (ibid.) *The History of the Franks X:15*, pp. 570-71.

390. George, Judith W., *Venantius Fortunatus* (Oxford: Clarendon Press, 1992) p. 67.

391. (ibid.) p. 32.

392. Gregory of Tours, tr. and intro. by Lewis Thorpe, *The History of the Franks* (op. cit.) p. 36.

393. (Book V, number 3)

394. *The History of the Franks* (op. cit.) p. 36.

395. (ibid.) p. 264.

396. George, Judith W., (op. cit.) p. 214.

397. (ibid.) pp. 129-130.

398. (ibid.) p. 130.

399. McGuire, Brian Patrick, *Friendship And Community* (op. cit.) p. 100.

400. (ibid.) p. 99.
He describes their separation but insists on how their love binds them together:
The Seine holds you back, while the Atlantic binds us
One love draws together those separated by their lands. (111.[26])

401.Waddell, Helen, trans., Coote, Stephen, ed., in *The Penguin Book of Homosexual Verse* (New York: Penguin Books, 1983) p. 112.

402. Holweck, F. G., (op. cit.) p. 1008.

403. Krautheimer, Richard, *Three Christian Capitals* (Berkeley.Los Angeles.London: University of California Press, 1983) p. 47.

404. d'Alverny, Marie-Thérèse, *Etudes sur le symbolisme de la Sagesse et sur l'iconographie* ed., Burnett, Charles, (Aldershot, Hampshire, Great Britain: Variorum, 1993) in an article entitled "Le symbolisme de la Sagesse et le Christ de Saint Dunstan", p. 238. She says, "Une seconde basilique était dédiée à la Dynamis". Thomas Schipflinger , likewise, claims that Constantine I built a Hagia Dynamis in Constantinople in *Sophia-Maria*(York Beach, ME: Samuel Weiser, Inc., 1998) p. 272. Michael Grant speaks of Constantine's church of Holy Power in *Constantine the Great: The Man and His Times* (New York: Maxwell Macmillan International, 1994) p. 201.

405. Also in 360, the Synod of Constantinople deposed the violent and arrogant Patriarch Macedonius I of Constantinople for a heresy, which came to be called Macedonianism. The Creed issued by the First Council of Nicaea had ended with the words, "...and in the Holy Spirit." Macedonius taught that the Son was like the Father all right, but that the Holy Spirit was quite unlike the Father. It was realized than that the Creed needed to be expanded on the subject of the Spirit. So the First Council of Constantinople was convened in 381 by Emperor Theodosius I and by the city's Patriarch at the time, St. Gregory of Nazianzus. The assembled bishops completed the Creed as it exists to this day by proclaiming the full divinity of the Holy Spirit and expamnding on the Spirit's relationship to the Creator and the Redeemer.

406. Constantinople was not the only city whose cathedral was dedicated to Holy Peace. At the end of the fourth century, during the time St. Augustine was bishop of North African Hippo Regius, its *Basilica Pacis* (Basilica of Peace) seems to have been his cathedral. cf. Bourke, Vernon J., *Augustine's Quest of Wisdom* (Albany, NY: Magi Books Inc., 1993) p. 140.

407. Grant, Michael, (op. cit.) pp. 177-78.

408. In John 20:21-22, Jesus not only greets his disciples with the word "Peace" but, simultaneously, bequeaths the Spirit by breathing on them.

409. Moorhead, John, (op. cit.) p. 51.

410. Mango, Cyril, "The Church of Saints Sergius and Bacchus at Constantinople and the Alleged Tradition of Octagonal Palatine Churches" (op. cit.) p. 192. Mango believes that "the church of Sts. Sergius and Bacchus is not a precursor, but a contemporary of St. Sophia (sic)". He states that Sts. Sergius and Bacchus was definitely built sometime between 527 and 536, but he is inclined towards the later rather than the earlier limit. The main reason he gives is that "Even if the Monophysite monastery was set up as early as 527, some time must have elapsed before it grew to the point of requiring a second church." But there seems to have been a large number of Monophysites who converged on the place as soon as it was safe to do so. Also, Mango does not take into consideration Justinian's determination to outdo Juliana as a builder of churches and to get even with her for outfoxing him in the matter of her gold - of which had nothing to do with the number of Monophysite monks in the Hormizdas Palace.

411. (ibid.) p. 157.

412. (ibid.) flyleaf.

413. Browning, Robert, *Justinian and Theodora* (New York: Praeger Publishers, 1971) pp. 122&124.

414. Moorhead, John, (op. cit.) p. 55.

415. Quoted from the "Narratio" by Mainstone, Rowland J., *Hagia Sophia* (New York: Thames and Hudson, 1988) p. 10.

416. Paton, W.R., translator, *The Greek Anthology* (Cambridge, MA: Harvard University Press, 1925) Loeb Classical Library Series, 67, pp. 9&11.

417. Harrison, Martin, (op. cit.) p. 8.

418. (ibid.) p. 137.

419. (ibid.) p. 9. Those desirous of seeing portraits of Anicia Juliana, Justinian I, and Theodora may find them in the following places. The only known authentic portrait of Anicia Juliana can be found in a detail from the frontispiece of the *Herbal* of Dioscorides, which was copied for her in ca. 512 and is now in Vienna (Nationalbibliothek, Cod. Vind. Med. gr. 1). A color reproduction can be found in Martin Harrison (op. cit.) pp. ^{31}-32. The same portrait is reproduced in color in Robert Browning (op. cit.) p. 93, along with reproductions of the famous portraits of Justinian (pp. ^{206}-7) and Theodora (pp 166-7) from the mosaics in San Vitale Church, in Ravenna.

420. Taylor, Jane, *Imperial Istanbul* (London: Weidenfeld and Nicolson, 1989) pp. 51-52.

421. Stiglmayr, Joseph, "Der sogennate Dionysius Areopagita und Severus von Antiochien," *Scholastik 3* (1928): 1-27, 161-89, mentioned by Jaroslav Pelikan in *Pseudo-Dionysius: The Complete Works* (New York: Paulist Press, 1987) p. 13.

422. (ibid.) *The Divine Names* VII:4, p. 109.

423. McGinn, Bernard, *The Foundations of Mysticism* Vol. I, (op. cit.) p. 159. Von Ivánka, Endre, "Plato Christianismus: Übernahme und Umgestaltung des Platonismus durch die Väter" (Einsiedln: Johannes-Verlag, 1964) pp. 228-42.

424. (ibid.) p. 160.

425. Uspensky, Nicholas, *Evening Worship in the Orthodox Church* (Crestwood, NY: St. Vladimir's Seminary Press, 1985) p. 143.

426. (ibid.) p. 152.

437. Cady, Susan, Ronan, Marian, and Taussig, Hal, *Sophia: the Future of Feminist Spirituality* (San Francisco: Harper & Row, 1986) p. 58. The quote if from Neale, J. M., and Littledale, R. F., *The Liturgies of Ss. Mark, James, Clement, Chrysostom, and Basil and the Church of Malabar* (London: Griffith Farran and Co. 1880), p. 130.

428. (ibid.) p. 57, quoting (ibid) p. 14.

429. (ibid.) p. 57, quoting (ibid) p. 77.

430. (ibid.) p. 57, quoting (ibid) p. 79.

431. d'Alverny, Marie-Thérèse, (op. cit.) p. 238.

432. Butler, Alfred J., *The Arab Conquest of Egypt and the Last Thirty Years of the Roman Dominion* (originally published in 1902) (Oxford: The Clarendon Press, 1998) p. 389.

433. d.Alverny, Marie-Thérèse, (op. cit.) p. 234.

434. Trubetskoi, Eugene N., *Icons: Theology in Color* (Crestwood, NY: St. Vladimir's Seminary Press, 1973) says her face was red (p. 87, n. 15). Evdokimov, Paul, (op. cit.) says her face was purple (p. 352).

435. (ibid.) pp. 86-7. "Russia and Her Icons" was first printed in one of the last issues of the journal *Russkaia Mysl'* (January/February, 1918).

436. (ibid.) pp. 52-3. "Two Worlds in Old-Russian Icon Paintings," originally published as a monograph in 1915.

437. Mainstone, Rowland J., (op. cit.) p. 133.

438. At Constantinople, Emperor Justinian II decided that since the last two general councils, the fifth and the sixth, had issued no disciplinary decrees, he would hold one to supply the deficiency. Justinian's Council is, therefore called the Quinisext (fifth-sixth). It was also called the Trullan Council because it was held in the same great domed hall of the Imperial Palace, the Trullus (*troullos* in Greek = coupola = *trullus* in late Latin), in which the Sixth Ecumenical Council (III Constantinople) had been held. The Trullan Council was rejected by Pope St. Sergius I (687-701) for several reasons, among them the decree which stated that the Church of Constantinople had the same rights as the Church of Rome. Brusher, Joseph S., S.J., *Popes Through the Ages* (New York: D. Van Norstrand Company, Inc., 1959) p. 168.

439. Evdokimov, Paul, (op. cit.) p. 346.

440. From the earliest Christian centuries, Abraham's three heavenly guests, whom he addressed as "Lord," were considered a foreshadowing of the Holy Trinity. Since it was not permitted to depict the invisible God in icons (except as God-made-visible/the Incarnate

Christ) the way iconographers solved the dilemma was by representing the Holy Trinity in its First Testament foreshadowing - the scene of Abraham giving hospitality to his three heavenly visitors.

441. Evdokimov, Paul, (op. cit.) p. 347.

442. Johnson, Elizabeth A., (op. cit.) pp. 166-67. She is quoting Reuther, "Feminist Theology and Spirituality," in *Christian Feminism*, 21.

443. Conway, Msgr. J.D., (op. cit.) p. 87.

444. Bahat, Dan, *Carta's Historical Atlas of Jerusalem* (Jerusalem: Carta, 1983) p. 43.

445. Mazar, Benjamin, *The Mountain of the Lord: Excavating in Jerusalem* (Garden City, NY: Doubleday & Company, Inc., 1975) p. 260.

446. Bahat, Dan, (op. cit.) p. 43.

447. Mango, Cyril, *The Art of the Byzantine Empire 312-1453* (op. cit.) p. 55.

448. (ibid.), pp. 55&57, n. 8.

449. Kuryluk, Eva, *Veronica and Her Cloth* (Cambridge, MA: Basil Blackwell, Inc., 1991) p. 46.

450. Palmer, Andrew, (op. cit.) pp. 10, 118, and named in the book's index.

451. Bilasov, W. A., *Cyrillus et Methodius Monumenta Diplomatica* (1868) (Amsterdam: Editions RODOPI, 1970) p. 239.

452. Lenhoff, Gail, *The Martyred Princes Boris and Gleb: A Socio-Cultural Study of the Cult and the Texts* (Columbus, OH: Slavica Publishers, Inc., 1989) p. 28.

453 Newman, Barbara, *God and the Goddesses* (Philadelphia, PA: University of Pennsylvania Press, 2003) p. 196.

454. Bousfield, Jonathan, and Richardson, Dan, *Bulgaria: The Rough Guide* (London: Penguin Books, 1996) p. 50.

455. Mango, Cyril, *Byzantine Architecture* (op. cit.) p. 203, f. 5. The source of this information is Bojadiev, S., *Sofijskata cérkva sw. Sofija* (Sofia: 1967)

456. Grant, Michael, (op. cit.) p. 119. The quote is from the *Fragmenta Historicum Graecorum*, IV, 189.

457 Nichol, Donald M. (op. cit.) p. 186.

458. Theoharidou, Kalliopi, *The Architecture of Hagia Sophia, Thessaloniki* (BAR International Series 399, 1988) p. 3.

459. Mango, Cyril, *Byzantine Architecture* (op. cit.), p. 96.

460. A role characterized by Alexios Comenos as "the mouth and the hand of the patriarch," technically archivist and librarian of the patriarchate. See Cavallo, Guglielmo, ed., *The Byzantines* (Chicago and London: University of Chicago Press, 1997) p. 212.

461. Procopiou, Angelo, *The Macedonian Question in Byzantine Painting* (Athens, Angelo Procopiou, 1956) p. 22.

462. Der Nersessian, Sirarpie, *Armenia and the Byzantine Empire* (op. cit.) p. 61.

463. Lancaster, Osbert, *Sailing to Byzantium: An Architectural Companion* (New York: Dorset Press, 1969) p. 127.

464. Runciman, Steven, *Byzantine Style and Civilization* (New York: Penguin Books, 1975) p. 165.

465. Hetherington, Paul, *Byzantine and Medieval Greece* (London: John Murray, 1991) p. 220.

466. Lancaster, Osbert, (op. cit.) p. 124.

467. Ostrogorsky, George, *History of the Byzantine State* (New Brunswick, NJ: Rutgers University Press, 1969) p. 567.

468. Symeon of Thessalonike, trans. by H.L.N. Simmons, *Treatise of Prayer* (Brookline, MA: Hellenic College Press, 1984) p. 44.

The Church is the dwelling of the living wisdom of God personified, which is why "Wisdom has built herself a house" (Pr 9:4) - the sacred body of the Church.

469. Alcuin, ed. Peter Godman, *The Bishops, Kings, and Saints of York*, vs. 1507-1520 (Oxford: Clarendon Press, 1982) pp. 119-121.

470. In the early Medieval period, the area called Kievan Rus' encompassed that part of the Slavic world along the Dnieper River which had Kiev as its cultural center. This territory is now found in Ukraine. As Christianity spread throughout Rus' and reached other towns like Novgorod, Pskov, and Vitebsk, these centers ended up loosely confederated, their Christianity being the bond which united them. Moscow did not emerge as an important force with which to reckon until the military hegemony established by Ivan III, "the Great" (d.1505) forced into being what would eventually be called Russia. So the use of words like Russia, Russian, Ukraine and Ukranian to describe these Medieval culture centers, their faith, and their art is both anachronistic and incorrect. Kievan Rus' is therefore the term we will use for the area and its art.

471. Since most Hagia Sophia churches in Rus' and later in Russia are usually referred to in English as St. Sophia - "St." being an abbreviation both from the Latin *Sanctus* and for the Russian *Swiet* - (both meaning "Holy,") I am honoring that custom in the Russian sections by using the abbreviation "St."

472. Ivanov, Father Vladimir *Russian Icons* (New York: Rizzoli, 1988) p. 11.

473. Gra, E.A., "The Trinity in the Old Testament". In *Symbols of Glory: The Stroganov Tradition* (Middle Green, Slough, England: St. Paul MultiMedia Productions, 1992) p. 17.

474. Kinross, Lord, *Hagia Sophia* (New York: Newsweek, 1979) pp. 60-61.

475. Zenkovsky, Serge A., ed., *Medieval Russia's Epics, Chronicles, and Tales* (New York: Meridian, 1974) p. 74.

476. (ibid.) p. 106.

477. (ibid.) p. 85.

478. Zenkovsky, Serge A. (ibid.), Metropolitan Hilarion: "Sermon on Law and Grace" p. 87.

479. (ibid.) p. 86.

480. Lowden, John, *Early Christian & Byzantine Art* (London: Phaidon Press Limited, 1997) pp. 156-61.

481. Acheimastou-Potamianou, Dr. Myrtali, ed., *Holy Image, Holy Space: Icons and Frescoes From Greece* (Athens: Greek Ministry of Culture. Byzantine Museum of Athens, 1998) pp. 108&193. Also in Monadadori, Arnoldo, ed., *The Icon* (New York: Dorset Press, 1987) p. 135.

482. Schipflinger, Thomas, *Sophia-Maria* (York Beach, ME: Samuel Weiser, Inc., 1998) p. 285.

483. (ibid.) p. 271, figure12, reproduced from Pavel Florenski's *La Colonne et le Fondement de la Vérité*. L'Age d'Homme, Lausanne, 1975).

484. (ibid.) p. 275, in a quote from Sergei Bulgakov.

485. (ibid.) p. 270.

486. Grekov, B., *Kiev Rus* (Moscow: Foreign Languages Publishing House, 1959) p. 498.

487. Voyce, Arthur, *The Art and Architecture of Medieval Russia* (Norman: University of Oklahoma Press, 1967) p. 92.

488. Grekov, B., (op. cit.) p. 531.

489. Trubetskoi, Eugene N., (op. cit.) p. 86.

490. Zenkovsky, Serge A., (op. cit.) "The Lay of Igor's Campaign VI" in p. 175.

491. (ibid.) "The Lay of Igor's Campaign X," p. 185

492. Grekov, B., (op. cit.) p. 499&548.

493. Zenkovsky, Serge A., (op. cit.) p. 239.

494. Grekov, B., (op. cit.) p. 498.

495. Trubetskoi, Eugene N., (op. cit.) p. 86.

496. Schipflinger, Thomas, (op. cit.) pp. 268&281.

497. Allen, Paul M. *Vladimir Soloviev: Russian Mystic* (Blauvelt, NY: Steinerbooks, 1978) p. 275.

498. Ivanov, (op. cit.) p. 27.

499. Ouspensky, Leonid, and Lossky, Vladimir, *The Meaning of Icons* (Crestwood, NY: St. Vladimir's Seminary Press, 1983) p. 45.

500. Gra, E.A., (op. cit.) p. 17.

501. (ibid.) p. 17.

502. Trubetskoi, Eugene N., (op. cit.) p. 74.

503. Ivanov, (op. cit.) pp. 31-32.

504. Evdokimov, Paul, (op. cit.) plate 11 and p. 345.

505. Gra, E. A., (op. cit.) p. 17.

506. Ivanov, (op. cit.) pp. 38&88).

507. (ibid.) pp. 122-24. This icon is presently in Moscow, at the Archaeology Office of the Ecclesiastical Academy.

508. Billington, James H., *The Icon and the Axe* (New York: Vintage Books, 1970) p. 46.

509. (ibid.) p. 64.

510. Karlinsky, Simon, "Russia's Gay History and Literature from the Eleventh to the Twentieth Centuries" in *Gay Roots*, ed. Leyland, Winston, (San Francisco: Gay Sunshine Press, 1991) p. 84.

511. (ibid.) p. 84, plus Billington, James H., (op. cit.) p. 65.

512. (ibid.) p. 84.

513. (ibid.) p. 85.

514. (ibid.) p. 84, and Billington, James H., (op. cit.) p. 65.

515. The other four were: "The Holy Trinity Vivifying Acting Force," "I believe in God the Omnipotent Father (Symbol of the Faith)," "Praise be the Lord of the skies (of liturgical nature)," and the Marian icon "It is worthy to praise Thee." Ivanov, (op. cit.) p. 70.

516. Karlinsky, Simon (op. cit.) p. 84.

517 Byne, Robert, and Romanoff, Nikita, *Ivan the Terrible* (NY: Thomas Y. Crowell Co.: 1975) p. 216.

518. Vzdornov, G., *Vologda* (Leningrad: Aurora Art Publishers, 1978) tr. Johnstone, Natasha, p. 12.

519. Logvinov, E. V., "The Praise of the Mother of God", in *Symbols of Glory: the Stroganov Icons* (Middle Green, Slough, England: St. Paul MultiMedia Publications, 1992) p. 24.

520. Trubetskoi, Eugene N., (op. cit.) p. 87.

521. Kostina, Inna, *Cathedrals of the Moscow Kremlin* (Moscow: Planeta Publishers Kuznetsky Most Ltd., 1993) p. 180.

522. Trubetskoi, Eugene N., (op. cit.) p. 87.

523. This refers to a passage in first of Isaiah's "Suffering Servant" Songs (Isaiah 42:1-7) which says, "He shall bring forth justice to the nations, not crying out, not shouting, not making his voice heard in the street."

524. Billington, James H., (op. cit.) pp. 173&175.

525. Hughes, Lindsey, *Sophia: Regent of Russia: 1657-1704* (New Haven and London: Yale University Press, 1990) p. 146.

526. (ibid.) pp. 23-24.

527. (ibid.) p. 66.

528. (ibid.) p. 140.

529. (ibid.) p. 263.

530.

531. Shlain, Leonard, (op. cit.) p. 400.

532. Billington, James H., (op. cit.) pp. 310-311.

533. (ibid.) p. 465.

534. Allen, Paul M. *Vladimir Soloviev: Russian Mystic* (Blauvelt, NY: Steiner Books, 1978) p. 42.

535. (ibid.) pp. 23-27.

536. Lubac, Henri de, S.J., *The Eternal Feminine* (London: William Collins Sons & Co. Ltd., 1971) pp. 39-40.

537. Billington, James H., (op. cit.) p. 465.

538. Solovyov, Vladimir, *Lectures on Divine Humanity* (Hudson, NY: Lindisfarne Press, 1995) p. VIII.

539. Allen, Paul M., (op. cit.) pp. 37&40.

540. Matthews, Caitlin, *Sophia: Goddess of Wisdom* (New York: Aquarian/Thorsons, 1992) p. 295.

541. Berdyaev, Nicolas, *The Russian Idea* (London: Bles - The Centenary Press, 1947) p. 176.

542. (ibid.) p. 466.

543. Allen, Paul M., (op. cit.) p. 273.

544. (ibid.) p. 274.

545. (ibid.) pp. 466-67.

546. Solovyov, Vladimir, (op. cit.) pp. 107-08.

547. Billington, James H., (op. cit.) p. 468.

548. Allen, Paul M., (op. cit.) p. 243.

549. Paplauskas-Ramunas, Antoine, *Dialogue entre Rome et Moscou* (Ottawa, Canada: Editions de L'Université D'Ottawa, 1966) p. 124.

550. Nichols, Aidan, O.P., *Theology In the Russian Diaspora* (Cambridge: Cambridge University Press, 1989) p. 28.

551. (ibid.) p. 468.

552. Solovyov, Vladimir, (op. cit.) p. VII, f. 1.

553. Allen, Paul M., (op. cit.) p. 140.

554. Leong, Albert, ed., *The Millenium: Christianity and Russia 988-1988* (Crestwood, NY: St. Vladimir's Seminary Press, 1990) p. xv.

555. Dostoevsky, Fyodor, *Crime and Punishment*, trans., Garnett, Constance (Toronto, New York: Bantam Books, 1982) p. 361, quoted by Kindlon, Paul, in his Ph.D. thesis *Anti-Platonic Affinity Between Nietzsche and Dostoevsky* (Chicago: University of Illinois at Chicago, 1991) p. 17.

556. (ibid.) p. 481.

557. Cavarnos, Constantine, (op. cit.) p. 99.

558. Unlike Sergei Vasilievich Rachmaninov (1873-1943), Pyotr Ilyich Tchaikovsky (1840-1893) was distinctive.

559. Berdyaev, Nicolas, (op. cit.) p. 175.

560 Karlinsky, Simon, *Marina Tsvetaeva* (Cambridge: Cambridge University Press, 1985) p. 50.

561 Aldrich, Robert, and Wotherspoon, Garry, ed. *Who's Who in Gay & Lesbian History* (London and New York: Routledge, 2001) p. 447.

562 Karlinsky, Simon, *Marina Tsvetaeva* (op. cit.) p. 211.

563 (ibid.) pp. 84-85.

564. Slesinski, Robert, *Pavel Florensky: A Metaphysics of Love* (Crestwood, NY: St. Vladimir's Seminary Press, 1996) p. 25.

565. The other co-founders were Valentin Pavlovich Sventsitsky (1879-1939), Vladimir Frantsevich Ern (1881-1917), and Aleksander Viktorovich Elchaninov (1881-1934).

566. Florenski, Pavel, *La Colonne de le Fondement de la Vérité*, translated from the Russian by Constantin Andronikov (Lausanne: L'Age d'Homme, 1975) p. 253.

567. Slesinski, Robert, (op. cit.) pp. 178-79.

568. Slesinski, Robert, (ibid.) p. 180.

569. Florenski, Pavel, (op. cit.) p. 349.

570. Slesinski, Robert, (op. cit.) p. 176.

571. Florenski, Pavel, (op. cit.) p. 227.

572. Slesinski, Robert, (op. cit.) p. 192.

573. "The law of praying (is) the law of believing" (i.e. As people pray, so they believe).

574. Slesinski, Robert, (op. cit.) p. 190.

575. (ibid.) p. 191.

576. (ibid.) p. 212.

577. (ibid.) p. 215.

578. House, Francis, *Millennium of Faith* (Crestwood, NY: St. Vladimir's Seminary Press, 1988) p. 40.

579. Matthews, Caitlín, *Sophia: Goddess of Wisdom* (op. cit.) p. 298.

580. Shipflinger, Thomas, (op. cit.) p. 273.

581. Hauke, M., *Women in the Priesthood? A Systematic Analysis in the Light of the Order of Creation and Redemption* (San Francisco: Ignatius Press, 1986) p. 269.

582. Matthews, Caitlín, (op. cit.) p. 299.

583. Boulgakov, Serge, *La Sagesse de Dieu* , *Resumé de Sophiologie*, Constantin Andronikov, trans. (Lausanne: L'Age d'Homme, 1983) pp. 8-9; 80-81. translated and quoted in Shipflinger, Thomas (op. cit.) p. 275.

584. Berdyaev, Nicolas, (op. cit.) p. 241.

585. Berdyaev, Nicolas, (ibid.) p. 241.

586. Berdyaev, Nicolas, (ibid.) p. 241.

587. Richardson, David Bonner, *Berdyaev's Philosophy of History* (The Hague: Martinus Nijhoff, 1968) p. 55.

588. Berdyaev, Nicolas, (op. cit.) p. 241.

589. Berdyaev, Nicolas, (ibid.) pp. 242-243.

590. Roerich, Nicholas, *Shambala* (New York: Nicholas Roerich Museum, 1985) p. 265.

591. Matthews, Caitlín, (op. cit.) p. 299.

592. Matthews, Caitlín, (ibid.) pp. 301 (description) and 311 (reproduction).

593. Matthews, Caitlin, (ibid.) pp. 300-301. Here the *Madonna Oriflamma* is both depicted and described.

594. Rosenthal, Bernice Glatzer, editor, *The Occult in Russian and Soviet Culture* (Ithaca and London: Cornell University Press, 1997) pp. 326-27.

595. (ibid.) pp. 336-37.

596. Roberts, Elizabeth, and Shukman, Ann, *Christianity for the Twenty-First Century* (New York: Continuum, 1996) p. 17.

597. Davis, Nathaniel, *A Long Walk to Church: A Contemporary History of Russian Orthodoxy* (Boulder, San Francisco, Oxford: Westview Press, 1995) p. 191.

598. Shlain, Leonard, (op. cit.) p. 402. Shlain writes, "The worship of Sophia (Mary's name in Russia) was execrated. Images came under assault."

599. Nouwen, Henri J. M., *Behold the Beauty of the Lord* (Notre Dame: Ave Maria Press, 1987) p. 47. He quotes from a narration by the Russian art historian and painter Vladimir Desyatnikov, in "The Russian Renaissance: Andrei Rublyov" (for the 625th anniversary of his birth, *Soviet Life*, Oct. 1985, p. 55.

600. Berrigan, Daniel, with icons by McNichols, William Hart, *The Bride* (New York: Orbis Books, 2000) p. 131.

601. Berrigan, Daniel, and McNichols, William Hart, (ibid.) p. 132.

602. Evdokimov, Paul, *La Femme et la Salut de Monde* (Tournai: Casterman, 1958) p. 265, trans. by Matthews, Caitlín, and published in (op. cit.) p. 302.

603. Roberts, Elizabeth, and Shukman, Ann, (op. cit) p. 16.

604. Roberts and Shukman, (ibid.) p. 17.

605 Men, Alexander, *About Christ and the Church* (Torrance, CA: Oakwood Publications, 1996) p. 17.

606. (ibid.) p. 21.

607. Roberts and Shukman, (ibid.) It was first published posthumously in *Kul'tura i dukhovnoe vozrozhdenie* (Moscow, 1992, pp. 378-413). pp. 107-108.

608. Roberts and Shukman (ibid.) pp. 120-121.

609. Men, Alexander, (op. cit) p. 34.

610. Slesinski, Robert, (op. cit.) p. 170.

612. Meyendorff, John, *Rome, Constantinople, Moscow* (St. Vladimir's Seminary Press, 1996) p. 181.

612 Essig, Laurie, *Queer in Russia* (Durham and London: Duke University Press, 1999) p. 58.

613 "Stonewall" refers to the reaction to police harassment which occurred at New York's Stonewall bar on the last week-end of June, 1969. It is said to have marked the beginning of gay liberation in the United States and is the reason for the annual Gay Pride parades throughout the world.

614. (ibid.) pp. 133-34.

615. (ibid.) p. 67.

616. Reported in PlanetOut News & Politics, Gay.com U.K., Friday, September 5, 2003 / 4:34 PM

617. Boswell, John, *Same-Sex Unions in Premodern Europe* (op. cit.) pp. 141-46, 154-55, 158, & 182.

618. October 22, 1998 was the 5th anniversary of The Living Circle's incorporation. The celebration was the culminating event of a month-long exhibit in the lobby of the Episcopal Diocesan Center of the art from The Living Circle's chapel

619. Among these parishes, 10 are Orthodox, 5 are Romanian Catholic, 10 are Melkite Catholic, 30 are Ukranian Catholic, and the rest are Reuthenian Catholic.

620. In 1999, this author was requested to write an abbreviated *Lives of the Saints*, for the feast days of the liturgical cycle of the Roman Catholic Church. Among the entries was the story of Polyeuct and Nearchus, accompanied by a copy of Robert Lentz's icon. This can be seen on the web page whose address is www.internetnpm.org. Since this was requested by World Library Publishing Company, who also prints Sunday bulletins for parishes, it is possible that it helped to inspire the icon printed by the Eastern Christian Bulletin Service. The icon, of recent vintage, comes from Greece and is part of a set of images of saints for every day of the year. The artist is not identified.

621. Eastern Christian Bulletin Service - P.O. Box 3909, Fairfax, VA 22038-3909. Phone (703) 407-2075 Fax: (703) 691-0513.

622 In the book *Same-Sex Unions in Pre-Modern Europe*, also called *The Marriage of Likeness*.

623 Gussow, Mel, *Conversations With Miller* (New York: Applause, 2002) p. 21.

624.Information on both the goddess and the saint can be found in Mary Condren's *The Serpent and the Goddess* (San Francisco: Harper, 1989) and in James J. Preston's *Mother Worship* (Chapel Hill: University of North Carolina Press, 1982), which contains an article entitled, "The Cult of Brigid: A Study of Pagan-Christian Syncretism in Ireland", by Donal O'Cathsaigh.

625.Toulson, Shirley, *The Celtic Alternative: A Reminder of the Christianity We Lost* (London: Rider, 1987) pp. 70,74, & 78.

626.D'Arcy, Mary Ryan, *The Saints of Ireland* (St. Paul, MN: Irish American Cultural Institute, 1974) p. 24.

627.Shepard, Paul, and Sanders, Barry, *The Sacred Paw* (New York: Arkana/Penguin, 1985) p. xiv.

628. Ashe, Geoffrey, *Dawn Behind the Dawn* (New York: Henry Holt and Company, 1992) p. 30.

629. Matthews, Caitlín, *Sophia: Goddess of Wisdom* (op. cit.) p. 214.

630. Furlong, Nicholas, *Dermot, King of Leinster and the Foreigners* (Tralee, Co. Kerry: Anvil Books, 1973) pp. 37-38.

631. The abbesses of Kildare were given the jurisdictional authority of bishops and the other Irish bishops seated themselves at her feet whenever they were all assembled until this custom was ended by the Synod of Kells in 1152, which had been called by Theobald, the first Archbishop of Canterbury to assume any such jurisdictional authority in Ireland. Like their counterparts in Ireland, the abbesses of St. Brigid's convent at Douglas, on the Isle of Man were considered peers of the realm and could maintain their own baronial courts until the Reformation closed the convent.

632. Dames, Michael, *Mythic Ireland* (London: Thames & Hudson Ltd., 1992) p. 15.

633. Ellis, Peter Berresford, *Celtic Women* (Grand Rapids, MI: Wm. B. Eerdmans Publishing Company, 1995) p. 146.

634.D'Arcy, Mary Ryan, (op. cit.) p. 25.

635.Pennick, Nigel, *Celtic Sacred Landscapes* (New York: Thames and Hudson, 1996) p. 173.

636 Schulenburg, Jane Tibbetts, *Forgetful of Their Sex* (Chicago and London: University of Chicago Press, 1998) p. 94.

637. (Ibid.) See K. Meyer, ed., *Tertia Vita*, in *Ancedota Oxoniensia* (Oxford: 1885), part 4.

638. Ellis, Peter Berresford, *Celtic Women* (op. cit.) p. 147.

639. (ibid.) p. 148.

640. Quoted in Condren, Mary, *The Serpent and the Goddess* (San Francisco: HarperSanFrancisco, 1989, p. 65.

641. MacDonald, Iain, *Saint Bride* (Edinburgh: Floris Books, 1992), p. 27.

642. Saltman, Avrom, *Theobald: Archbishop of Canterbury* (New York: Greenwood Press, Publishers, 1969) p. 136.

643. It is ironic that, by the time the abbess of Kildare was demoted in 1152, it was no longer the only monastic establishment in the Church whose abbess had episcopal jurisdiction. In 1101, Robert d'Arbrissel (d. 1120) established the Order and abbey of Fontevraut, whose first abbess (d.1149) was Pétronille de Chemillé. She and the abbesses who succeeded her (many of whom had French royal blood) down to the time of the French Revolution had jurisdictional authority over the monks as well as the nuns. (Tunc, Suzanne, *Les Femmes Au Pouvoir* (Paris: Les Éditions Du Cerf, 1993) pp. 14-16.)

Later in the same century, after the demotion of Kildare, the Royal Monastery of Las Huelgas was established by King Alfonso VIII of Castile's Queen, Eleanor, the daughter of Henry II of England's Queen, Eleanor of Aquitaine. It was a convent to which only women of the highest rank were admitted. While its abbess was not head of an Order, as at Fontevraut, she was a princess-Palatine, second only to the queen, and as *señora de horca y cuchillo* lady of gallows and knife), possessed powers of life and death over 51 manors. The abbesses insisted that they were Cistercian, but that they would not obey the general chapter at Cîteaux in which no woman was allowed to sit. Las Huelgas became the burial place of the royalty of Castile. With all of this going on in the same century, one might wonder why Rome chose to demote Kildare. The answer can only be that Rome, which had long resented the authority which the Celtic Church accorded women, was now in a position to do so. Not long before Kildare's demotion, King Henry II had presumed he had the right to give authority over Ireland to the only English Pope in history, Adrian IV (Nicholas Breakspeare), who presumed that the had the authority to take it. Ireland was being dismantled by the cooperative predatory actions of England and Rome. The abbeys of France, Spain, and Italy, on the other hand, had the power of royal backing.

Episcopal jurisdictional authority was bestowed on the abbesses of the Abbey of Conversano In the thirteenth century. (Tunc, Suzanne, (ibid.) p. 16)

> It was in the year 1266 that a community of Cistercian nuns arrived in Brindisi as refugees from the Convent of Saint Maria de Verga, Montone, Rumania. Abbess Dameta Paleologus was of the imperial family of Constantinople. By ordinance of Pope Clement IV, she was given the monastery and territory of Saint Benedict in Conversano, Apulia. From the very beginning the abbess and the community were established as exempt by papal decree so that they did not come under the jurisdiction of the Bishop of Conversano, but were directly dependent on the Holy See. The Abbess Dameta, as also the abbesses that followed her, had therefore a quasi-episcopal jurisdiction....which included reception of the miter. (Morris, Joan, *Against Nature and God* (London and Oxford: Mowbrays, 1973) p. 69)

644. Schulenburg, Jane Tibbetts, (op. cit.) p. 323.

645.Reeves, William, *The Culdees of the British Islands* (Dublin: M. H. Gill, 1864) p. 53.

646. Sellner, Edward C., *Wisdom of the Celtic Saints* (Notre Dame, IN: Ave Maria Press, 1993) p. 73.

647. Moorhouse, Geoffrey, *Sun Dancing: A Vision of Medieval Ireland* (New York: Harcourt, Brace & Company, 1997) p. 206.

648. O'Donohue, John, *Anam-Cara: Spiritual Wisdom from the Celtic World* (New York: Bantam Press, 1997) p. 35.

649. Schulenberg, Jane Tibbits, (op. cit.) p. 355.

650. Baring-Gould, Rev. Sabine, in *The Lives of the Saints, Vol. 2* (New York: Longmans, Green & Co., 1898), pp. 22-23.

651. Cherici, Peter, *Celtic Sexuality* (London: Duckworth, 1994) pp. 114-15.

652. Ellis, Peter Berresford, *Celtic Women* (op. cit.) p. 149.

653. Lucie Smith, Edward A., *Joan of Arc (New York: W.W.Norton Company Inc., 1977) p. 186.*
Here Edward A. Lucie Smith has writes about the recorded testimony of eyewitnesses that she preferred to sleep with younger women and opines, therefore 'from this we may perhaps deduce an element of homosexual attraction, though noting that it was certainly unconscious.'

654. MacDonald, Iain, *Saint Bride* (op. cit.) pp. 36-7.

655. Butler, Rev. Dugald, M.A., *The Ancient Church and Parish of Abernethy* (Edinburgh: H. Blackwood & Sons, 1897) p. 63. Similar to the nineteen fire-tending nuns of Kildare were the Nine Maidens, daughters of St. Donevald (Donald), to whom the Pictish King Garnard gave a lodging and oratory at Abernethy at the beginning of the eighth century, at a place called "Holy Oaks" There was also a holy well dedicated to the Nine Maidens. Both the oaks and the well there were much frequented by pilgrims until the Reformation. (ibid.) pp. 147-48.

656. Baring-Gould, Rev. Sabine, (op. cit.) p. 23.

657. Bitel, Lisa M., *Land of Women: Tales of Sex and Gender from Early Ireland* (Ithaca and London: Cornell University Press, 1996) p. 86.

658. Foster mothers trained young women and men in many ways, even sometimes in military ways; and many Christian abbesses would assume this role. St. Ita (Deirdre) (d. 570) would come to be called the "Brigid of the West" and the forster-mother of the saints of Ireland, because she taught so many of them in her famous school at Killeady. Other famous "foster-mothers" who headed schools which produced many saints and scholars were Brigid's contemporary and friend, St. Moninne (Modwena, Edana, Mo-edana) of Killeavy (and of Edinburgh) (516), St. Hild (Hilda) of Whitby (d.680) and St. Samthann (Safan) of Clonbroney (d.739)

659. O'hOgain, Dr. Daithi, *Myth, Legend, and Romance* (New York: Prentice Hall Press, 1991) p. 63.

660. Gregory, Lady, *A Book of Saints and Wonders* (Gerrards Cross, Buckinghamshire: Colin Smythe Limited, 1972) pp. 19-20.

661. Minehan, Rita, CSB, *Rekindling the Flame* (Kildare, Ireland: Solas Bhríde Community, 1999) p. 14.

662. Veronica Morrison, Barbara O'Neill, Dennis O'Neill, and Stephen Starr.

663. Brenneman, Walter L., and Mary G., *Crossing the Circle at the Holy Wells of Ireland* (Charlottesville and London: The University Press of Virginia, 1995) pp. 77-78.

664. Meehan, Bernard, *The Book of Kells* (London: Thames and Hudson, 1994) p. 50.

665. Baruffa, Antonio, *The Catacombs of St. Callixtus* (Vatican City: Libreria Editrice Vaticana, 2000) p. 151.

666. Vienne is a city 27 kilometers southeast of Lyons.

667. Guerin, Mgr. Paul, *Les Petites Bollandistes Vies Des Saints* (Paris: Bloud et Barral, 1880) Vol. 4, p. 581, where the French phrase used is "étroite amitié."

668. Butler, Rev. Alban, *Lives of the Fathers, Martyrs, and Other Principal Saints*, (Boston, Massachusetts: The Stratford Co., 1926) Vol. II, p. 31.

669. (ibid.), p. 32.

670. Gregory of Tours, St. *Glory of the Martyrs* (op. cit.) p. 73.

671. Gregory of Tours, St. trans. and intro. by Lewis Thorpe, *The History of the Franks* (op. cit.) p. 11.

672. Holweck, F.G., (op. cit.) p. 1011.

673. Boswell, John, *Same-Sex Unions in Premodern Europe* (op. cit.) p. 140. to thēlu autōn paraxēlōn dia tōn thēríou / sexui earum etiam de bestia aemulatus.

674. Salisbury, Joyce E., *Perpetua's Passion: The Death and Memory of a Young Roman Woman* (New York and London: Routledge, 1997) p. 143.

675. (ibid.) p. 170.

676. (ibid.) p. 170.

677. (ibid.) p. 171.

678. (ibid.) p. 176.

679. (ibid.) p. 171.

680. (ibid.) p. 176.

681. The majority of contemporary investigators think that the first draft of *The Primary Chronicle* was composed between 1037 and 1039. From 1060 to 1073, it was continued by Nikon, a monk at the Kievan Crypt Monastery, who was an eyewitness to much that he recorded. From 1093 to 1095, this version was reworked at the same monastery. Around 1113, another monk there named Nestor rewrote it and added the introduction with its historical and philosophical discussions. And the text underwent another redaction at the same location between 1117 and 1118. Zenkovsky, Serge A. ed., *Medieval Russia's Epics, Chronicles, and Tales* (New York: Meridian (Penguin), 1974.

682. Grekov, B., *Kiev Rus* (Moscow: Foreign Languages Publishing House, 1959) p. 553.

683. (ibid.) p. 555.

684. Simon Karlinsky is professor emeritus in the Department of Slavic Languages and Literatures at the University of California, Berkeley.

685. Karlinsky, Simon, "Russia's Gay History and Literature from the Eleventh to the Twentieth Centuries," in *Gay Roots: Twenty Years of Gay Sunshine* (San Francisco: Gay Sunshine Press, 1991) ed. Winston Leyland, p. 83.

686. His feast day is July 26 in Russia.

687. Karlinsky, (op. cit.) p. 83.

688. (ibid.) p. 83.

689. Volkoff, Vladimir, *Vladimir the Russian Viking* (Woodstock, N Y: The Overlook Press, 1985) p. 299.

690. Demshuk, (op. cit.) p. 49.

691. (ibid.) p. 49.

692. This same Sadko is the subject of "Sadko, a Musical Picture," Opus 5. Composed in 1867 by Nicolai Rimsky-Korsakov, is was the first Russian symphonic poem.

693. Grekov, B., (op. cit.) p. 554.

694. (ibid.) p. 554.

695. (ibid.) p. 554. The feasts were on May 2, May 20, July 24, August 11, August 12, and September 5.

696. Demshuk, (op. cit..) p. 51.

697. The translation, by Samuel H. Cross, reads thus: "...they fell upon him like wild beasts about the tent, and overcame him by piercing him with lances. They also overpowered his servant, who cast himself upon his body. For he was beloved of Boris. He was a servant of Hungrian race, George by name, to whom Boris was greatly attached. The prince had given him a large gold necklace which he wore while serving him. They also killed many other servants of Boris. But since they could not quickly take the necklace from George's neck, they cut off his head and thus obtained it. For this reason his body was not recognized later among the corpses." Zenkovsky, Serge A. (op. cit.) pp. 102-03. When the author of this book wrote to Simon Karlinsky to inquire about the differences in translation, he replied, in a letter dated November 5, 2000, "I got my text on St. Boris and George the Hungarian in the same place Serge A. Zenkovsky got his: the Legend of Boris and Gleb (in my own translation). However, Zenkovsky chose not to cite George's words, either because he didn't see their significance or because he preferred to omit them.

698. Lenhoff, Gail, *The Martyred Princes: Boris and Gleb: A Socio-Cultural Study of the Cult and the Texts* (Columbus, OH: Slavica Publishers, Inc., 1989) UCLA Slavic Studies, Vol. 19, p. 128, n. 21 .

> *(The boy also) saw the retainer (Georgij), who had fallen on the blessed Boris (in order to shield*
> *him from Svjatopolk's men), holding a candle in front of the saints...*

699. Popova, Olga, "Russian Icons at the Time of St. Sergius", found in Swift, Anne Marie, *Contemplating the Mystery: Saint Sergius and Rublev* (Slough, England: St. Paul MultiMedia Productions, 1996) pp. 5&6. It is also depicted in detail in Alpatov, Mihail, "The Icons of Russia" in "The Icon" (New York: Dorset Press, 1987), pp. 260-61.

700. Trubetskoi, Eugene N., *Icons: Theology in Color* (op. cit.) p. 19.

701. Quenot, Michel, *The Icon: Window on the Kingdom* (Crestwood, NY: St. Vladimir's Seminary Press, 1991) p. 29

702. Talbot Rice, David and Tamara, *Icons and Their History* (Woodstock, NY: The Overlook Press, 1974) p. 103.

703. Nathanael, Bishop of Vienna and Austria, "St. Andrei Rublev", from *Orthodox Life* (Jordanville, NY: Holy Trinity Monastery, 1978) Issue No. 5, pp. 2-3.

704. Ivanov, (op. cit.) p. 57.

705 Bigham, Fr. Steven, *Heroes of the Icon* (Torrance, CA: Oakwood Publications, 1998) pp. 123-25.

706 Plugin, Vladimir, *Masters of World Painting: Andrei Rublev* (Leningrad: Aurora Art Publishers, 1987) p. 7.

707 Ibid. p. 8.

708. Semler, Helen Boldyreff, *Discovering Moscow* (New York: Hippocrene Books, 1987) p. 125.

709. Nathanael, (op. cit.) pp. 2-3.

710. Joseph Sanin (d. 1515), after some years of monastic life, was elected abbot at Borovsk. After this, he instituted a monastic reform by becoming founder and hegumen of Volokolamsk, was "the last and most articulate of the great monastic pioneers". His monastery was in the Novgorod diocese. He was a strong supporter of Archbishop Gennady's inquisitorial treatment of heretics and greatly contributed the ideology behind the Muscovite Czardom. Billington, James H., (op. cit.) p. 63.

711 Plugin, Vladimir (op. cit.) p. 3

712 St. Joseph of Volokolamsk, quoted from, in, Bigham, Fr. Steven, (op. cit.) p. 124.

713 Pachomius the Logothete, quoted in , (ibid.) p. 181.

714 (ibid.) p. 124.

715 *Synaxaire 1*, quoted in (ibid.) p. 124.

716 Ouspensky, Leonid, and Lossky, Vladimir, *The Meaning of Icons* (Crestwood, NY: St. Vladimir Seminary Press, 1982) pp. 46-47.